Social Work with Disadvantaged and Marginalised People

Sara Miller McCune founded SAGE Publishing in 1965 to support the dissemination of usable knowledge and educate a global community. SAGE publishes more than 1000 journals and over 800 new books each year, spanning a wide range of subject areas. Our growing selection of library products includes archives, data, case studies and video. SAGE remains majority owned by our founder and after her lifetime will become owned by a charitable trust that secures the company's continued independence.

Los Angeles | London | New Delhi | Singapore | Washington DC | Melbourne

Social Work with Disadvantaged and Marginalised People

Jonathan Parker
Sara Ashencaen Crabtree

Learning Matters
An imprint of SAGE Publications Ltd
1 Oliver's Yard
55 City Road
London EC1Y 1SP

SAGE Publications Inc.
2455 Teller Road
Thousand Oaks, California 91320

SAGE Publications India Pvt Ltd
B 1/I 1 Mohan Cooperative Industrial Area
Mathura Road
New Delhi 110 044

SAGE Publications Asia-Pacific Pte Ltd
3 Church Street
#10-04 Samsung Hub
Singapore 049483

© Jonathan Parker and Sara Ashencaen Crabtree
2018

First published 2018

Editor: Kate Keers
Production controller: Chris Marke
Project management: Swales & Willis Ltd,
Exeter, Devon
Marketing manager: Camille Richmond
Cover design: Wendy Scott
Typeset by: C&M Digitals (P) Ltd, Chennai, India
Printed in the UK

Library of Congress Control Number: 2017954828

British Library Cataloguing in Publication Data

A catalogue record for this book is available from the
British Library

ISBN 978-1-4739-9457-7
ISBN 978-1-4739-9458-4 (pbk)

We would like to dedicate this book to our children, Isabel and Miranda, and to all the service users, clients and families we worked with when we too were once social workers. And as the pseudo-Latin phrase goes: *illegitimi non carborundum*!

Contents

Series editor's preface   viii

Acknowledgements   ix

Introduction   x

Part I: Understanding disadvantage and marginalisation   1

1   Understanding the concepts   3

2   Who are the disadvantaged and marginalised people?   22

3   The processes: how people become marginalised
     and disadvantaged   45

4   The impact: how disadvantage and marginalisation
     are experienced   63

Part II: Knowledge and skills   79

5   Factual and interpretive knowledge   81

6   Skills   98

7   Professional knowledge and skills   115

Part III: Practising ethically and reflexively   133

8   Using the law and policy   135

9   Ethical dilemmas in practice   152

10   Reflections and conclusions   168

References   172

Index   191

Series editor's preface

We have witnessed significant changes and shocks in recent years. These have resulted in numerous challenges for the wider world, and for all four countries of the UK (England, Northern Ireland, Scotland and Wales). These include political shifts to the 'popular' Right, a growing antipathy to care and support and dealing with lies and 'alternative truths' in our daily lives. Alongside this is the need to address the impact of an increasingly ageing population with its attendant social care needs and working with the financial implications that such a changing demography brings. At the other end of the lifespan the need for high-quality childcare, welfare and safeguarding services has been highlighted as society develops and responds to the changing complexion. As demand rises, so do the costs and the unquestioned assumption that austerity measures are necessary continues to create tensions in services, policies and expectations.

Migration has developed as a global phenomenon and we now live and work with the implications of international issues in our everyday and local lives. Often these issues influence how we construct our social services and determine what services we need to offer. It is likely that as a social worker you will work with a diverse range of people throughout your career, many of whom have experienced significant, even traumatic, events that require a professional and caring response. As well as working with individuals, however, you may be required to respond to the needs of a particular community disadvantaged by world events or excluded within local communities because of assumptions made about them.

The importance of high-quality social work education remains if we are to address adequately the complexities of modern life. We should continually strive for excellence in education as this allows us to focus clearly on what knowledge it is useful to engage with when learning to be a social worker. Questioning everything, especially from a position of knowledge, is central to social work.

The books in this series respond to the agendas driven by changes brought about by professional bodies, governments and disciplinary reviews. They aim to build on and offer introductory texts based on up-to-date knowledge and to help communicate this in an accessible way, so preparing the ground for future study and for encouraging good practice as you develop your social work career. The books are written by people passionate about social work and social services and aim to instil that passion in others. The current text introduces core social work themes that all practitioners will face. Working with marginalisation and disadvantage is something that is core to the profession.

Professor Jonathan Parker

Acknowledgements

We are most grateful to our students, colleagues and service users and carers we have worked with for the time and passion spent discussing ideas and thoughts that in some sense have made their way into this book. In this regard we would like to thank Susi, Terry and Muriel in particular. We hope we have done justice to everyone in this process. We would also like to acknowledge the great support provided by Kate Keers at SAGE who has been fundamental in kick-starting the project and encouraging its completion.

Introduction

In this introduction we will introduce you to the rationale underlying the book, setting the scene for understanding contemporary social work by offering a brief history of its growth and expansion and drawing on the development of ethical and value statements for practice over time. Whilst acknowledging the many forms of social work and its multiple foci, the book will emphasise the political and personal aspects of social work in practising with people at the edges of or excluded from society. The focus for understanding will primarily be on English social work but the discussion of concepts, discourses and practices transfers across countries and administrations. We will, therefore, use examples from international social work that illustrate core themes, thinking and practices without losing sight of organisational, contextual and practice differences across countries. Subsequently, at the end of this introduction, we provide an overview of the coverage of the book, introducing each part and chapter.

A rationale for the book

There are a range of texts that deal with issues of marginalisation and disadvantage (Burke and Parker, 2007; Sheppard, 2012; Matthies and Uggerhøj, 2014; Al Krenawi et al., 2016), anti-discriminatory and anti-oppressive practice (Dominelli, 2002, 2008; Dalrymple and Burke, 2006; Laird, 2008; Bhatti-Sinclair, 2011; Bartoli, 2013; Thompson, 2016; Williams and Graham, 2016) and social justice and human rights (Ferguson, 2008; Lundy, 2011; Dominelli, 2012; Austin, 2014). So it is important to ask why we need a book that deals with such seemingly central issues to social work practice. First of all we need a word or two about the title of the book. When proposing this title we wanted to consider all people, individuals and groups, who are in some way marginalised from or out of step with their wider society. However, the phraseology highlights a number of questions that we need to address. For instance, who or what marginalises whom? how does that take place? is it always negative? and, do people who are marginalised necessarily experience disadvantage? The direction of actions leading to marginalisation is also central to understanding what it is we are trying to address. Some of these debates are fluid and set in history and so will change over time. Some are more rooted within philosophical, political and ethical structures through which social work carefully treads.

We will deal more fully with the concept of marginalisation in the first chapter. However, it is important to recognise that marginalisation, in the context in which we are using it, refers to something – in this case a person or group of people – being pushed to the edges of society or the living context of those people. Sometimes being a part of society may not be a 'good' thing, and this is recognised too. Marginalisation is something that can be done or not done to a person or group of people by others. It can be intentional, a deliberate action or omission to create differences in treatment. For instance, in the early twentieth century we can point to the lack of voting rights for women as a means of continuing specific gendered inequalities and reinforcing men's primary positions in politics. It can also be unintentional, in which unspoken assumptions about the way things should be or how people should act are taken for granted and applied to people regardless of background and context. An example of this can be seen in the ways in which assumptions about a child's gender may influence the types of presents he or she receives – a toy gun for a boy and a doll for a girl. This can unintentionally have negative consequences for children who buck these norms and can lead to them being considered 'odd' or 'different' – reflecting the beginnings of a process of marginalisation.

The concept of society, as we intimated above, is a complex one. It is often a taken-for-granted term that, it is assumed, refers to something we all know. This easy assumption was brought into sharp relief some years ago in 1987 when the UK Prime Minister of the time, Margaret Thatcher, took issue with the phrase, drawing a distinction between reliance on the state and self-reliance for support and welfare issues in an interview and turning the tide from collective responsibility to individual responsibility (Thatcher, 1993). This had great implications for social work at the time that have permeated the profession ever since and, through political shifts, have encouraged a return to a focus that sees a person's situation to be more about individual pathology than social conditions and structures.

Social workers, whatever their specialisms, employing organisations or interests, practise with people at the margins of our society. Binary questions of personal versus collective responsibility, of individual pathology versus structure, intertwine with social work's contexts and influence practice. Social workers, however, stand alongside those who are disenfranchised, ostracised and treated unfairly by the taken-for-granted processes maintaining social order and functioning, by embedded social structures and by others with vested interests in maintaining the current functioning of that society. They need a critical understanding of what people experience, how they experience it and why these conditions arise. These are complex areas and no single explanation is adequate, of course. The processes of disadvantage and marginalisation do not just occur at the structural level of society but also operate within communities, work and school cultures, and at the interpersonal level of families. From labelling and discourse theories, amongst others, we can surmise that experience of these processes may also lead to the acceptance of intrapersonal experiences of disadvantage by individuals.

Thus, student social workers need to command fluency with the processes that lead to disadvantage and marginalisation, how this is experienced and the consequences such may have for individuals, groups, families and communities. Social workers also need to be critically reflective at both personal and political levels in working to counter marginalisation and alleviating negative consequences and disadvantage. The processes and consequences of disadvantage and marginalisation are faced by all social workers in practice, and it is something taught throughout all programmes leading to a social work qualification.

Contemporary social work and its contexts

Since 1948 and the implementation of the Welfare State in Britain, social work has been guided by legislation and latterly regulated by it. Legislation both acts to include and protect people who are in need or vulnerable in society and to proscribe, punish and marginalise through behavioural regulation. Social workers require the knowledge, skills and values to be able to tread a path through a complex political and personal landscape of potential traps. The Equality Act 2010, the Welfare Reform Act 2012, the Welfare Reform and Work Act 2016, the Care Act 2014, the Counter-Terrorism and Security Act 2015, the Children and Social Work Act 2017, and the 2016 UK referendum on European Union (EU) membership provide a glimpse of the changing landscape of legislation that makes this book central to social work education in England and the other countries of the UK in respect of their own parallel legislation. Using legislation to ensure fair treatment, to prevent and address marginalisation and disadvantage is important for social workers but it is not always enough. The laws cannot be assumed to be benign and the political whim and values underpinning them need to be seen clearly and critiqued. Social workers therefore stand betwixt and between two, sometimes opposing, perspectives of law to help people who are marginalised and law to constrain and enforce unspoken norms that perpetuate disadvantage.

As social work in the UK sought to 'professionalise' – a loaded and contested term that in itself created problems – the focus shifted from the relational and radical to the politically prescribed and popular (Parker and Doel, 2013a). It may not always seem that social work practice is 'popular', but policy makers and politicians directing social work's development draw on such thinking to inform practice and its organisation. It is also the case that there has never been a 'golden age' in social work where relational practice and radical politics infused it (Payne, 2005). However, expansions in the 1960s and 1970s of civil rights movements and anti-discrimination legislation and the subsequent development of radical social work based on Marxist approaches provided a much-needed challenge to the individualistic, therapeutic developments of psychoanalytic casework (Corrigan and Leonard, 1978). The professionalising tendency begun under the Conservative Governments of the 1980s and 1990s was continued through the 'modernising agenda' of the New Labour Government of 1997. This acted as a funnel that squeezed social work into local authority work, societal maintenance and policing and restrained extra-political action as employer need and value for money gained the ascendency.

Alongside these changes, devolution in regulation and registration and education and training allowed social work to develop differently in each UK administration from 2003 to 2004. In England there has been an increasing turn towards safeguarding (a term that encompasses protection but, perhaps, cloaks the emphasis with a seemingly more palatable approach that includes wider wellbeing, however the latter may be defined). Social work in England, as a soft form of social policing which is necessary and important, concerns the protection of people considered vulnerable, in need or at risk – valuable work, often intense and demanding. The focus has, to an extent, redefined social work and removed its critical and radical perspective. This too is necessary if those who are marginalised and disadvantaged from and by society are to be assisted in their lives.

As the International Federation of Social Workers (IFSW) and International Association of Schools of Social Work (IASSW) *Global Standards for the Education and Training of the Social Work Profession* (2012) and the IFSW (2014) *Global Definition of Social Work* indicate, the global challenges of disadvantage and marginalisation enacted through poverty, gender, sexuality, age, health status, ethnicity, religious faith or belief provide an international context in which social work is located. These socio-structural issues played out in individual lives render this book essential reading now and into the future.

What is social work?

When we pose the question *What is social work?*, we expose ourselves to a morass of interpretation and associated questions. Does the question imply that there is a single, peculiar entity, job or profession that we call by the name of social work? And, if so, is social work a global phenomenon or does it relate solely to particular nations at specific periods in their development? The redefinition we posed above in respect of English social work is important in this discussion.

When we come to analyse the questions of definition still further we see that the practices of social work vary, not only across the countries of the world – something that may well be expected given the local circumstances in which social workers operate – but also within the UK itself. Within the four administrations in the UK, the regulation of social work by professional bodies differs and legislation underpinning social work practice varies, especially between England and Wales, and Scotland. If what we do as social workers portrays what we are in the eyes of the public, and if what we do is determined by legislation that is singular to a country or region, then we have a range of social work types.

It is an empirical fact that social work is not a homogeneous entity. The complexities of social work practice and the diverse meanings associated with it across the world, and even intra-nationally, such as in the four countries of the UK, are acknowledged in the literature (Hutchings and Taylor, 2007). But the acceptance of the broad IFSW (2014) definition of social work may be indicative of similarities and standards, which is further shown within a shared approach to aspects of social work curricula, methods, practices and legislation and administration (Parker et al., 2012a; Parker, 2017):

> *Social work is a practice-based profession and an academic discipline that promotes social change and development, social cohesion, and the empowerment and liberation of people. Principles of social justice, human rights, collective responsibility and respect for diversities are central to social work. Underpinned by theories of social work, social sciences, humanities and indigenous knowledge, social work engages people and structures to address life challenges and enhance wellbeing.*
>
> *The above definition may be amplified at national and/or regional levels.*

(IFSW, 2014)

Elsewhere, we have argued that shared approaches to the design and delivery of social work may stem from colonial histories and represent neo-colonial actions enacted in indigenous terms (Parker and Doel, 2013b). Earlier definitions also seemed somewhat reductive rather than expansive and inclusive. The 2014 definition included above offers the chance for individual countries or administrations to add to, not detract from, the definition to make it indigenously appropriate. However, as a challenge to contemporary English social work, the core focus concerns communities and societies' collective responsibilities for the welfare and care of their citizens or people for whom they have political responsibility.

Our focus in this text is to locate social work in England and the rest of the UK, recognising organisational and political alignment with social work structures in the West, and offering, not imposing or assuming, perspectives that may be useful where systems are developing in different ways.

Structure of the book

This book deals with contemporary issues common to social work around the world and considers the experiences of disadvantage and marginalisation. The book is unique in that it also addresses the processes by which people become marginalised and examines social work responses at three levels: the intrapersonal and interpersonal, the organisational and community, and the societal or structural levels.

It is:

1. contemporary
2. personal and political
3. practical
4. theorised.

The book is written in three core parts. The first part introduces the complex yet ubiquitous concepts of disadvantage and marginalisation and explores the processes that work to push people to the edges of society at a societal, organisational and community level and how this operates between individual people and between individuals and organisations/institutions. The ways in which people experience marginalisation and disadvantage are considered and who might represent a disadvantaged or marginalised person is explored.

The conceptual overview in Part I is followed in Part II by an examination of the knowledge and skills that social workers need to practise appropriately and sensitively in this area. In this section we consider the importance of dealing with the self as both part of that society which creates the conditions for the marginalisation of people, together with being part of the solution to work with such people, society itself and working to alleviate intolerable situations.

Part III follows from the reflection on social work's ambiguous position in respect of disadvantage and marginalisation. It introduces ways in which social workers are required to practise through use of legislation and policy, the expectations of social work from local authority/statutory and from third-sector and specific-interest group perspectives, and ways in which social workers can enhance their practice through personal and political reflection concerning the values on which the profession is predicated.

Part I: Understanding disadvantage and marginalisation

The first part of the book presents theoretical and research material introducing the focal concepts of the book. The context of social work is set out in the introduction and the first four chapters outline what we understand by disadvantage and marginalisation, which groups and individuals may be considered to be disadvantaged and marginalised, how they become so and what consequences this might have for them. This sets the scene for Parts II and III, which relate specifically to social work and the knowledge, skills and values for working with people who have been disadvantaged or marginalised.

Having set the historical context of social work briefly here, Chapter 1 introduces the core concepts of disadvantage and marginalisation, exploring their meanings in contemporary society. Following on from the first chapter, the second chapter examines who and which groups may be described as disadvantaged or marginalised and in what ways. We consider both socio-cultural and psycho-social factors, including: poverty, ethnicity and migration status; educational attainment and capacity; (un)employment status; health status; (dis)abilities; gender and sexualities; systems of belief and culture (religious, behavioural and political); subcultural involvement; intra-familial marginalisation, bullying, abuse and self-marginalisation. This overview leads into the next chapter, which seeks to understand how and why people become disadvantaged or marginalised. Marginalisation and disadvantage are theorised from the perspectives of functionalism, which would apportion the blame to individuals and groups themselves and using labelling theory, strain theory, deviance theories, conflict theories and everyday practices to understand the processes in a critical way.

Having identified what constitutes disadvantage and marginalisation, those people and groups who may be classed as being as such and the processes that lead to it, we are in a position, in Chapter 4, to outline some of the ways in which this might be experienced by people. The potential consequences of these experiences are outlined.

Part II: Knowledge and skills

Having outlined the core concepts, definition and theoretical bases for the book we move in the second part to exploring the knowledge and skills needed to work with disadvantaged and marginalised people and groups. We look at this through different lenses – the lens of wider factual knowledge, the lens of skills and, finally, that of professional knowledge and practice wisdom.

The knowledge base for working with people and groups who are disadvantaged and marginalised is wide ranging. In Chapter 5 we debate a range of factual knowledges – knowledge that exists and is interpreted in the social world inhabited by social workers and those with whom they work. These range from the very practical understanding and use of legislation, of organisational policy and procedure, through understanding wider world events having an impact on people, groups and communities, to theoretical understandings of working with difference, diversity, discrimination and disadvantage, values and ethics.

Chapter 6 explores the knowledge base for practice with people and groups who have been disadvantaged and/or marginalised and provides the underpinning social workers need and from which they can exploit their skills in order to work constructively alongside people towards change.

The final chapter in this section, Chapter 7, draws together the knowledge and skills by looking at developing social workers. Through their practice social workers develop practice wisdom, an intuitive and 'felt' way of responding to people, groups, situations and events. The final part of this chapter will focus on vulnerability, resilience and looking after oneself as a social worker, developing the skills and emotional hardiness to deal with complex, emotionally draining and traumatic events and stories in others.

Part III: Practising ethically and reflexively

The third and final substantive part of the book develops the ethical and reflexive approach to social work by exploring how law and policy can be employed and what kinds of ethical dilemma might be encountered in practice with people who have been disadvantaged and/or marginalised.

Chapter 8 differs from Chapter 5 in Part II, shifting from knowledge to practice, to the use of the law with people, groups and communities. This includes making others aware of the legislation and assisting their use of it to enable change, and directly challenging the legislation – acting politically as a social worker. This prepares the way for the next chapter, which examines the ethical dilemmas that may arise in working with people and groups who are marginalised and/or disadvantaged. This includes discussion of some of the following:

- when the law acts to marginalise and disadvantage people, groups and communities;
- when agency policies and procedure conflicts with your moral sense;
- when the resources aren't there;
- when communities collide with each other;
- when those who use social work challenge your moral sensibilities;
- when cultural/individual values and practices challenge your value base.

Finally, a short concluding chapter revisits the content of the book and conceptual discussion of social work and the mechanics and processes of disadvantage and discrimination, summarising how social workers may practise and what issues and problems they may encounter.

In summary, this book addresses the experience of disadvantage and marginalisation and the processes by which people become marginalised, areas which represent the focus of professional contemporary social work itself underpinned by a commitment to social justice and the promotion of dignity, human worth and wellbeing.

Part I

Understanding disadvantage and marginalisation

Chapters 1–4 outline the context and environments in which social work is practised with people who are marginalised in and disadvantaged by society. Theoretical models for understanding marginalisation and disadvantage and who may experience such alongside the ways people become marginalised and the impacts of this are discussed.

1: Understanding the concepts

Achieving a social work degree

This chapter will help you to develop the following capabilities, to the appropriate level, from the Professional Capabilities Framework.

Diversity

Understand how an individual's identity is informed by factors such as culture, economic status, family composition, life experiences and characteristics, and take account of these to understand their experiences, questioning assumptions where necessary.

Rights, justice and economic wellbeing

Understand, identify and apply in practice the principles of social justice, inclusion and equality.

Recognise the impact of poverty and social exclusion and promote enhanced economic status through access to education, work, housing, health services and welfare benefits.

Knowledge

Understand forms of harm and their impact on people, and the implications for practice, drawing on concepts of strength, resilience, vulnerability, risk and resistance, and apply to practice.

(Continued)

(Continued)

It will also introduce you to the following academic standards as set out in the social work subject benchmark statement.

5.2.i, iv, ix Social work theory
5.3.vi Values and ethics
5.4.i–v Service users and carers

Introduction

This chapter will introduce you to the core concepts of disadvantage and marginalisation, exploring their meanings in contemporary society and the bearing they have on people's lives. The changing and fluid concept of social work is stated in the introduction and some beginning understandings of our core concepts have been outlined. The complexities of disadvantage and marginalisation will be developed in this chapter in more depth using the explanatory concepts of intersectionality and super-diversity to explore the interrelationships between people's experiences and drawing on the wealth of social work thinking concerning anti-discriminatory and anti-oppressive practice. There will also be some discussion of cognate ideas and terms which expand or refine the definitions that we are using. Throughout the chapter we will illustrate the concepts using specific examples and ask you as the reader to engage with some of the understandings emerging from the discussion.

What is disadvantage?

In tennis a player gains advantage when she or he has won a point, needing only one more to win a game. One might consider the other player to be disadvantaged but would not consider this to have moral, social or political connotations. The concept, when taken apart from sport, is much more complex. Indeed, when we consider the idea of an advantage it may be taken as having more of a certain property, more options and/or resources, and importantly, more legitimation from others. It is multi-faceted and dependent on the context and those who have the power to set the terms of the argument.

Activity 1.1

Think of a time when you believe you were disadvantaged. Make a list of what this disadvantage consisted of, what the effects of it were and how you dealt with it.

Comment

There are many possible ways that this activity can be undertaken and the ways in which you have completed it will say something about you and your understanding of and approach to matters of disadvantage and marginalisation. These will be important to remember and reflect on when practising as a social worker. By way of comment we draw your attention to the following case study of Ann, Jane and Mark, social workers who qualified together and who now work in the same local authority.

Case study

Ann has been qualified as a social worker for six years. She has worked in a number of jobs and roles since qualifying, including working in an intake team and undertaking complex investigations and assessments until moving into a job she has wanted to do since training to become a social worker, working in a fostering and permanence team. She feels lucky to have got this job, although she has been told by older colleagues that it is *a dead end* for her career, meaning that she is less likely to be considered for management and leadership roles in the future.

Ann qualified alongside two colleagues she works with in the local authority. Jane remains in the intake team in which she started six years previously, having had one period of maternity leave, and is now working half-time. Jane is happy in her position and believes it offers her flexibility in respect of her family but realises that being in a part-time position and having a young child she is unlikely to progress rapidly in career terms. Mark is a team leader in a looked-after children team who is earmarked for area management roles and sometimes stands in for the existing manager when she is unavailable. Mark misses some of the individual and direct work he used to complete with children and young people and their parents but he is pleased with the way his career has progressed.

All three social workers may be seen to be disadvantaged in some way: Ann through her choices of work, although she may not feel so; Mark in respect of losing enjoyable aspects of his role; and Jane through her lifestyle and working choices. An unspoken aspect of disadvantage may be the result of different approaches taken to each person on the basis of their gender and their commitments (Parker and Ashencaen Crabtree, 2014a). This is likely also to have an impact on their earning potential in the future. The personal aspects of choices are influenced by structural assumptions about roles, careers and gender and this type of disadvantage may reinforce positions of power in the future.

In some respects we all try to achieve an advantage in various ways. For instance, if we have more money, greater access to books and more support from family, friends or influential people we may be able to succeed in our studies or careers more easily or more speedily than others. Of course, this requires an unequal system which is also open to conflict and abuse and where advantages are preciously guarded and controlled, being dispensed to those in favour or holding particular beliefs or ways of living. Our society is particularly unequal in this respect (Wilkinson and Pickett, 2010). Differences and inequalities in people's abilities, wants, wishes and likes are, of course, part of the social world and add richness to it. However, the favouring of certain people or groups above others may add an inequity alongside inequality that begins to disadvantage people on the basis of their position, characteristics and innate qualities rather than the wider social and individual differences that comprise a varied social world.

Activity 1.2

What do you think the differences are between inequity and inequality? Make a list of these.

Comment

You may have listed a range of differences that are partly based on values and questions of morality, those based on economics, heritage and nationality, health status, gender, age, geography and so on. Inequalities might be due to differences between people and their preferences whereas you may have written that inequities concern the intentional or unintentional unfavourable treatment that people experience as a result of their differences. Whatever examples you wrote down, it is clear that the difference between the two terms is important. Inequities result from avoidable differential treatment of characteristics and conditions that are often deliberately continued, although they create unfair disadvantage in favour of or against certain characteristics held by individuals or groups. Inequalities refer to those differences that occur in the distribution of certain characteristics or resources that are beyond immediate control. Schofield (2015) provides examples from health sociology to demonstrate these distinctions. Whilst both create disadvantages and need to be countered, the deliberate creation of unfair disadvantages is something that social workers may more easily identify and challenge.

So there are economic and resource disadvantages that we need to be aware of but there are also disadvantages that are physical, social, political and spatial. Like economic disadvantages, these other types of disadvantage are structurally determined and imposed from normative positions of power. That is, they are set by the existing political structures and social systems that are accepted as the norm in society. These are often unchallenged and simply assumed, and they are organised and promoted by those who have the power to set those norms (although we must recognise this is often unconscious). It must be remembered too that the structures have an influencing effect on those in power and those on the receiving end of it, creating a view of what 'should be', or the norm. The following case study provides an example.

Case study

A local community resource centre was seeking funding to make its building accessible to all people wishing to use it. It was a small building, set back from a local playing field, built in the early 1950s and having small doorways and steps up to the main entrance. A campaign had been launched by a disability rights group who wanted to use the building. The community committee worked alongside them to put together a bid to secure development funding from the council. The application was rejected because of reduced financing of social projects resulting from austerity measures and because it was said there was already a council-owned building nearby that people with disabilities and wheelchair users could use. The campaign group and community committee challenged this decision as members of the group wanted to enjoy the same facilities and resources as everyone else in the community.

We are discussing here unfair disadvantages, those which are calculated to have a negative effect on specific people and groups and to favour others. The council's assumption that, because there is already a building that can be used, there is no need to alter the community resource is founded on the basis of social norms and the ability to exercise power. The disability rights claim challenges these assumptions and demands fair and equal access regardless of personal characteristics. The use of equality legislation (see Chapters 5 and 8) also stresses the centrality of treating all people fairly rather than on the basis of a disability. Social work's role is to counter such unfair disadvantage, which results in unfair discrimination. The notion of fair play is an important one, which we will come back to when considering legislation and policy, but permeates much of our discussion.

This inequality in treatment may be behaviourally based which, at first glance, may be seen to be something with which most people would agree. Consider the members of a youth football team who offer the reward of a trip to the cinema and a meal for those who score the most goals in a season. This may seem a good thing to do, to celebrate success and achievement. However, such rewards automatically advantage those players in forward and attacking positions and disadvantage goalkeepers, fullbacks and often midfielders. When we explore this more deeply we can see that it sends a clear message that some players and positions within the team are more valued than others and begins to create a distinction between team members of advantage and disadvantage, opening opportunities for some and closing them down for others.

Whilst this relates to a game, similar advantages and disadvantages are created in other areas of society. For instance, a family reliant on benefits is unlikely to be able to afford a school trip to Spain to learn about the culture and language without a great deal of difficulty. This may be more within the reach of a family in which both parents are working in professional jobs. What this means is that the child in the first family is likely to be disadvantaged in his or her education and more likely to repeat those disadvantages later in his or her family whereas the converse is true for the second family (Hills, 2017). The unspoken message given is that people in poverty are worth less than those who are not so. This represents unfair disadvantage that social workers need to keep at the forefront of their mind when working with people. As we know, social workers practise with people who are economically disadvantaged more than others, and those people often experience increased mental illness, drug and alcohol problems, accommodation problems and so on.

The examples we have considered so far give some indication of how the term 'disadvantage' is understood and embedded in people's lives, but there are often very serious consequences resulting from them. The location of the disadvantage and the potential for blame are important. We can take a lead from the social model of disability to recognise that disadvantages are not qualities that are necessarily inherent within an individual, although others may use someone's particular characteristics to disadvantage them or to create the conditions in which the person with disabilities may experience disadvantage or limitations not endured by others. It is crucial to rehearse the view that disadvantages are imposed structurally, organisationally or interpersonally and that a moral discourse may often be developed at the same time which legitimates the disadvantage and allows those without it to regard themselves as the norm from which other people's life chances may be judged. So, when we use the term 'disadvantage' in this book we are referring to those conditions imposed externally to people which restrict or curtail the potential of those individuals, without there necessarily being any 'fault' whatsoever in them. The association with inequity is central to this understanding.

The concept of disadvantage, however, is contested and not without problems. When we were developing the outline for this book we received some very useful feedback concerning the use of the term 'disadvantage' and how some people, groups or communities may not view themselves as disadvantaged or, indeed, may regard the application of the label of disadvantage as problematic or wrong. This is important and we need to consider how the impact of such terms can affect the lives and chances of individuals (see the discussion of labelling in Chapter 3). We recognise the problematic aspects of disadvantage but, taken together with marginalisation and the ways in which we have set out its use, believe it to be important for beginning social workers to consider disadvantage and inequity in their work with people and structures. Before we move to a discussion of marginalisation, read the following research summary which sets out some of the ways in which the terms have meaning.

Research summary

The complexity of the expressions used to describe people who are 'on the margins of society', 'excluded', 'disadvantaged' or any of the plethora of terms available is expressed well by Foster (2000) in her study examining the relationship between social exclusion, drugs and crime. She draws upon the important debate between agency and structure, or the relative importance of individual characteristics, personality and faults versus the influence and impact of social structures, thinking and assumptions. Her work was set at the time the then Labour Government of the UK was concerned with social exclusion and developing ways of minimising it in the context of increased neoliberal policies that had reduced the UK's industrial base and effected profound changes in society. This resulted in the 'exclusion' of large numbers of White working-class men, especially in the North of England (see Sibley's (1995) *geographies of exclusion*). This largely forgotten, disparate group of people exemplified the intersection of social characteristics and/or divisions and the centrality of aspects of social exclusion.

However, Foster's (2000) focus on this group brought to the fore questions of disadvantage and individual blame, as well as some of the wider questions. Politically charged as these concepts are, we cannot avoid grappling with them. Disadvantage is a problematic concept and can suggest that the fault lies with the individual rather than outside of the person by focusing on behaviours and characteristics and by association with the US concept of the *underclass* (Murray, 1994). Foster's position, using Lewis's (1968) much-criticised *culture of poverty* thesis reminds us that, when the structures of society force people into the margins, people's expectations are affected and a 'learned helplessness' can set in that alters their behaviours and attitudes. In this way there is an interaction between the structural and the agency (or individual).

Disadvantage in social, economic and personal life can lead to marginalisation, to which we shall now turn.

What is marginalisation?

We often think of margins in books we are reading or writing in: the spaces at the sides where there is no writing. There is a blankness which can be ignored because we want to concentrate on what is written or where we have to write. In respect of people being marginalised we can take the metaphor further, seeing these individuals as pushed to the side-lines of life, made invisible and therefore their wants, wishes and needs can be ignored. However, margins are not simply negative spaces but areas which can look into the mainstream, in which interpretations can be made or written and changes proposed. Later in this section we will look at the notes that may be created on the margins, the voices of marginalised people who add a commentary to contemporary social and political life.

We need to ensure there is a balance between the negative and the potentially challenging aspects when we consider marginalisation. We also need to understand the processes through which people become marginalised (see Chapter 3). These again are complex and not necessarily unidirectional. On occasions people may remove themselves to the margins deliberately. Also, we must remember that it is not always a good thing to bring someone back into society: societies may be unjust, unfair or debilitating and taking oneself to the margins can be protective and positive.

Activity 1.3

Write down what you think is meant by the term 'marginalisation'.

Consider a time when you or someone you know has been marginalised. What did this consist of and how did it feel at the time?

Comment

Whilst we will all have written something different here, our experiences are unique and the ways in which we make meaning of them is individual to each of us and our lives so far. However, it is likely that you will have written about being excluded, pushed to one side, ignored and made invisible. These experiences can demoralise and it is possible to experience a kind of *learned helplessness* (Maier and Seligman, 1976), a feeling and belief that whatever you do it will not be recognised and certainly will not improve your lot, so better to do nothing. However, for some people being marginalised can make them very angry, prone to outbursts and even violence. At times these outbursts may be considered self-defence against the violence of a system that has pushed people to the limits.

It is important that you note carefully how writing about your own experiences, or those of someone you know, made you feel. Reflect on these and keep this in mind when working with people who have experienced being marginalised. It can help guard against the further marginalisation as a result of behaviour that is labelled without looking to its context and its causes (see Chapter 3).

Socio-spatial marginalisation

Geography can be implicated in a person's or a group's marginalisation (Sibley, 1995). At the international level, we have seen a geographical divide between the Global North and the

Global South, where wealth, resource and the power to set the terms of arguments rest more closely with the Global North than the Global South (Hugman, 2010). In turn this reflects a historical marginalisation in which the geographies of power have been determined by prior colonial and post-colonial experiences (Razack, 2009; Parker et al., 2016a). Whilst most social workers will be able to do little within their roles to reduce this marginalisation at a structural level, it is important to be aware of the wider geographies of marginalisation, as you are likely to be working with people from disadvantaged global communities and need to understand the way the world is organised and how the situation has come about, acknowledge what people are experiencing and to seek redress on an individual level for those with whom you are working (see Chapter 5). You also need an awareness of your own advantage and privilege in these contexts. Whatever your social, economic, geographical and ethnic background you will be in a position of significant authority as a social worker.

The geographies of marginalisation are not solely located at the global level, however. In Europe we can note the disadvantages experienced by some countries as opposed to others and the ways in which some of these are structured, such as the situation in Greece and the debt crisis engendered by austerity measures (Ioakimidis, 2013; Varoufakis, 2017). It is also closer to home as well, considering urban/rural divides, distinctions between the countries of the UK (Scott et al., 2007) or divisions between the North and South of England (Robbins, 2005). It may also relate to the geographical dispersal of the rich and the poor (McDuff, 2017). You may be wondering what this has to do with social work and we will consider this next in terms of political marginalisation.

Political marginalisation

In Foster's paper in the earlier research summary, she noted the disadvantages that communities in the North-East of England had experienced. These are replicated throughout the North of England, where employment and opportunities are less, where investment appears low, where many refugees and asylum seekers have been housed. Rightly or wrongly, there is a perception of marginalisation by Westminster. This perception spills into the emotional and behavioural patterns of communities, leading to tensions, as we have seen in the early years of the century (Žižek, 2011). Social workers tread a pathway through the concerns, perceptions and lived experiences of marginalisation to foster community cohesion, to work with those who are disadvantaged, who adopt lives on the edges and who, sometimes, reject a society they feel has done violence to them.

Young people, who became, to an extent, more politicised following the 2016 referendum vote, have expressed feelings of alienation and marginalisation, a topic discussed in more detail in Chapter 4. Other people in more traditional Labour-voting communities rejected these traditions and turned towards more extremist political parties, believing their voices had been neglected in the homogenised atmosphere of UK politics that seemingly sought to defend itself rather than serve the public. Being on the political margins, however, can lead to a reigniting of resistance, something that social workers need to work with in order to effect change (Guo and Tsui, 2010).

Sexual marginalisation

Marginalisation on the basis of sexuality or gender remains rife despite the development of equality legislation and the legacy of gay rights campaigners such as Peter Tatchell, and second-wave feminism from the late 1960s onwards (Ahmed, 2017). Social work is a profession in which most qualified and registered practitioners are women and most students entering education are women. It remains an occupation in which many managers and those in policy direction, education and academic positions are men, disproportionately so (Ashencaen Crabtree and Parker, 2014; Parker and Ashencaen Crabtree, 2014a). Social work itself remains plagued by sexism, which reflects wider society and becomes part of the assumed worlds people inhabit. Bringing this to light is important so that, as social workers, we can allow those with whom we work to take action. The inherent sexism in social work – and wider society no doubt – is more complex, however. In our research concerning male social work students the unspoken, taken-for-granted perspectives played out in considering those male students to be deviant, potentially predatory and interested in power (Ashencaen Crabtree and Parker, 2014; Parker and Ashencaen Crabtree, 2014a), a topic we revisit in Chapter 4.

Marginalisation on the basis of gender or sexuality is an important field in which social workers can engage, exposing assumptions and campaigning for equality. This is something that you as student social workers can also be active in countering. Consider the following case study.

Case study

Maggie was programme leader of a social work course at a large urban university in England. The student group were predominantly female, in line with other programmes around the country. Out of seven staff she was one of only two women. At a meeting that she called in order to explain recent changes to the programmes to the student and staff group, she noticed that when greeting the students they acknowledged this very simply and went immediately to say hello to the male staff members and to shake their hands. When the meeting began the student group were seen to be looking towards the male staff for confirmation of what was being said. Maggie spoke to her colleagues about her perceptions of being pushed to the margins. They all noticed this and recognised that something had to be done to challenge this unspoken and no doubt unconscious privileging of the male staff group.

Marginalia

When we began this section, we mentioned the margins of a book, suggesting these are the blank spaces we do not see. Of course, this is not always the case, as we acknowledged, and it is helpful to draw a parallel with the marginalia employed in many texts that add interpretation, understanding and illumination to them. It is possible to understand marginalisation as providing an opportunity for the construction of socio-political marginalia. As a social worker having a responsibility for illuminating the experiences of those on the margins and interpreting them through the lenses of those people, you can inscribe and/or read the human notes in the margins of society and publish these widely. Social work is, as we argue throughout this book, a political activity and becoming marginal is often necessary for seeking a *liberation perspective* (Freire, 1972). Whilst this may sound romantic, the pain and distress that people experience must be our guide to action, and seeking their alleviation through political, social, community and individual change is our role as social workers.

Marginalisation expands the lexicon of thinking that we have about people's experiences and the social divisions that contribute to these. It allows a more nuanced understanding of the different ways varied social divisions interact and contribute to the experiences of individuals, families, groups and communities. Like Ahmed and Rogers (2016), we understand the concept to move beyond previous explanatory frameworks which tended to focus on normative approaches to social divisions such as race/ethnicity, gender and sexuality and class to acknowledge complexity. Whilst focusing primarily on health and social care, they state:

> We use the term 'marginalisation' to denote the dynamics and processes which makes experiences of accessing health and social care services problematic for less heard groups in society, but it has wider application. Marginalisation also relates to social status, and can arise through being born into particular groupings in society (for example, ethnic group), but for others it can be acquired through becoming disabled or by changes in the economic system.
>
> (Ahmed and Rogers, 2016:12)

It is this wider use that we take in this book.

There are links between marginalisation and the concepts of discrimination and oppression, the latter of which are well traversed in social work. In the next section we will consider these and then move forward to discuss the associated discourses of intersectionality and super-diversity, illustrating how they relate to the core concepts that we are using: disadvantage and marginalisation.

Discrimination, oppression, intersectionality and super-diversity

It is often assumed without question that discrimination is wrong. However, it is important to remember that discrimination is value-neutral: there is both legitimate and unfair discrimination (Benatar, 2012). An example will help illustrate this idea. Think of a fine artist developing her colour palette and seeking to choose the best shade of pink to show the late-evening sky. This artist would discriminate between the various shades until she found the right one. So, discrimination is concerned with choosing and privileging the choices made. It is in the act of privileging that discrimination can become unfair if the treatment meted out to one individual is different to that given to another if the criterion for judging and offering that treatment is based on a social or cultural characteristic or division. Again, an example will help here.

Case study

Bahija was a young mother with a toddler, Yehya, who was expressing a range of behavioural difficulties. He had tantrums that often ended with him being aggressive and biting and kicking his mother and young friends at the local toddler group. This had become so concerning that other parents were withdrawing from contact and Bahija was feeling isolated. She agreed to a referral to the social services department for some help in managing his behaviour. Jadwiga was experiencing similar difficulties with Stefan and had also agreed to a referral for support.

Both Bahija and Jadwiga were offered a visit from social worker Tom. Both accepted and Bahija's husband took time off work to meet Tom when he visited. Jadwiga's partner was unable to attend as he was working away at the time. Tom was able to offer both Bahija and Jadwiga a one-to-one programme of behavioural work. However, he could only undertake this at certain times and Bahija was unable to accept because her husband could not be there at the time. The social work team was very busy and there were no other female workers available. It was not possible to offer her support at this time although it was possible to offer support to Jadwiga. Bahija was asked to remove Yehya from the toddler group because he was disrupting the other children too much.

Whilst both mothers were offered help and support, Bahija's cultural needs to work with a woman could not be accommodated, meaning that she got less of a service than Jadwiga, for whom working with a man was acceptable. Bahija's and Yehya's needs were not met and on the basis of a cultural characteristic that support was unavailable. This represents unfair discrimination regardless of the good intentions of Tom and the social work team.

Discussions concerning discrimination can become quite controversial, complex and difficult to deal with. Try to think through some of the issues in the following activity.

Activity 1.4

Read the following case study and follow the hyperlink to the newspaper article: http://www.guardian.co.uk/society/2012/nov/26/ukip-fostering-row-couple-apology. After you have read the case and article consider:

1. Were the actions of the social worker justifiable?
2. Was the social worker discriminatory and if so, was this discrimination fair or unfair?
3. How might a social worker act in a complex and contested situation such as this?

In November 2012 two foster parents from South Yorkshire had three foster children removed from them after the social worker discovered they were members of UKIP. The social worker was concerned that the children would be at risk of psycho-social harm if they were exposed to racist ideology and believed that UKIP presented such a risk. The couple complained, and the actions of the social worker were subject to question by political leaders of different parties and the matter was investigated by the council.

Comment

This is a complex case and your duty as a social worker is to ensure the safety and wellbeing of the children. This means protection from psychological harm and damage as much as from physical harm. The case was extremely complex and the social worker took action to ensure that the children's cultural and ethnic needs were preserved. However, whatever we may think of UKIP and its destructive ideologies concerning ethnicity and immigration, it is a legal political party in the UK and a decision to bar someone from foster care on the basis of membership alone would constitute unfair discrimination, although it would not be unfair to prevent someone who expressed pernicious and racist views becoming a foster carer.

The questions attached to this activity are designed to make you think and reflect. There are no easy answers and, as social workers, we must return to the ethical and moral base on which social work rests and seek professional and supervisory support when faced with complex cases such as this one.

Thompson (2016) recognises that discrimination is in itself a neutral term and that, as we have noted, it is *unfair* discrimination that is generally considered in the social work literature. Recognised differences become the basis for differential and disadvantageous treatment of people as a result of the evaluation of certain characteristics. Thompson adds the complex concept of power to this mix, which allows him to develop his holistic model of discrimination and oppression that acknowledges the interaction of psychological/personal prejudices, cultural and organisation perspectives and the embedded assumptions within social structures. Before we move to explore Thompson's (2016) personal/cultural/social (PCS) model, it is sufficient to say that oppression at these levels leads to the marginalisation of individuals from a place in society in which they may exert influence or have a say.

Personal/cultural/social aspects of discrimination

Neil Thompson developed an interactive and intertwined model of discrimination and oppression in which, importantly, he pointed out that it was not just the personal prejudices of individuals that could be labelled as sexist, racist or ageist and other social characteristics. Rather, he explained that racism, sexism, ageism and disablism were ingrained within the structures of society which influence the cultures and communities that people live in and that both of these influenced individual behaviours and beliefs. He also indicated that this was multi-directional. That is, personal beliefs also reflect back on organisations and communities developing a particular ethos within them and individuals and communities or cultures reflect back on society and the ways in which the structures of society are reimagined (Thompson, 2016). Sometimes the impact of community and personal prejudices is seen in nationalism, populism and reactions to it. For instance, note the rise in right-wing populism throughout Europe since the introduction of austerity measures in 2008 and in particular in England during the 2016 referendum on membership of the European Union. However, more often this recursive form of social construction influences individual, community and societal thought and behaviour in more subtle ways in which it is difficult to unravel the complex origins of taken-for-granted approaches to a range of social characteristics and divisions.

Anti-oppressive practice

Another important approach to working with structural causes of unfair treatment stems from anti-oppressive practice. The work of Lena Dominelli and Neil Thompson has been seminal in embedding this within the repertoire of social workers in the UK and beyond, but it is worth exploring where this has come from. Social work has a long history of concern for oppressed people across a range of areas. Throughout the literature one can see a transformation in the latter half of the twentieth century. Social work has shifted from individually focused methods and casework (Perlman, 1957; Biestek, 1961; Hollis, 1964), approaches that now underpin a much-needed contemporary focus on the human, through to a more overtly political, predominantly Marxist, approach, labelled *radical social work* (Bailey and Brake, 1975;

Corrigan and Leonard, 1978). This has had a resurgence recently through the neo-Marxist work of Lavalette (2011) and Ferguson (2008) and spawned the critical perspectives school (Ife, 1997; Fook, 2016). Interspersed between the relational and political has been an emphasis on particular aspects of discrimination such as anti-racism (Dominelli, 2008; Bartoli, 2013), feminist perspectives in social work (Dominelli and McLeod, 1989; Langan and Day, 1992; Milner, 2001) and ageism (Thompson, 2005).

The concept that draws much of this thinking and practice together is formulated as anti-discriminatory or anti-oppressive practice. The terms are distinct rather than synonymous but are often used interchangeably (Dalrymple and Burke, 2006; Clifford and Burke, 2009; Parker, 2010). Anti-discriminatory practice tends to focus on specific characteristics and issues experienced by people but, as we will see later, individuals experience the world in multifarious ways depending on their life histories and biographies; people are not focused on a single issue. Thus anti-oppressive practice tends to consider people's negative experiences of power, its abuse, in intersecting, non-hierarchical ways. This understanding helps us conceptualise marginalisation in terms of power disadvantages resulting from societal, organisational and individual responses to social characteristics and divisions (see Thompson, 2016 and the PCS model above).

This approach to understanding the positions and contexts of those who are marginalised within and from society and others is expanded and taken further by emerging models of intersectionality and super-diversity, to which we will now turn.

Intersectionality

Romero (2017) argues that previous one-dimensional approaches to social discrimination and inequality, those that focus just on one characteristic or part of a person's identity and experience, are no longer viable. One can question whether such understandings were ever viable, although it is important to acknowledge the need to focus on particularly pertinent social differences at specific times as long as the interplay of others is not ignored. Romero says that we need to consider the dynamic interplay of all systems of social disadvantage and discrimination to understand how these interact within individuals, forming their experiences of life, and the impacts they have on them. The importance of this understanding is emphasised by Hill Collins and Bilge (2016), building on the earlier work of Anderson and Hill Collins (2007), who focus primarily on the intersection and interaction of race, class and gender, describing this as a *matrix of domination*:

> *A matrix of domination posits multiple, interlocking levels of domination that stem from the societal configuration of race, class and gender relations.*

> (Romero, 2017:5)

As Fook (2016) explains, the term 'intersectionality' is a fairly recent introduction into the lexicon of discrimination and disadvantage. Indeed, she recognises that it was first attributed to Crenshaw (1991), when looking at the ways race and gender interacted to compound the negative social experiences of Black American women. Ahmed and Rogers (2016) expand it as a means of understanding how the range of different social positions people occupy overlap, forming multiple layers of experience and identity construction. They consider intersectionality to be very useful when looking at marginalisation and how this can be understood for a variety of perspectives. The concept of multiple oppressions and the tensions perceived in respect of hierarchical approaches has been debated overtly within social work since the 1990s in ways which extended the range of intersecting categories of inequality and oppression (Dalrymple and Burke, 2006; Parker, 2010). Unfortunately, some of these debates have tended to drive certain groups to the margins or to claim an enduring special status for one group or another, but not to see the multiplying effects of interlocking social divisions.

A useful addition to the debate, cited by Fook, comes from the sociologist Nasar Meer (2014), who usefully separates structural intersectionality, which concerns inequalities between different social groups, and political intersectionality, which relates to the political agendas that stem from multiple structural inequalities. Unfortunately, of course, many of those political agendas may attempt to divert attention away from the structural aspects of a person's, group's or community's oppression and marginalisation.

Super-diversity

The concept of super-diversity came to prominence in 2007 when Stephen Vertovec (2007a, b) employed it as a summary term in the context of global changing migration patterns, indicating that these changes are wider than simply identifying expanding numbers of ethnicities, languages and countries of origin within a host country, but also include

> a multiplication of significant variables that affect where, how and with whom people live. In the last decade the proliferation and mutually conditioning effects of a range of new and changing migration variables shows that it is not enough to see 'diversity' only in terms of ethnicity, as is regularly the case both in social science and the wider public sphere. In order to understand and more fully address the complex nature of contemporary, migration-driven diversity, additional variables need to be better recognized by social scientists, policy-makers, practitioners and the public. These include: differential legal statuses and their concomitant conditions, divergent labour market experiences, discrete configurations of gender and age, patterns of spatial distribution, and mixed local area responses by service providers and residents. The dynamic interaction of these variables is what is meant by 'super-diversity'.

(Vertovec, 2007a:1025)

The concept has grown in significance, as Vertovec (2014) highlights that over 300 publications have employed the term 'super-diversity' since 2007. Use has been global, spanning many different disciplines and used in many different ways, from expanding focus on ethnicities to complex and multi-layered concerns with contemporary society. Indeed, at the University of Birmingham there is a research institute, IRiS, dedicated to studies of super-diversity (**http://www.birmingham.ac.uk/research/activity/superdiversity-institute/ index.aspx**). Vertovec identifies that the term is used in many different ways, from referring to increased diversity, increased ethnic distinctions, moving beyond ethnicities, recognising the changed socio-political conditions in which diversity is experienced and responded to, or relating to complexity in contemporary life. Expanding the concept further, Meissner and Vertovec (2015) edited a special journal collection that explores the developing uses of the concept of super-diversity.

This multi-layered complex concept of super-diversity helps us in understanding the culture of social work practice. It can no longer be seen as a means of either supporting and enabling or regulating one section of a society or one group of people. It offers a perspective in which social work can challenge its privileged position in society in order to campaign against the disadvantage and marginalisation of the 'other'. It helps to offer a path to social work in moving towards a complex understanding of diverse groups of peoples presenting perhaps at a macro and meso level particular ethnicities, genders, sexualities, chronicities, capabilities, religions, spiritualities, and so forth.

We have argued elsewhere, however, that the danger of uncritical application of a super-diversity concept occurs when complex, varied differences are accepted without critique as explanations of behaviour when there are clear dangers for individuals and families (Parker et al., forthcoming). The lack of questioning and critique was highlighted, for instance, as far back as the Climbié Inquiry (Laming, 2003), in which the failure to challenge dangerous cultural beliefs was implicated in the circumstances that led to the tragic death of Victoria. Again, as we stress throughout this book, the importance of reflexivity on behalf of the practitioner is important if we are to offset such potential problems.

Super-diversity shares much, as you will note, with intersectionality and anti-oppressive practices in that these concepts seem to move beyond the simple, single-focus ideas of race and ethnicity, age, gender and capability. There is a recognition of complexity, something that all social workers need to bear in mind when working on today's complex world of work, service users and socio-political demands.

When we start to apply our understanding to the ways in which people become marginalised, much of the preceding discussion can be understood using the thinking of the influential French social theorist Pierre Bourdieu concerning social practices (1977). He posited a complex interrelationship of *habitus* (long-lasting ways of thinking and doing that come from life experience), capital (the different resources and capabilities one has in different circumstances), field (the areas in which one lives and operates) and *doxa* (the unspoken assumptions that often guide our thoughts and behaviours) (Bourdieu, 1977; Bourdieu and Wacquant, 1999). These are explored in greater depth when we come to look at the processes by which people become marginalised in Chapter 3.

Why do disadvantage and marginalisation matter to social workers?

To be disadvantaged is, as we have seen, perhaps something that many people would not wish to consider themselves to be. However, it is intimately connected with marginalisation, both leading to it and flowing from it. To be disadvantaged implies the removal from a person of that which is necessary to function in ways that other people can and do expect from others.

As we will be exploring throughout the book, social workers often stand out because they stand alongside others in vulnerable and liminal positions (Parker, 2007). Indeed, it may be argued that social workers represent a group, potentially, of marginalised people (see Chapter 2), although this is more complex, given the power and authority that people who use social work services recognise within social workers. Social workers, rather like the Roman god of two faces, Janus, are both on the edges of and integral to contemporary social structures and systems.

Chapter summary

In this chapter we have explored the core concepts of disadvantage and marginalisation, examining a range of meanings in contemporary society and looking at the impact these experiences may have on the lives of individuals and groups. Alongside our examination of disadvantage and marginalisation we have considered wider concepts of anti-discriminatory and anti-oppressive practice, intersectionality and super-diversity to explore the interrelationships between people's experiences. We are using the term 'disadvantage' to refer to unfair disadvantages calculated to have a negative effect on specific people and groups and to favour others. It is associated with inequity in treatment imposed externally to the person and not the result of an inherent deficit. Our exploration of marginalisation led to understanding the concept as moving beyond previous explanatory frameworks, which tended to focus on normative and often singular approaches to social divisions on the basis of race/ethnicity, gender and sexuality, and class, to acknowledge complexity in individuals' lives. In the following chapter we consider who might be marginalised or disadvantaged before looking at how this might occur.

Further reading

Ahmed, A. and Rogers, M. (eds.) (2016) *Working with Marginalised Groups*. Basingstoke: Palgrave.

This excellent, short edited collection brings a range of practical and theoretical insights into our understanding of marginalisation and offers ways of working with people who find themselves on the edges of society.

Thompson, N. (2016) *Anti-Discriminatory Practice*, 6th ed. Basingstoke: Palgrave.

The latest edition of Thompson's seminal work explores the PCS model in depth and applies it to various social divisions commonly encountered in social work practice. Thompson's clear and erudite approach makes this a useful starting point when considering anti-discriminatory and anti-oppressive practice.

2: Who are the disadvantaged and marginalised people?

Achieving a social work degree

This chapter will help you to develop the following capabilities, to the appropriate level, from the Professional Capabilities Framework.

Professionalism

Recognise your professional limitations and how to seek advice.

Values and ethics

Manage potentially conflicting or competing values, and, with guidance, recognise, reflect on and work with ethical dilemmas.

Diversity

Understand how an individual's identity is informed by factors such as culture, economic status, family composition, life experiences and characteristics, and take account of these to understand their experiences, questioning assumptions where necessary.

Rights, justice and economic wellbeing

Recognise the impact of poverty and social exclusion and promote enhanced economic status through access to education, work, housing, health services and welfare benefits.

Knowledge

Recognise the short- and long-term impact of psychological, socio-economic, environmental and physiological factors on people's lives, taking into account age and development, and how this informs practice.

It will also introduce you to the following academic standards as set out in the social work subject benchmark statement.

5.2.iii Social work theory
5.3vi Values and ethics
5.4.i–v Service users and carers
5.5 The nature of social work practice

In this chapter we examine who and which groups may be described as disadvantaged or marginalised and in what ways. We explore socio-cultural and psycho-social factors, including: poverty, ethnicity and migration status; educational attainment and capacity; (un)employment status; health status; (dis)abilities; gender and sexualities; systems of belief and culture (religious, behavioural and political); subcultural involvement; intra-familial marginalisation, bullying, abuse and self-marginalisation. This overview leads into the next chapter, which seeks to understand why people become disadvantaged or marginalised. However, prior to that we will take a brief historical tour to understand where contemporary British social work is located in the long continuum of care in the community relating to how need was constructed and how the needy themselves were viewed.

Changes in British social work

If one were to ask the general public what kind of people British social workers work with, it is quite likely that their guess would be reasonably accurate in mentioning children, older people and probably people with disabilities or infirmities of various sorts. Open any social work textbook and there is a fair chance that many similarities would be observed over the years in terms of professional interventions and the groups of people/groups in receipt of them. This is not altogether surprising as the problems that beset people today, to the extent of calling for or receiving outside help, are not so very far removed from the problems that people have often experienced over time.

What has changed is how such care is framed in politicised discourses and how regulated and controlled care provision is as doled out in contemporary society. Social work in Britain is not a discipline that delights in taking a retrospective look, if only to see where it has come from in order to plot where it is going. More's the pity, as it is hard to learn from past lessons when these are not really known; consequently we would argue that a historical understanding of social need and social welfare is key knowledge for informed and empowered social workers.

Instead, owing to a highly restrictive social work curriculum, which, like a Chinese panda, boasts a great appetite for a very narrow diet, there are often neat and false divisions made between social work as academic and social work as practice. Elevating the practical and pragmatic aspects of the social work job is one that recent governments and local authorities emphasise, usually by downplaying and denigrating the intellectual, philosophical aspects of this otherwise complex and nuanced profession. One can easily see why that should be: social workers, by the very virtue of their role, and social work itself in straddling so many fault lines in a society riven by inequities, may both be viewed by their very nature as subversive.

Being subversive is an excellent thing to be, when there are clearly so many wrongs to right, and where those wrongs are ingrained at institutional, structural levels. However, it also represents a threat to the established order and thus taming social work into a dull and compliant workforce seems the main aim of much of the government critique that has been aimed at social work education and social workers from political parties. A 'pragmatic' (uncritical), 'efficient' (uncreative/unimaginative) social services of practitioners dutifully gluing down the fraying corners and seams of society, and daily keeping bureaucratic local authority engines stoked up, regardless of the quality and the purpose of what adulterated products are being generated and for whom, is a comforting idea to some maybe. To social workers and those who use their services, hopefully such a vision is anathema and one to be resisted.

Social work has never been about being comfortable. It has been and should remain a proudly maverick profession. One that at times walks a thorny path and is often confronted by perplexing crossroads, where failures will occur from time to time, as is to be expected in any domain of human, not supernatural, agency; but much more often progress and success will feature large in our undertakings.

In Chapter 1 we raised the somewhat controversial notion of social workers as also representing a group of marginalised people. While clearly debatable, this is not a metaphor too far. The social work role has always been one of contradiction and paradox. Social workers act as advocates and also police people. They serve as access points to services and help to reimagine the lives of under-privileged service users. At the same time they act as gatekeepers to those services by 'assessing needs', which in reality means that only those whose needs meet a certain threshold or are viewed as legitimised will be met. In Britain, the majority of social workers will work in state-run services, rather than the independent and non-government sector. Consequently, social workers also occupy a troubled and contested space in both working for the state and seeking to temper its greater injustices and inequities.

The stigmatisation of social work derives in large part from its direct association with those generally deemed as under-privileged people: the perceived deviant, the lost and the ill.

Those seen as marginal survivors and outcasts tend to generate discomfiting feelings in others – a normal human empathic response. In a positive fashion this can energise our social conscience and give rise to active remedies to help others or ameliorate suffering. An alternative response is that the witnessing or hearing of suffering in turn can create such conflicting emotions in individuals that aversion and avoidance result. Or indeed sometimes a mixture of the two occurs, which charities (corporatised businesses in themselves) exploit by seeking to create discomfort in viewers with miserable images of pain, which are soothed by the application of £5 electronically sent. In social workers (and other personnel involved in emotional labour) empathic distress created by too much or intense exposure to service user pain and suffering lies at the root of emotional 'burn-out' (Wacker and Dziobek, 2016), leading to stress and illness.

Activity 2.1

Has there ever been a time, whether at home, school or university or in the workplace, that you felt you really should speak out about something going on that you knew to be not right? Think back about the way you acted then and why. Would you do the same again?

Comment

Now and again we have second-hand information or find ourselves in situations where we feel uncomfortable that perhaps something is happening that is not quite right. If this takes place in a social work/social care context then one obvious option could be to fall back on both our professional values and our professional codes of ethics to help us decide what to do. However, there are also reasons why professionals decide not to act: sometimes it is because of our worries about getting a colleague into trouble; sometimes it is because of an unspoken professional 'rule' of the need for professionals to 'close ranks' if problems loom; and again, it may be because 'whistle blowers' have been punished for their deeds by being labelled as troublemakers and not infrequently sacked.

The stigma of social work, however, is not solely attributed to those who dedicate themselves to working with those inhabiting the interstices of affluent society. Individually, of course, some social workers may be viewed as contemporary saints by those who know them, but social work is not regarded in itself as saintly, for all the reasons previously outlined. Its remit is too contradictory, its roles are too ambivalent and, as a social institution, it is too ambiguous for easy and unalloyed public approval. Social workers must therefore find within themselves and collectively ways of negotiating these uncertainties in their development of professional skills, wisdom and harnessed human compassion – a topic we consider in greater depth in Chapter 6.

Who are they? Living at the margins

The rich man in the castle

The poor man at his gate

God made them high or lowly

And ordered their estate

(All Things Bright and Beautiful, 1848)

The poor, as Mark's Gospel (14:7) points out, have always been with us – so too the sick, the infirm, the friendless and the homeless. This apparently inevitable state of affairs is pithily summed up in the otherwise cheerful Victorian hymn, *All Things Bright and Beautiful*, where poverty is so permanent a feature of human society that it is ascribed to divine will. This is not to say that the permanent presence of human suffering has been tolerated with indifference throughout time; there have been numerous ways in which succour (help) has been offered and received. In his history of social work Payne (2005) notes that the established nexus of help in medieval England was monasteries and churches which were essential to the Christian duty of mercy, as exemplified by the figure of Jesus Christ in his care of outcast and sick people, and in specific references to the stories of his miracle healing of the sick. Monasteries provided shelter, food and skilled herbal remedies – the very beginnings of a kind of hospital care. However, at that time in Andalusia, the medieval European capital of cultural civilisation, medical specialisms and organised hospitals had already been established by the Arab Moors for their multi-faith citizens (Ashencaen Crabtree et al., 2016).

Ecclesiastical care continued up until the time of the dissolution of the monasteries under Henry VIII's Reformation period. This deliberately paved the way for the deposing of Henry's old Queen, Catherine of Aragon, to install his new Queen, Anne Boleyn, by rupturing the ties of former Catholic England to Rome. This heralded in Protestantism, which then permitted Henry's divorce to proceed. Monasteries were wealthy places and so idleness and corruption were levied as excuses against the monks, but once these places of sanctuary were closed to the vulnerable people they served, it was no longer only the monks who were left destitute and helpless.

New measures were called for and from the fifteenth to the nineteenth centuries sweeping changes were made to the institutionalisation of formal relief. Following the Reformation, the gap in welfare left by the monasteries required some organised response from authorities. This now revolved around the local parish, where once again an important ecclesiastical presence, in the form of the main neighbourhood church, provided the boundaries for eligibility of care. Thus the parish related to those communities served by particular churches, and the parish itself became an institutionalised hub, which allocated whatever community relief of poverty, and related ills, was deemed necessary to relieve those who lived in it.

Despite the hardships of poverty and the reaping by high mortality rates, the population grew immensely from 1801 (Jackson, 1998). In 100 years the population rose from just about 10 million people in England and Wales (the majority of whom were rurally based) to 35 million, the majority of whom were urban dwellers (Jackson, 1998; Harris, 2004). The exponential demographic changes brought sharp rises in the numbers of the poor, leading to a demand for welfare reform.

Immense social upheaval in England had brought in the Poor Laws, which continued to be revised periodically right up until the nineteenth century. The more enlightened Elizabethan Poor Law, in comparison to later harsher changes, provided a relatively liberal interpretation of how the parish needy should be assisted by its community (Fraser, 2009). For example, 'outdoor relief' (with two minor exceptions) and the early Georgian Speenhamland system, which was designed to supplement the low wages of agricultural workers, were swept away (Harris, 2004; Fraser, 2009). Individuals and families who petitioned for parish help would now be classified according to need, with the assumption that the community had a moral and religious responsibility to care for its own during times of trouble.

Under the Elizabethan Poor Laws this categorisation had demarcated potential recipients of parish support into 'impotent' (helpless) and 'potent' (able-bodied) groups. The impotent were those such as the elderly impoverished, infirm, sick, the insane[1] and orphans – none of whom could reasonably be expected to look after themselves. The able-bodied 'potent' were expected to support themselves through gainful livelihoods, while it was recognised that poor harvests and unemployment caused temporary but severe hardship that required local support. Almshouses (a form of early supported lodgings), workhouses, apprenticing of orphans to a trade (a most important security measure for future skilled employment) and 'outdoor relief' were all applied as remedial support. For those deemed to be 'potent' but wilfully idle and recidivist, the House of Correction would provide basic subsistence along with a 'sharp shock' remedy (Rothman and Morris, 1995).

The amended Poor Law of 1834 saw a much stricter welfare policy than the liberal, rural-focused Elizabethan one. This now became based on a highly censorious moral position that viewed destitution as a personal failing rather than the later interpretation of being primarily structural, or the earlier interpretation as just an inevitable feature of life's exigencies. These new reforms swept away 'outdoor relief', where families once received support in the form of basic provision: food, clothing as well as money, which enabled them to remain at home. Now whole families would be accommodated in the dreaded workhouse, where husbands would be separated from wives and children from parents in the punitive 'care' and rehabilitation of the incorrigible poor (Fraser, 2009). As Charles Dickens points out in *A Christmas Carol* (1843), some preferred to die of starvation rather than resort to the workhouse, so appalling

---

[1] Bethlehem Hospital, later notoriously known as Bedlam, then a semi-rural institution on the outskirts of a small London, was established as a Tudor institution for the insane.

and stigmatising was its reputation. Nineteenth-century fiction routinely emphasised the fundamental punitive degradation of the workhouse, where, for instance, the forlorn and abandoned Fanny Robin, in Thomas Hardy's *Far from the Madding Crowd*, dies in childbirth in Casterbridge. The same fate is reserved for Oliver Twist's ill-used but genteel young mother (Dickens, 1838). The Houses of Correction, such as Bridewell Prison in London, were retained for both men and women, imposing hard labour for those deemed 'underserving' as well as being a disciplinary sentence for a variety of offenders.

The Poor Laws were premised upon classification of petitioners for institutionalised (meaning organised, not just institutionally based) support. The concepts of 'deserving' and 'underserving' were viewed as important yardsticks by which to measure the need, and particularly the needy themselves. While this moral positioning has been strongly critiqued, arguably it remains firmly entrenched, with very clear overtones found in contemporary social policy discourses on welfare provision. The miseries of the new forms of urban poverty in the nineteenth century and the ramifications of the Industrial Revolution, as well as rural, agricultural poverty (the source of the Tolpuddle Martyrs' discontent) were clearly not addressed by the changes to the Poor Law Act of 1834. It would not be until much later, following the Beveridge Report of 1942, that the entire reshaping of the welfare landscape of post-war Britain would take place.

Prior to that, the scourges of cholera and typhus due to contamination of water supplies by human and animal waste led to greatly improved sanitation measures through the same splendid Victorian engineering feats that drain public waste today (Black, 1996). The earlier findings of the 1833 Factory Commission Report began the gradual reprieve of the exposure of young children to extremely long hours of arduous and often dangerous work in factories (Fraser, 2009). However, the exploitation of and cruelty towards child domestic servants (as depicted in the early twentieth-century children's novel, *A Little Princess*, by Frances Hodgson Burnett, published in 1905) were not addressed by factory reform legislation.

Other social welfare reforms were often led by the earnest and often fiery Christian sensibilities of middle-class reformers campaigning on leading issues of the day. Thus the Quaker, Elizabeth Fry, led prison reforms; and Josephine Butler campaigned on the scandalous issues of child prostitution and sexual health (including oppressive measures targeting women) (Payne, 2005). Social housing was strongly campaigned for by Octavia Hill, who was appalled by the disease-laden squalour and overcrowding of accommodation for the urban poor (Harris, 2004). It was during the Victorian period that so many well-known charities commenced, including the Royal Society for the Protection of Cruelty against Animals (RSPCA), the Young Men's Christian Association (YMCA), Royal National Lifeboat Institution (RNLI), Dr Barnardo's and the Salvation Army. Several decades elapsed before the National Society for the Prevention of Cruelty to Children (NSPCC) came into being following the establishment of the RSPCA – a telling point regarding social values of the time.

So prolific was the rise of charitable bodies that by 1861 there were 640 charitable bodies in London alone (Fraser, 2009). The bewildering number and overlapping remit of these charities gave rise to a concern for a more efficient and effective system of charitable relief. In 1869 the Charities Organisation Society (COS), generally known as the forerunner of modern social casework, was founded (Orme, 2001). However, its original title provides an insight into the moral stance that COS stood for: Society for the Organisation of Charitable Relief and Repressing Mendicity (*mendicity* means idleness, rather than the similar-sounding but very different word, *mendacity*[2]).

The main aims of COS were threefold: preventing the duplication of the work of local charities (organisation); investigating and assessing genuine cases of need (social casework); and finally, the education and reform of recipients of charity to prevent welfare dependency (rehabilitation).

Nominally working in harness with the Poor Law, the COS brought a certain accountability to charitable welfare through their organised approach and investigation of the backgrounds of recipients (the detection of 'welfare scroungers' of the day); the moral high ground of power and control remained firmly in the hands of COS rather than recipients. In J.B. Priestley's (1945) famous play of moral retribution, *An Inspector Calls*, the plot gradually reveals, through the interrogation by the enigmatic inspector, the damning sequence of events, based on prejudice and power, that lead to the suicide of a wronged young woman turned callously from charitable help in her hour of greatest need.

Charity alone was entirely incapable of addressing the levels of under-privilege in a nation state of such great industrial might, which was only equalled by great welfare need. Studies of entrenched, absolute poverty challenged the COS assumption that moral rectitude and self-sufficiency, with the occasional charitable helping hand, were sufficient to overcome 'want' (poverty). Death by starvation had been portrayed in the nineteenth-century novels of Elizabeth Gaskell, such as the novel *Mary Barton* (1848), where she wrote of the privations of working-class families in Northern manufacturing towns. Factual information, however, required social investigation in the form of household visits and surveys. A more systematic understanding of the needs of impoverished families was required, along with the development of theoretical concepts and classifications of poverty, which arose from many of these early studies.

A form of social case study was first exemplified in Scotland by the impassioned and charismatic church minister, Thomas Chalmers, founder of the Free Church of Scotland, who brought mission zeal to his parish work in Glasgow in 1815 (Payne, 2005). Chalmers' concern for his impoverished parishioners motivated, among other good works, home visits to each one of over 2,000

---

[2]The playwright Tennessee Williams (1955) sums up the definition of 'mendicity' in his play *Cat on a Hot Tin Roof*, where the main character, Brick, refers to 'mendicity' as referring to 'lies and liars' – which, in connection with the manipulations of politicians, is now notoriously renamed 'alternative facts'.

households under his ecclesiastical care. In London William Booth, founder of the Salvation Army, undertook surveys of Tower Hamlets, East London and Hackney in 1886 and 1887, developing the concept of a 'poverty line' in consequence. His work drew shocking comparisons between the levels of care given to working animals (cab horses) and the far inferior care of millions of contemporary Britons (Fraser, 2009). As Prochaska (2006) points out, Victorian social welfare and the early inquiries into need were both intimately bound up with Christian fidelity to their faith and the desire to demonstrate Christianity in action by alleviating suffering.

Commensurately, at the turn of the century, a scion of the wealthy Quaker confectionery family, Seebohm Rowntree undertook a study of poverty in York in 1901 (published as *Poverty: A Study of Town Life*), where his figures tallied with that of Charles Booth's investigation of London poverty, in estimating that around a third of the urban population lived in marked poverty. Still later, following the conflagration of the First World War, the millions of subsequent deaths from Spanish flu and the agonies of the Depression, George Orwell wrote his polemic, *The Road to Wigan Pier* (1937), drawing on a rich tradition of social inquiry to detail the poverty and miseries of the mining families he visited in Lancashire in the 1930s. The notion that individual fecklessness or personal bad luck was largely responsible for poverty was shown to be a deeply inadequate explanation for the ragged armies of the poor nationally.

If the First World War left in its wake only a new lexicon of muted agony at the scale of carnage and loss, accompanied by the death of the optimism and opulence of the Edwardian era, it was the end of the Second World War that saw a marked determination to create a better world in the form of a blueprint for a new welfare state, paid for through social insurance – an idea borrowed from Bismarck's Germany (Fraser, 2009). War was once again waged, but this time under a new Labour Government against the five so-called giants of need: want, disease, squalour, ignorance and idleness.

Today the Welfare State in Britain totters on shaky legs, heavily attacked by successive right-wing governments, supported limply by those on the Left – and publicly mourned by many. Those who can recall the new post-war dawn of Beveridge's Welfare State are now among the oldest of the old in British society. Yet to try to understand how very different life had been for poor families before the National Health Service (NHS) takes a leap of imagination today when contemporary privations seem harsh enough, but where access to free health care is still available to the greatest majority.

Case study

Muriel is a 95-year-old woman who enjoys telling her younger visitors about her working-class childhood in the Wirral, where she left school at 14 to work in the factory of the Lever Brothers in Port Sunlight, gluing the tops on cardboard bottles of Vim. A dead-end job by anyone's standards, yet Muriel knew she was lucky to see her 14th year at all, for when she was 12

Muriel developed sharp pains in her abdomen, which became excruciatingly painful over the next few hours. Her parents hovered around her anxiously for hours but dared not call a doctor to attend her because they simply couldn't afford to pay the doctor's bill. Despite Muriel being the baby of the family, and having already lost Muriel's elder sister in an accident, her parents hesitated so long that by the time they finally called for help, Muriel's appendix had ruptured and the arriving doctor immediately rushed her to hospital. Before the availability of antibiotics, Muriel's life hung delicately in the balance for three long days until she was pronounced out of immediate danger, with a long period of convalescence following. Her parents later told her that during that time she lay in the same ward and indeed in the very next bed to the one her elder sister had died in some years before at the same young age. Muriel later grew up to become a nurse serving in the new NHS.

'Vulnerable' people

It seems only right and fair that scarce social care resources should be allocated to those who really need them and it is in this spirit that one could approach the entire issue of vulnerability and eligibility criteria: that this person, rather than that person, is 'vulnerable' and will therefore receive help. The language of social care encourages this kind of discrimination (to use the word in its proper sense) in order to weigh up levels of need that may be met with an appropriate service, as opposed to types of need that will not receive help. Professional jargon used uncritically can lead to the view that vulnerability is a state of being, an attribute even, and one that belongs only to some and not to others. It becomes logical then that these few are entitled to services and maybe even 'deserve' services – and thus a judgement is made that is designed to sift out the chaff of the many down to the few grains that are left in the sieve, who may now receive services.

The conceptualisation of vulnerability is critically explored by Penhale and Parker (2008), who analyse the term and note that the (now replaced) Care Standards Act 2000 defined vulnerability as applying to those living in care or nursing homes. In addition, this definition includes those who live in their own home and receive domiciliary services and those who receive particular prescribed medical services. In short, it is the professional criteria used which define who is vulnerable, rather than the experience of vulnerability itself; after all, most of us have felt vulnerable at some point. It is little wonder that the term is not used in the Care Act 2014.

Conversely, the label of vulnerability may be applied to individuals regardless of whether they feel vulnerable or not. Thus the question of 'vulnerability' is not only used as a yardstick measurement but also as a label, with all the attendant concerns of reduction to an object and stigma that labelling implies. The act of labelling someone vulnerable can increase that person's vulnerability, while service provision, such as care homes, can create situations of personal vulnerability (see Chapters 3 and 4).

People with learning disabilities

The term 'vulnerable adult' therefore is a loaded one, laden with the burden of professional expectations and agendas that may have little to do with the perceptions of the individual or that person's particular situation. The term itself creates boundaries between need and the obligation to respond if vulnerability is not recognised. The gap between being known, in an abstract sense, to be vulnerable and receiving the levels of support that address vulnerability can be wide. The horrifying case of Steven Hoskin illustrates this well: Steven was a man with learning disabilities who was murdered in 2006 by the 'gang' who had taken up with him. Prior to leading a more independent life, Hoskin lived with his mother in a rural community. Leaving the area, Steven fell in with dangerous company that cruelly preyed upon him. His disreputable new lifestyle, where he seemed to have little control over his own life, even in his own bedsit, seems to have contributed to disguise to the authorities his level of real vulnerability, until it was too late.

Tragically, a not dissimilar case was seen in 2009. Michael Gilbert was another vulnerable man with learning disabilities, who fell in with a terrifyingly abusive family who forcibly imprisoned him and kept him as a grossly maltreated slave up to the point when they murdered him (Jones, 2010).

Finally, we come to the most recent case of Jimmy Prout, yet another vulnerable man with learning disabilities, who was horrifically tortured and then murdered by a group of four people in 2016. His body was dumped and not found for many months. The ring leader of this horrible crime, Zahid Zaman, was described by the sentencing judge as an *evil, vindictive, manipulative and devious man* (BBC, 2017a). A notable aspect of the case that severely challenges our concepts of vulnerability is that Zahid is himself disabled and confined to a wheelchair, but this apparently did not serve to inspire any mercy for his victim; he apparently had no connection of solidarity with his victim from both being vulnerable men.

In the cases of Hoskin and Gilbert, the police and social services were aware of concerns regarding the welfare of these two individuals. Equally, in both cases it seemed that the seriousness of their plight was not understood properly in respect of their learning disabilities, the men's limited understanding of the danger they were in and what options for help might be available to them (Independent Police Complaints Commission, 2011).

A final example of the under-estimation of the dangers facing this group is that of Fiona Pilkington, a woman with learning disabilities, who killed herself and her profoundly learning-disabled daughter in 2007, after years of being terrorised and their home being besieged by aggressive local youths. Once again the Independent Police Complaints Commission found failures in the police and borough council responses, which failed to view the family as vulnerable and to provide an orchestrated robust response to protect them (Walker, 2011).

Such crimes of victimisation fall into the loose category of hate crimes, and people with disabilities and autism are common targets of such crimes as well as exploitation, so-called 'mate crimes', where people are typically bullied and robbed by those they are led to believe are their friends. Steven Hoskin, Michael Gilbert and Jimmy Prout were subject to this kind of abuse early on in the relationships of abuse that served to entrap them further.

The Crown Prosecution Service has since attempted to create a criminal justice action plan that seeks to offer a joined-up approach to improve prosecution rates of offenders and to support disabled victims and witnesses. However, the prejudice shown to people with learning disabilities is clearly a serious concern. We hypothesise that, perhaps owing to a lack of other obvious physical disabilities that might inhibit aggression (although this is by no means always the case or to suggest that many forms of abuse are not visited on people with physical disabilities), people with learning disabilities are too often the easy targets or scapegoats of malicious intent.

Thus, public education is an important aspect to address the stigma of disability (and also mental health). However, tackling prejudice effectively needs to be thought through carefully to avoid reinforcing it. MENCAP'S 2017 campaign forms a prime example of this problem, where they have recently launched a series of photographs as part of their public campaign to alter public perceptions of learning disabilities. The character 'Joe' features in one such photograph. 'Joe' is a young man with, one assumes, developmental disabilities, posed in a deliberately belligerent attitude: lips set, eyes staring, hands in the 'come on, then!' street fighter's beckoning gesture, who is apparently spoiling for a brawl. Whatever the original intentions of MENCAP, this image creates an unfortunate suggestion to the viewer that intellectual disabilities can be associated with mindless thuggishness; and thereby the message both underplays the issue of personal vulnerability and replaces it with another questionable association.

A recruit into a new area of social work specialism, one of the authors in a previous incarnation as a social work practitioner, was warned by colleagues that social work with learning disabilities was regarded as low-status compared to child protection or mental health, for example, which was considered much more high-profile and complex work. It was an interesting initiation into understanding the underlying view that the apparent simplicity of people with learning disabilities as individuals was equally translated as being an area of social work practice that must in turn be simple. Moral dilemmas abound in all types of social work and this area is no different from any other. It is true that people with learning disabilities are likely to become 'revolving door' clients, returning for social work support at times throughout their lives, as they reach lifespan milestones, such as leaving home, forming intimate relationships, parenthood and old age.

The levels of vulnerability individuals may experience can overlap with their sense of self and autonomy, and the decisions and choices they may make. As in the case of Michael

Gilbert, poor life decisions do not negate the responsibility of professionals to work with such individuals, even if weak personal insight results in an attempt to cancel the very services, as Steven Hoskin did, that may keep those people a little safer. How, why and what consequences arise from such life decisions by client groups requires critical reflection, which is the hallmark of good social work practice.

Some people with learning disabilities have complex needs and in terms of health and bio-psycho-social concerns a common additional factor among affected people may be mental health problems and substance/alcohol abuse. Galvani and Thurnham (2014) note that not only is the area of substance and alcohol misuse a highly marginal area in social work education, services are also uneven across the two forms of dependence and where the strategy for alcohol misuse is (if the pun will be forgiven) watered down compared to that of substance misuse. The stigma of dependency is viewed as one reason why this area of need is not given much weighting in social work (Galvani and Thurnham, 2014). One could also hypothesise that the condition may well be viewed by professionals as not comparable with disability, for example, and is much more about the consequences of the poor lifestyle choice of autonomous beings. This line of thought inevitably brings us back to the old moral questions of individual fecklessness and desert. This is not to say that such moral questions are irrelevant, but rather that the underlying assumptions of free will, moral agency, consequence, reward and retribution, upon which judgements of the deserving and undeserving rest, need to be thought through critically in relation to the amoral realities of modern welfare, questions of citizenship, provision of and access to health and social care services.

Rough sleepers

An example of the selectiveness of social services relates to that of rough sleepers. This is a conspicuous and growing area of need and we in Britain have become used to the sight of bagged bodies in shop doorways and underpasses, piled together like so much refuse. This sight, probably common enough to our Victorian urban ancestors, is certainly an aspect of late society that even only a few decades ago would not have been so apparent. Once most of the destitute were more likely to be perennial 'gentlemen of the road' who tramped their routes seeking casual work as they went. The poet, Laurie Lee (1969), writes of leaving his home pre-war as a young man from deeply rural Gloucestershire to seek his fortune in London in his delightful autobiography, *As I Walked Out One Midsummer Morning*. Unused to being away from his mother and village, Laurie luckily falls in with Alf, a professional tramp, padded with newspaper and layers of cloth, clanking with paraphernalia, who teaches the *poor little bleeder* how to survive and explains his annual peregrinations around the country, which are as timed to the season as a migrating bird. Orwell (1933) too squeezes a literary, if less lyrical, experience out of his enforced short time on the road in which he spends his time with another forlorn companion, seeking odd jobs and *tea and a slice* (bread and margarine) from housewives while endlessly pacing the byways to find temporary overnight accommodation.

Today's rough sleepers are still much more likely to be men than women, often homeless due to relationship breakdowns, but are now much more numerous than formerly. Few could be described as proper tramps in having opted for or adapted to homelessness; many are young, although the average life expectancy of male rough sleepers is only 47 years old, and for women even younger, at 43 (Crisis, 2011). Vulnerability to addiction, violence, suicide, exploitation, traffic accidents and mental illness are ubiquitous hazards facing rough sleepers (Crisis, 2011).

Asylum seekers

Destitution is a common fate threatening refugees and asylum seekers entering the UK and the response of social workers to this humanitarian need depends largely on how receptive local authorities are to processing this human flotsam and jetsam. Funding care for asylum seekers is clearly an issue that social workers deal with at the sharp end of local authority financial constraints – a most unwelcome and soul-destroying aspect of the professional remit. Fine calculations can be found on the internet to work out the cost of accommodating children by local authorities, but these overall costs are likely to be considerably higher than the £30,000 the Home Office has provided for unaccompanied child asylum seekers.

Ad hoc 'boxing-and-coxing' strategies to accommodate those asylum seekers lucky enough to be allowed to remain in the country are key social and political concerns in the UK, where the Home Office – usually most deservedly – receives much bad press for decisions that on the face of it are frankly heartless, inhumane and seemingly subject to much capricious, bureaucratic, ill judgement. The international Dublin Regulations sought in turn to clarify the processes by which asylum seekers can claim refugee status in particular countries according to a set of criteria, and thus aimed to prevent countries from being able to reject refugee applications sequentially.

In the UK many asylum seekers arrive in Kent and are then dispersed to large, profit-making, private housing organisations, which are mostly located in the North of England. Refugees are not permitted to work to support themselves and the delay between processing their applications, required for recourse to public support, and the daily realities of survival is partially bridged by charitable organisations like the British Red Cross through remedial, emergency, hand-to-mouth provision. This fragmentary provision means that, while newspapers report the scandal of vermin-infested accommodation into which asylum seekers are herded (Travis, 2017a), faith-based charities along with some local authorities, like Shropshire, have been urging the British public with room to spare to take on the role of a supported lodging carer to look after unaccompanied refugee minors entering the country, whose arrival and care can be highly haphazard and chaotic.

Case study

Afsar, an Afghan minor of 17, entered the UK following the closure of the Calais refugee camp. Under the international Dublin Regulations, the Home Office plan was to reunite him with his uncle and family, also asylum seekers living in the South-West of England. The Red Cross brought Afsar to the local social services duty social worker under Section 17 of the Children Act 1989 to make the handover to Afsar's extended family, who had agreed to accommodate Afsar temporarily only, owing to their uncertain and overcrowded accommodation. Afsar would now be one of six children, together with his aunt and uncle, living in a three-bedroomed rented house.

The duty social worker did not make an additional assessment of need but simply brought him to his uncle's house in the middle of the night and made the exchange on the doorstep with a promise of a domiciliary visit in the near future – a visit that failed to materialise. Afsar does not have recourse to public welfare and without that will not be able to access further support once he reaches his majority, and is currently entirely dependent on his uncle's precarious help. Since Afsar was placed with his uncle the family has been evicted from their rented accommodation and their appeal to the local authorities for help has only resulted in the offer of taking all the children into care if the parents are destitute. This is an unacceptable offer that is viewed by the family as a deterrent against them seeking further local authority help.

Few asylum seekers are free from the taint of stigma that accompanies destitution and desperation on the doorstep of usually unknown host countries. The policy of accepting limited quotas of unaccompanied refugee children has meant that affluent counties like Dorset are only responsible for taking in 54 such children. In turn, herding asylum-seeking families towards privatised housing companies has meant a concentration of such families in certain areas, which may benefit some families through informal help giving, but also creates a high level of exposure demographically, which may not always be welcome within local communities. The highly dubious card played by the Brexit political lobby regarding immigration restrictions must give us pause for thought regarding how to integrate asylum seekers into communities in ways that seek to welcome them and give them dignity and a place at the table of the community. In other words, to be seen as in-coming assets to British society rather than cap-in-hand, beggared petitioners.

Such questions may remain academic, for now the arrival of more children like Afsar has been deliberately blocked by the current Prime Minister, Theresa May, and her government, bringing to an end the 'Dubs' scheme, named after its proponent, Lord Alf Dubs, with the aim of rescuing around 3,000 children from the filth and cold of refugee camps in France, Italy and Greece by bringing them to comparative safety in the UK. Ultimately the British government begrudgingly agreed to take a mere 350 refugee children under the scheme (Travis and Taylor, 2017), although without doubt much more could have been done to help, including concerted motivation galvanising the general public to help actively, however modest their abilities to do so.

Lord Dub's attempt to motivate the British government into making a desperately needed humanitarian gesture arose from his own experiences as a *Kindertransport* refugee child. To return to a comparison of how UK governments have responded to serious refugee crises, compare this shameful political response announced in February 2017 to that made by former Prime Minister Stanley Baldwin in December 1938, following the infamous *Kristallnacht* Nazi pogrom in Germany the month before. Over £522,000 (a colossal sum then) was raised in answer to the call from the concerned, ecumenical British public to help European Jewish children. This provided the impetus for the famous *Kindertransport* movement that sought to rescue endangered children up to the eve of war, when this lifeline was cut by the Nazi invasion of Holland. Prior to that, Prime Minister Neville Chamberlain's government permitted an unlimited number of unaccompanied Jewish children to enter the country under the private sponsorship of ordinary British families who were willing and able to donate £50 (a considerable amount of money then) for each child helped. Many of these 10,000 saved *Kindertransport* children grew up to make a huge contribution to their adopted country and others, among whom were two future Nobel prize winners (Ashencaen Crabtree and Parker, 2013).

Poverty: a social work concern?

The question of poverty no longer appears to be a central theme in social work, although of course it is closely connected to neglect and various other forms of abuse in families. The categorisation of practice areas (safeguarding adults, safeguarding children and so on) tends to obscure the fact that so much of social work has always been involved in attempting to ameliorate poverty and prevent its worst evils. The loss of community work as a central plank to social work, along with probation, has ensured that the topic and consequences of poverty are pushed to the peripheries of social work direct action, where the topic has become almost as marginalised as those who experience poverty (Popple, 2000).

Working with poverty seems to have gone into reverse, where it is once again the concern of charities (and other non-government agencies) offering a modern form of Poor Law 'outdoor relief' in the shape of food banks – resources increasingly being drawn on by a range of people who live in or have fallen on hard times. One of the biggest is the Trussell Trust, which operates over 400 food banks nationally. Their statistics report that 500,000 three-day emergency food packs were delivered in the first half of 2016 – a 2% increase on the previous year (Valadez and Hirsch, 2016).

Food banks directly help impoverished families, where one in four children are now growing up in relative poverty in the UK. The highest numbers are located in the big cities, with London holding the greatest number of children living in poverty (in 2015 Tower Hamlets had the highest number of children in poverty of all the local authorities). Beyond London, Manchester follows, with Birmingham bringing up the rear. Scotland appears to fare reasonably well in relation to child poverty as, perhaps unsurprisingly, do many of the Home Counties (Valadez and Hirsch, 2016).

Urban poverty is arguably more visible and recognised than its rural counterpart. It is easily spotted in its concrete ugliness and graffiti murals, in the squalour of grimy, neglected terraces huddling by main arterial routes; seen in the forlorn and dismal playgrounds cowering in the shadows of encircling post-war tower blocks; found in the boarded-up high streets taken over by cash lenders, budget food shops and second-hand clothing outlets. These are the hallmarks of urban poverty, but cities also contain important infrastructure, outlets, services and facilities that can be accessed relatively cheaply by most people without travelling too far.

Rural poverty is a very different matter: the markers of poverty are less apparent, the countryside has traditionally been viewed as the playground of wealthier classes, and plump and pleasant landscapes viewed from passing trains and cars serve to conceal the hard realities of rural life (Jones, 2013). Poverty in rural areas can be a very different experience from that of the urban conurbations.

Case study

Sherborne is a beautiful and ancient market town, built of mellow, golden stone, standing on the borders of Dorset and Somerset. The town's most glorious son, Sir Walter Raleigh, was, in his time, a well-known advocate for the Sherborne poor. Apart from its two castles, Sherborne is also the home of two famous public schools and a magnificent abbey with probably the best medieval, stone-vaulted ceiling in Europe.

More to the point, Sherborne boasts over 600 years of unbroken community care of the aged and infirm in the form of its lovely St John's Almshouse, where since 1437 a benevolent history continues to embrace its aged local residents with residential care, and has done so each day unfailingly throughout the centuries, regardless of social unrest, civil turbulence and war (Parker et al., 2016b).

All in all, Sherborne is simply a splendid gem of a town in England's crown. Yet, despite its beauty and obvious affluence, as well as being a Tory stronghold, it is a quiet corner of deep rural poverty. From Sherborne Abbey a food bank is organised and delivers around 200 food parcels each month to needy local families, and this need continues to grow.

Delivery is an unusual practice for a food bank but in Sherborne it is a necessity, for there are only two days on which buses will make village runs and outside of those times, if you do not have a car at your disposal, you are effectively cut off from supermarkets, general practitioners, libraries, cinemas, larger schools and colleges, parks and theatres, sport and youth clubs, areas of natural beauty (beyond immediate fields), the famous Dorset coastline, and even the abbey itself, where services of worship run throughout the week.

Moreover, where for the urban poor the internet provides some access to a bigger world and its wealth of information – and can be gained, if only through a public library – by contrast, in rural areas like Sherborne, Wi-Fi reception, even if available, can be so weak that the internet barely works. Thus is rural poverty in all its economic, social, educational and cultural deprivation, where the urban/rural divide is as acute as it ever was, with little sense of effective reprieve given the continual cuts in local services.

Communities on the margin

So far we have considered some groups that fall outside the immediate focus of social work, as it has become in England and Wales, but who nonetheless represent new forms of need as well as representing a hoary continuation of human suffering that welfare responses have long recognised and worked to ameliorate. Now we consider the issue of marginalisation in relation to under-privileged minority groups. Clearly a close and detailed examination of this area lies beyond the boundaries of this book, which here represents not the scope of this topic, but raises representative aspects with implications for social work.

In the novel *Anna Karenina*, Tolstoy (1877) declares that *All happy families are alike; each unhappy family is unhappy in its own way*. We could paraphrase this well-known quote to observe that, while relative privilege is similarly experienced across society, there are different ways in which under-privileged circumstances affect particular groups. Thus to speak of one group does not necessarily infer that other under-privileged groups are subject to the same experiences. With this caveat in mind, we mention two very different but specific groups who can both be regarded as belonging to under-privileged people: Roma Gypsy Travellers and Muslim ethnic minority groups in Britain.

European Gypsy Roma, British Romany and Traveller groups form distinctive groups that are often treated in a similar way and are some of the few remaining groups in the UK (and in other countries as well) who are subject to overt discrimination with impunity in society (Heaslip et al., 2016; Scullion and Brown, 2016).

The question of indigeneity is bound up with some of these issues where, despite current xenophobic nationalist exclusionary discourses, it has to be asserted that the UK is a mongrel nation that has no identifiable indigenous people within it. We could look to the earliest Britons as indigenous, but who were these Neolithic people other than various tribal groups arriving at certain historical moments by walking over the land masses that joined Britain to the rest of continental Europe, or later on by bravely sailing from various hazardous points of embarcation? We could look to the Romano-British prior to the Saxon invasion, but who were they? Various Celtic groups occupying certain parts of the island, who were oppressed by the invading Romans and eventually mixed their blood with Roman settlers. Celtic groups too, of course, were widespread in Europe, having been inveterate migrants themselves, and maybe in so doing displacing earlier settlers. So, in short, we have no indigenous people in Britain; we are all made up of waves of migration who look with welcome, curiosity, askance or with open hostility at the next wave joining us.

If there are no indigenous people in Britain, to make up for it there are many ethnic groups and culturally based lifestyles, some of which have the oldest of pedigrees. Among these are the nomadic Gypsy Roma Travellers, numbering around 58,000 in the UK (Heaslip et al., 2016), who have not only been part of the British landscape for centuries but have for virtually as long been subject to stigma, rejection and, of course, alarming fable.

> My mother says I never should
>
> Play with the gypsies in the wood
>
> If I should, she would say
>
> 'Naughty girl to disobey!
>
> You hair won't curl, your shoes won't shine.
>
> You gypsy girl, you shan't be mine!'

(Traditional children's rhyme)

The old stories of Gypsies as child enticers, or worse, stealers of Christian children form the basis of the famous tale by Victor Hugo (1831) of Quasimodo, the hunchback who lives in the sanctuary of the great Parisian cathedral of Notre Dame. Hugo juxtaposes the story of Quasimodo's hopelessly unrequited love for the beautiful and kindly Gypsy girl, Esmeralda, in opposition to the cruel, destructive lusts of the antagonist that eventually result in her death.

Stigma and prejudice towards Gypsy Roma Travellers are easily detected at the interpersonal level as well as being found in institutional racism (Ashencaen Crabtree, 2017a). Derogatory language, such as 'pikey', is a highly offensive racist term, but nonetheless bandied around with impunity in the way that has been more or less publicly stamped out in respect of abhorrent racist terms like 'Paki' and 'nigger'.

The lifestyles of the Roma are subject to exclusionary and prejudicial tactics. It is commonplace to find height-restricting barriers on public car parks to prevent taller vans and caravans from entering, and potentially leading to camping. Other sites that could be used for camping are subject to a variety of restrictions regarding lighting fires (a key part of Roma culture through an oral tradition of knowledge passed on communally around a camp fire).

Restrictions arbitrarily applied by local authorities keen to discourage nomads are applied regarding water access, toileting and hygiene, preventing people from being able to manage bodily functions properly. Most of these restrictions are framed within the petty bureaucracy of local authority policies and by-laws in their attempt to impose dominant group normativity (what is and should be permitted), which are actually malicious in intent in preventing nomads from being able to use areas that are unused for other purposes (Heaslip et al., 2016). This is institutional racism in action, and in the case of these people, as inferred from Heaslip et al.'s (2016) work, actually constitutes a form of cultural genocide. As such it therefore forms another concern for practitioners as an affront to social work values and principles.

Other aspects of institutional racism include the culturally inflexible state systems, which are not geared up to dealing with the education of Gypsy Roma Travelling children, because this firstly involves getting to grips with how formal education may be understood, valued or used within the cultural framework of their beliefs and expectations. Secondly, it involves adapting education for such groups through specifically mobile and flexibly accessible educational systems.

Health systems too fail to adapt to the needs of Roma groups, to understand their interpersonal communication styles, which may be interpreted as rudeness or belligerence and can thereby be easily denied to those in need. Roma Traveller lifestyles may preclude individuals being able to offer a set home address to a disapproving medical receptionist (Heaslip et al., 2016). Anxiety may be very high among such groups concerning dealing with unsympathetic bureaucrats and alarming health professionals, both of whom are likely to make paternalistic decisions about them in which they have no say, having apparently no obvious place at the table of power in the country where they reside, because they attract little political interest in general.

Another group of people we consider here as subject to under-privilege has, by contrast to Gypsy Roma Travellers, been subject to far greater political and media interest than they could possibly wish for or deserve. We refer of course to British Muslims, whose experiences of migration, social integration and Islamophobic prejudice have relegated this heterogeneous group as likely to experience conspicuous health and social welfare need (Heath and Li, 2014). Although there has been a welcome increase in tertiary-level education for young British Muslims over the past few years (Muslim Council of Great Britain, 2015), there is still a disproportionately high level of income disparity, unemployment and, notably, poorer health affecting Muslim minority ethnic groups in the UK (Laird et al., 2007; Ashencaen Crabtree et al., 2016) in comparison with White Britons and all other minority ethnic groups (Muslim Council of Great Britain, 2015).

Discrimination on the grounds of race/ethnicity has been an ugly facet of society for centuries in one form or another, but is also an unthinking prejudice that has been generally curbed over time by education, legislation and liberal religious interpretation. Such beliefs culminated in modern history in the Holocaust, the genocide of European Jewry under the Third Reich. This stands as both a symbolic and factual monument to the evils of such gross prejudice. It is therefore deeply worrying that once again people are being openly discriminated against on the grounds of their ethnicity and faith.

Accordingly many negative associations have been made against Muslims in the UK, where an almost casual association is made between ordinary Muslims and 'terrorists'. Recent populist propaganda stirring up xenophobic hatred in the UK reminds us of an earlier witch hunt – the rabid paranoia about communism in 1950s America (the 'Red-under-the-bed' syndrome). Today's counterpart serves to fuel anti-immigration feelings and hate crimes by stirring up paranoid notions of the covert Jihadist masquerading as a desperate Syrian refugee fleeing Daesh, for example.

The battle between the Trump administration and the US judiciary has also been carefully monitored, regarding the former's attempt to ban entry of people from particular Middle Eastern countries with the excuse of preventing terrorism. The intention has clearly been to discriminate against Muslims entering the USA, but with the clear ramifications of such a policy for the exclusion and rejection of US Muslims. Despite the objections raised by many in the US judiciary, since the policy came into the public domain a random variety of people, including Muslims and non-Muslims of many different nationalities, have been subject to intimidating and humiliating interrogation by hostile immigration officials, with some refused entry and others very begrudgingly permitted in.

As Orwell (1949) shows us in his book, *1984*, an identified and symbolic scapegoat is a handy strategy for diverting public attention away from the internal problems of state governance and bad political decisions. In this sense, contemporary Muslims are forced to play a useful role in Western politics; although certainly this is not to exonerate or overlook any problems within minority ethnic communities that cause harm to others, as Ashencaen Crabtree et al. (2016) discuss in depth. It is made all the harder, however, to tackle these effectively when the waters are muddied by prejudice and bigotry – and where labelling tars all with the same brush.

Such prejudice towards Muslims *per se* is commonly referred to as 'Islamophobia'. This is a term in common currency since the UK Runnymede Trust report of 1977, and sadly, Islamophobia has sharply increased in terms of prejudice and hate crimes in Britain, the USA and the Global North in general within the past two decades. The brunt of the impact has fallen heavily upon families and communities, which have often been viewed as generally segregationist, religiously fanatical, benighted and a hotbed of radicalism. The fear of Islamist extremists has become totally disproportionate to the probable actual numbers owing to the dangers such individuals can pose to the public, where tragically indiscriminate blood lust seems to have been the dominant motive in some recent and appalling terrorist attacks. This is, however, a far cry from assuming that such views are shared by the greatest number of Muslims, for whom Islamist extremists are probably one of the greater threats to Islam. The refusal by 130 Imams to observe the funeral rites for the London Bridge Islamist murderers was a hugely significant display of public revulsion and Muslim rejection of the atrocities (Sherwood, 2017).

In the meantime, the highly controversial Prevent programme continues to be enacted in schools, universities and other public service spaces. The Prevent strategy arguably forms a far greater danger to social cohesion and multiculturalism than the threat to society that it is designed to prevent (Ashencaen Crabtree, 2017a, b).

'Collective stigmatisation' is the topic of a paper by Louise Ryan (2011), which explores how Muslim women understand and respond to negative, gendered portrayals and the construction of Muslims as risks for enhanced securitisation measures. Furthermore, Ashencaen Crabtree and Husain (2012) offer an intercultural feminist analysis deconstructing the false dichotomies constructed of Muslim versus 'Western' (non-Muslim) women, seen in sexist and racist discourses as passive carriers of patriarchal cultural values.

Finally, for a more in-depth focus on contemporary issues affecting the lives of Muslim service users in terms of the socio-political, religio-cultural context of Islam, readers are directed to Ashencaen Crabtree et al.'s (2016) *Islam and Social Work*, where they will find a full discussion of the impact of oppressive attitudes and practices towards Muslim minority ethnic communities as well as those that are enacted within them upon members of such communities.

Chapter summary

This chapter has undertaken a broad historical sweep of British social work and social issues to outline the context for our exploration of who might be the marginalised or disadvantaged people we are focusing on in this book. Having set the scene, we considered a range of people who have experienced different but fundamental political, social and individual circumstances that mark them out from society and attract attention that is not always welcome, often, as we shall see in the next chapter, based on unspoken and unquestioned assumptions. The first two chapters have prepared the ground for us now to turn to some of the ways in which marginalisation takes place, the processes by which it is internalised in society and within individuals.

Further reading

Ahmed, A. and Rogers, M. (eds.) (2016) *Working with Marginalised Groups.* Basingstoke: Palgrave.

This excellent, short edited collection brings a range of practical and theoretical insights into our understanding of marginalisation and offers ways of working with people who find themselves on the edges of society.

Ashencaen Crabtree, S., Husain, F. and Spalek, B. (2016) *Islam and Social Work: Culturally Sensitive Practice in a Diverse World*, 2nd ed. Bristol: Policy Press.

This volume explores some of the ways in which Muslims have experienced disenfranchisement and marginalisation in contemporary society, something that links to other faiths and cultural groups and helps us to explore social reactions and the ways in which people are affected by labels and myths.

Novels offer a good way into people's experiences; for instance:

Bradman, T. (ed.) (2007) *Give Me Shelter: An Asylum Seeker Anthology.* London: Frances Lincoln.

This book draws together a collection of short stories that explore what it is like to be a child refugee. It is moving and heart warming.

Steinbeck, J. (1939/2000) *The Grapes of Wrath.* London: Penguin Classics.

A *tour de force* describing the impact of the Great Depression in 1930s USA.

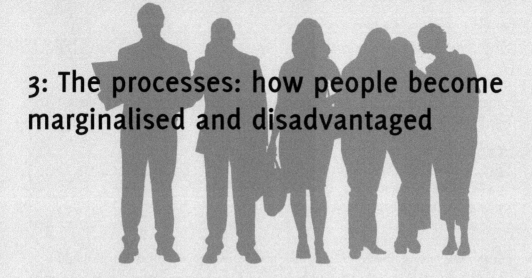

3: The processes: how people become marginalised and disadvantaged

(Continued)

It will also introduce you to the following academic standards as set out in the social work subject benchmark statement.

5.2.iv Social work theory

5.3.iv, x Values and ethics

5.4 i–v Service users and carers

5.5.v, vi The nature of social work

In the last two chapters we have considered what marginalisation and disadvantage might mean for people, how the concepts are defined and who these people, groups and communities might be. In this chapter will consider how people become disadvantaged and marginalised from one another, from social structures and from society itself. The different levels of marginalisation and disadvantage will be explored and the ways in which this happens will be theorised. We will examine the perspectives of functionalism which would apportion the blame to individuals and groups themselves and, using labelling theory, strain theory, deviance theories and conflict theories, we will explore in a critical way the ways in which marginalisation and disadvantage happen and the pathways towards them. Alongside these theoretical approaches to understanding the processes we will look at everyday practices and psycho-social performances to understand them further.

Functionalist sociology and the pathologisation of individuals and groups

Systems thinking and functionalist approaches

One of the first major schools of sociological thought derived from one of the founding figures in sociology, Emile Durkheim, and was further developed in the mid-twentieth century in the USA by figures such as Talcott Parsons and Robert K. Merton. Durkheim took a broad historical approach to understanding the ways in which societies developed, functioned and survived (Mooney et al., 2016). He considered social solidarity to be important in this and described the functioning of earlier societies as employing a mechanical solidarity in which rules were clear and adhered to in order to maintain families, reproduction and order. As societies developed these tacitly assumed ties were weakened, but Durkheim suggested that a more organic solidarity allowed them to continue to function. This organic solidarity maintained social structures through transactions between people, families and work settings.

Parsons developed this thinking in reference to the function of the various roles that people assume in society, seeing social interactions and roles as a kind of system in which the interactions between sub-systems maintained the functioning and order of the whole. Merton also advanced on Durkheim's earlier work by delineating two separate functions of institutions and phenomena within society: a manifest function, which describes the overt or intended functions and the latent functions, which are not immediately apparent. We will explore below some of the ways in which these theories can be used to explain the processes by which people become marginalised and disadvantaged by the allocation of assumed roles within a given social system. We will explore the unpalatable notions that marginalisation, disadvantage and exclusion might serve important functions in maintaining social order and equilibrium. We will do this through case examples.

Parsons' sick role and mental health

When individuals are sick it seems reasonable to assume that they are not going to be preoccupied with thinking about the role and function they have taken on by being sick. That individual is, one expects, focusing on feeling better and resuming everyday life. Talcott Parsons was instrumental in identifying the important role, function and obligations expected of people when they are sick, and the roles and functions this demands in those around that person. Parsons (1951), in his seminal work concerning systems and the sick role, described how being sick was a form of deviance from the expected norms of behaviour but one which was positively rather than negatively seen. Indeed, the changed behavioural patterns and functions that one is ascribed when sick are legitimised once they are sanctioned or approved by a member of the medical professions. For instance, not turning up to work is generally frowned upon, at the very least. However, if you are sick and have visited a doctor who says you should take time off, this behaviour is reinterpreted as positive and functional within that social context.

Parsons' theory seems only to consider acute spells of sickness and ill health as the legitimate deviation from everyday obligations and the adoption of new behaviours are assumed to be temporary. Also, it does seem to dismiss a person's agency or potential for change and development. The Equality Act 2010, as we will see in Chapters 5 and 8, focuses on the need for reasonable adjustments to allow people to complete tasks they are prevented from doing because of the way in which society is structured rather than to consider people who are sick or have a disability as helpless, as suggested by Parsons' sick role theory. In terms of this theory people are marginalised as they move from a legitimated role, where sickness is treated and time off sanctioned, to a deviant one in which the role no longer allows the individual to have access to the expected entitlements of society – a job, a social life, for instance.

The family and sexuality

Traditional functionalist approaches to the family again owe much to Talcott Parsons and to his contemporary, George K. Murdoch (Newman, 2009). Being functionalists, they both focus on the roles and functions of families in maintaining social order and nurturing the individuals within those family systems.

The functionalist approach to families is optimistic and positive in its perception of families. It does not allow for families which are abusive or not the nurturing safe harbours that Murdoch and Parsons suggest. Also, the research took place in fairly localised areas of the USA, amongst a homogeneous group of mainly middle-class, White families and is limited representatively. A feminist critique considering these criticisms would also draw attention to its unquestioned assumption of hetero-normative, patriarchal structures (Robertson Elliot, 1996).

It is clear that functionalist approaches to the family are liable to marginalise those individuals who do not conform to the accepted normative standard of living in a family and finding the family a unit of satisfaction. We know this is not the case and we also know that a rigid functionalist approach would have stifled change, such as the greater acceptance of non-heterosexual families, reconstituted families, and so on. People would be marginalised if they were not able to demonstrate their compliance with the norms of society. Where people had experienced abuse in a family setting or when coming from a culture in which family norms are different, the potential for marginalisation is increased. It is also likely that families would experience disadvantage resulting from laws and social policies that bolster the normative composition and functioning of families. Those who are different would attract differential treatment.

There are many criticisms of the functionalist approach to sociology, especially the lack of explanatory power these ideas have in explaining change and shifts in the way social institutions work or fail to do so (Layder, 2006; Mooney et al., 2016). Alongside this there is a lack of concern for people as individuals who are seen only in terms of their roles and functions as part of a bigger picture. This means that the actions of individuals are not fully explained and, when a singular person is excluded, marginalised and facing disadvantage, it does not help in explaining fully the idiosyncrasies of that individual's position, actions and the response of others to him or her. We need to consider other theories to gain a wider perspective of the processes involved.

Strain theory, labelling, deviance theory

We can draw on important sociological theories developed to help explain crime, criminal behaviour and deviance to understand some of the ways in which people become marginalised in society. These theories help to explain why certain beliefs about people become embedded and taken for granted, why people become labelled in certain ways, how this becomes a self-fulfilling prophecy and how those people at the margins of society accept these positions and sometimes reproduce these themselves.

The Chicago School of Sociology has exerted a significant influence on our thinking about how social pressures, structures and interactions sway the ways we act and behave and the positions we occupy in society. Chamberlain (2015) identifies two distinct phases in the thinking of the Chicago School, which are important to understand the processes by which people are marginalised in society. The first is influenced by Durkheim's work on the concept of anomie, the psycho-social strain resulting from this and the impact of urban space on social relations and behaviours. The second influential approach derived from symbolic interactionism, resulting in labelling theories, and is associated with the work of thinkers such as George Herbert Mead (1934), John Dewey (1935) and especially Herbert Blumer (1969), who coined the term and brought the concepts together in a coherent whole.

Durkheim's seminal work, *The Rules of Sociological Method*, expressed the notion that when people organise as social groupings – large or small – they develop shared behaviours, rules and norms (Durkheim, 1895). These ways of operating socially become embodied as taken-for-granted assumptions within the social and political systems that come to govern social life outside individuals, thinking that has influenced later writers such as Bourdieu (1977). The norms remain unquestioned and present a way of seeing the world around us, distinguishing between what and who is acceptable and unacceptable. Those individuals who violate the collective consciousness of assumed ideas, or the mechanical solidarity, are punished by and ostracised from society.

This perspective, however, offers us a more historical understanding where social order is simpler in form. As society becomes more complex in its organisation, diversity of views and opinions, and interdependence between different groups, increase, which, in turn, allows wider parameters concerning what is acceptable or not. To an extent this mitigates some of the potential for marginalisation experienced by individuals. It can lead to the conditions necessary for anomie when societies are in transition from traditionally accepted norms and agreed new norms have not yet been established (Chamberlain, 2015). These ideas are taken to underpin social understandings of crime and criminal behaviour but they are equally helpful in understanding social marginalisation and disadvantage in other contexts.

Strain theory

The US sociologist Robert Merton (1938) suggests that anomie represents the gap between the goals and values of a society and the means or resources that people have to achieve these, which produces strain in those individuals. This strain may lead to conformity and playing by the rules as people accept the way society is and attempt to achieve agreed goals, even though they have unequal resource to others in order to do so. It may lead to a reinterpretation of the goals for the individual who deigns to accept less because the rules of society represent the important condition, rather than individual achievement of the goals or what society values. This is disadvantaging if not marginalising, although the individual does seem to be marginalising him- or herself.

> ## Case study
>
> James and his friend Robbie grew up on the same housing estate in a large Northern town that experienced the collapse of its manufacturing industries and a significant rise in long-term unemployment. James wanted to earn a living that would allow him to buy a small house and move out of the area. He studied as much as he could at school, although he found it hard, and gained an apprenticeship and employment as a plumber. Robbie also found it difficult to study and felt too much was expected of him and that it was unlikely that he would ever get a job in any case. He failed his exams, and thought it best that he 'accept his lot' and not be disappointed if he could not find work. Ten years after they left school, James had fulfilled his ambition and just put down a deposit on a small terraced house; Robbie remained unemployed.

There are also deviant adaptations that people adopt, whether that concerns the ways some individuals employ of beating the system, such as tax evasion, or of moving into crime as a means of offsetting strain and tension in achieving those things that are desired. However, others occupy either a 'retreat' position, dropping out from mainstream society into drug addiction or homelessness, and still others rebel against the core values that cause the strain and seek to change the social structures.

> ## Case study
>
> A fellow pupil at the school that James and Robbie attended, Martin, found it lucrative to sell on some of the skunk (hydroponically farmed cannabis) that he bought for himself. This gave him a growing income and a degree of popularity that he did not believe he could get elsewhere. However, questions were being asked about where he got his money, given that he worked in a local café for low wages.
>
> Gillian, who had attended the same school and lived on the estate, had not been able to find work but volunteered at a radical outreach centre with rough sleepers. Their experiences challenged her views about society and she remained on the edges of her society, undertaking protests disrupting local council meetings and opening up unused buildings as squats.

Merton is criticised for a rigid application of his adaptation types to different social groups without addressing issues of power and control, such as who has the power to name and label different social positions or behaviours. Later, Robert Agnew (2006) took up the concept of strain theory, developing a general approach to include not only strains that are experienced in society, but those that are anticipated by individuals according to their social positions and vicarious strains that are felt by association with others. These strains all remove the potential for positive achievements and interactions in society or, at the very least, threaten them (see the cases of Martin and Gillian above). Different people have different ways of coping; some of those adaptations are to remove oneself from the general workings of society, to retreat to the margins or to reject society's operating structures and become 'deviant'.

Labelling

Labelling theory helps us to understand further how people become marginalised. Labels are an integral part of everyday life. We see labels on clothing and sports equipment. Labels are attached to material things to explain what they are, what their use is and to give us information. As we write, the plug for the computer displays a label that indicates it has been through an electronic safety test. So, in a sense, we can see labels as benign descriptions that help us make sense of, predict and order our social world.

However, there are other ways in which labels are applied. Consider the following conversation between two students.

George: Oh, you've got Sandra as your dissertation supervisor, I see. She's great; always gives you great support. I think she probably does more than any of the others.

Sam: Wow! I didn't realise. Who've you got?

George: I've got Tom – don't really know him except for that lecture on substance use.

Sam: Oh dear!

George: What?

Sam: Well, he was my tutor in the first year but, you know, he was staring at me, at my chest! I had to change my tutor.

George: What a sexist pig! I hope you've warned the others? That sort shouldn't be allowed in a university. I'll talk to the office and get him changed now.

Whilst this is an imaginary and rather superficially constructed conversation it begins to show a different side to labelling and demonstrates how the application of negative labels may lead to marginalising people on the basis of assumed characteristics and attributes. We do not know a great deal about the situation, but Sam certainly felt uncomfortable enough to change her tutor. It may be that an important conversation was had about Tom that could lead to students being able to lodge a complaint and to protect themselves from Tom's advances. However, we need more evidence before taking action. George was seeking to amplify the effects of the 'label' that he read from Sam's description of Tom's untrustworthiness and potential danger to women. If unjustified by the evidence, this could have led to unwarranted marginalisation of a member of staff. The situation shows how labels and labelling can be very 'messy' and that a critically analytic approach is needed as a social worker to work through their implications and meanings, which may be very serious indeed.

When writing about labelling theory earlier, one of us suggested that the crucial issue is the reaction of those people in the surrounding environment to the person who is labelled as deviant rather than the act itself (Parker and Randall, 1997). Being deviant in this context means that one transgresses agreed or commonly accepted rules of social behaviour. These rules create expectations of behaviour from people in society but also labelling deviation from these rules creates expectations from those who are labelled as deviant. Labelling theory describes the processes through which a person who breaks the rules passes from a member of society to label to deviant and outsider.

Chamberlain (2015) describes labelling theory's theoretical development from symbolic interactionism. This school of thought suggests that people behave towards things according to the meanings that these things hold for them and that the meanings themselves are the products of prior social interactions or interpreted social experiences. However, the meanings change according to the individual, who has his or her own ways of interpreting them. The process is two-way and the meanings that are changed by the individual's approach to them also influence and change the ways in which that individual sees the world, and what it means for that person. Our meanings are socially constructed by the external social environment but we also influence that social world by developing certain roles and behaviours. The labels which we place on these external roles, behaviours and people are important signifiers of what we expect and how we believe we 'ought' to behave.

This theoretical background influenced the development of Lemert's (1967) theory of deviance. He separated the concept into two types – primary and secondary deviance. Primary deviance represents an initial act or behaviour that transgresses the accepted rules of behaviour but is perhaps a one-off and may not necessarily have a major impact on a person's life. For instance, a teenager caught shoplifting may be subject to a caution by the police; she may have upset her family considerably but is not likely to be labelled a criminal nor incarcerated as a result. However, the act may bring her into contact with social institutions that raise the prospect of secondary deviance. For instance, contact with the police could subject that teenager to a degree of shame, degradation, stigma and humiliation. When such becomes society's response to a person's deviance and this is reinforced by punishment for transgression of the social norms, fundamental changes are caused to that person's life. This is secondary deviance.

Lemert's contribution was to show how the process leading from primary to secondary deviance is not immediate but unfolds over time. A primary deviant is subject to the controlling rituals of stigmatisation and degradation, and life becomes organised around a master status as a deviant, depending on the reaction of others and the adjustment of that particular person to these reactions. For instance, the young asylum seeker already accepting his 'deviance' from the norms of society by his need to flee is likely to reinterpret his status if subject to detention, processed through the rituals of being investigated, of not being believed, of not being able to work, of having to report to the authorities on a regular basis. Once this individual engages with the label of 'asylum seeker' used by the popular media, by politicians or by the general public, he is likely to internalise the negative, stigmatising aspects as part of his status and may behave according to the presentations this label suggests.

Another labelling theorist, Howard Becker (1963), brought out the implications of this, suggesting that deviance is not an act or a quality inherent within an individual; it is a consequence of the reaction of society to certain acts that transgress the assumed social rules. In fact, deviance itself is a label that has been created through the formation and acceptance of the social rules and accompanying rituals that support them, e.g. detention for asylum seekers whilst they are 'processed'. Becker's articulation of the labelling process and of people becoming *outsiders* is especially pertinent to social work in this area. A later paper by Becker (1967) demonstrated how institutions dealing with social control, including social services, education and public health, disproportionately label the powerless, the marginalised and the disadvantaged. This develops into an 'us and them' view of the social world and its organisation, which may help us understand some of the ways in which the labels we apply to negotiate the world can exert such power as to marginalise.

In 1974 Thomas Scheff wrote an important article that considered labelling theory in the context of mental health. Scheff argues that labelling theory has an important role in sensitising us to alternative ways of understanding the process of being diagnosed with a mental health problem. He draws attention to two important studies. The first suggested that psychiatrists and clinical psychologists were prone to influence in making diagnoses (Temerlin, 1968), although the setting for the research was artificial. Rosenhan's (1973) study, however, took place in 12 hospitals and involved eight people who feigned psychotic symptoms to gain admission to them. Once these 'pseudo-patients' were in hospital they stopped any symptomatic behaviour and behaved in ordinary ways. However, once admitted they struggled to convince the psychiatric authorities that they did not have a mental illness, suggesting that behaviour and person were interpreted by the label rather than what was actually observed.

Rosenhan's work has important connotations for social work practice. You will often be working with people who are introduced to you or described by a label, which in turn is usually pejorative. It is crucial to your practice to recognise the power of the label and to see the person first.

In respect of mental health, the anti-psychiatry school have much to add to our understanding of the processes by which people can become marginalised. Whilst functionalism and the sick role theory seem limited in considering sickness temporary and deviant, they also allow some of the beneficial aspects of family relationships to come out. The anti-psychiatry school sees 'madness' as a sane reaction to some of the pressures and contorted interpersonal relations of contemporary society.

Marx and critical theories

The theoretical work of Karl Marx has great relevance to understanding some of the processes through which people become marginalised. Indeed, alienation formed the focus of his earlier work and continues to represent a key element of his work. It has similarities to anomie, discussed earlier, but is rooted in relations between sectional groups – in Marx's writing it was class, but it could equally be ethnicity, health status, age or gender.

According to Marx, alienation took place when a person was separated from the creative and meaningful aspects of making a living seen to have taken place in the Industrial Revolution. This economic alienation was bound up with class and ownership, the exploitation of one group by another and the conflict necessary to change things. The dehumanising conditions of work and social life were made possible through capitalist exploitation of those who had only their labour to trade as a resource. This would be likely to lead to dissatisfaction and conflict and to change in the organising structures and political, legal and customary institutions – a revolution (Layder, 2006).

This view of alienation was based on Marx's view of social systems comprising two core elements: a base or substructure and a superstructure. The base concerned the economic and class relations of the time, the ways in which people organised production and the relationships between different groups who either produced through their labour or who owned and controlled the production. The superstructure, as we hinted above, related to the legal, political and customary institutions that supported the means of production at the base. Unlike functionalist and earlier sociological thought, this did not represent a consensual and benign social system but one that was rooted in conflict and likely, through what Marx termed *historical materialism*, to result in turbulent or revolutionary movements for change.

Of course, we know from human history post-Marx that his historical predictions of global revolution against capitalist systems and replacement by a system of advanced communal property and living did not come to fruition. However, his focus on the conflict between different sectional groups and the importance of alienation by exploitation and imposition of the ideologies of those with power remains important in analysing how people become marginalised and, in certain analytic terms, disadvantaged by society. Let us revisit the lives of James and his friends.

Case study

Veronique met James on a night out two years ago. She trained as a teacher and was working in a local primary school near James's house. They got on well and moved in together a year later. James kept contact with Robbie despite their different lifestyles. Veronique and Robbie tried hard to get on because of James but Veronique could not understand why he would not take any job he could find and why he was so comfortable living on benefits. Robbie, on the other hand, considered Veronique to be one of the causes of his situation, saying to James, 'it is posh people like her that expect us to take the menial stuff just so they can enjoy their lives the way they want.'

Marxist thought also offers a hopeful element for social work with people who are marginalised and exploited in society, taken up elsewhere in sociological thought (Habermas, 1987). Conflict is something which occurs in societies and is expected between groups who have differential access to resources, power and voice. Through the clash of views, groups and positions, conflict can produce positive change – a new way of engaging in social and economic production. This dialectic can be harnessed by marginalised people acting on their own behalf with social workers walking alongside them. This may bring you as a social worker into some degree of conflict with your employers, of course, and perhaps reflects the idea that you as a social worker, by virtue of the work you do, may also be marginalised.

Everyday practices and performances

The idea of 'everyday practices' is important for understanding social actions and relationships. The concept of practices derives from a continuing debate originating in family studies that suggests the daily practices of family members actually constitute what that family is and how it sees itself. These ideas are applicable more generally to the ways in which everyday practices construct and adapt all social relations and we can apply them to our understanding of how people become marginalised.

The theory of practices

The beginnings of a concern with everyday practices lie with Bourdieu's (1977) theory of practice, as we alluded to in Chapter 1. He attempts to explain how the external world is internalised by individuals and how this is reflected back on the world, not dissimilar to the processes identified in labelling theory. The resulting structures are constitutive of a particular type of environment, and produce what Bourdieu terms *habitus*. Habitus are systems of lasting dispositions which are exchangeable across the different contexts in which people live. They provide a blueprint for the generation and structure of practices, or what we do, at an everyday level. The individual is, at one and the same time, the producer and reproducer of objective meaning, whilst his or her actions and words are often the product of unconscious assumptions and internalisation of external social relations. Individuals and social structures influence one another. In respect of the ways in which people become marginalised, the beliefs that have arisen through life experience will guide everyday behaviours and will be responded to in ways that reflect wider social interactions. So, refugees placed in a town in the Midlands may expect to be moved and processed by authorities because of their prior experiences and believe this is how societies function. The social response, however, may have been influenced by the concerns of local residents worried that refugees will take their jobs, commit acts of terrorism or other unsavoury and unlikely deeds. Whilst these will not be presented overtly as policies, there may well be increased surveillance and monitoring of refugees and an insistence on continued and burdensome bureaucracy to 'manage' the situation. Such a situation creates marginalisation within the structures of that society or community and this is responded to by acceptance and compliance according to the habitus of the individual refugee.

One of the effects of the habitus is the production, therefore, of a common-sense world endowed with objectivity, which is secured by a consensus view of the meaning of certain everyday practices or *doxa*. Bourdieu (1996) applies his ideas to the family which constructed views about the correct way to 'do' or 'perform' family life. This itself can help to explain why some people become marginalised if they sit outside these norms of behaviour, but it can be widened into other areas of life.

Let us consider, for instance, counterterrorism. Using Bourdieu's analysis, counterterrorism can be understood as an objective social category or a *structuring structure*; this is one that helps to create what it is and how it is understood. However, it can also be seen as a subjective social category, or a *structured structure*, which is one created by the objective social category. In this sense counterterrorism (the objective social category) helps to order the actions and ideas of individuals that in turn reflect back and reproduce the objective social category. So, counterterrorist policy and the Prevent strategy (HM Government, 2015) act as a means of creating a view of what terrorism comprises, where the risks lie, with whom, and what we must do in order to counter the threat. Following from this, some of the ways in which terrorism is construed are played out within those groups alienated from mainstream society and may reflect back some of the expected practices. In this way there is a connection with earlier labelling theory. Individuals and groups meeting some of the assumptions underlying other people's thoughts and actions about what a potential terrorist is like may, therefore, be ostracised from communities and support and treated with deep suspicion. Bourdieu (1977) suggested that in this way daily practices, how we act, may result in a group habitus of expectations associated with particular social entities:

> *As an acquired system of generative schemes objectively adjusted to the particular conditions in which it is constituted, the habitus engenders all the thoughts, all the perceptions and all the actions consistent with those conditions, and no others.*

> (Bourdieu, 1977:95)

Whilst Bourdieu's theory of practice accounts for the reproduction of social entities, it has been criticised for not fully accounting for the possibilities of change and challenge to existing belief systems (Morgan, 1999).

Smith's (1987) feminist sociological analysis sees practices in a broadly similar way to Bourdieu as on-going, co-ordering of activities that bring the world into being. She adds the important point, however, that the researcher is also part of the world in which these practices take place, and that knowledge gained or created becomes part of that world. This is important for social workers, because it is equally the case that you will contribute to the production and reproduction of social entities by your practice, and by the interactions between you and those people you are working alongside.

Activity 3.1

If you have already undertaken a practice placement, bring to mind some of the ways in which you practised. If you have not yet undertaken a placement, draw on previous voluntary or paid work that you have participated in.

Think of some of the specific ways you acted, behaved and thought when working alongside someone. What guided you? Why do you think you practised in this way? What messages did your actions send to those with whom you were working?

Comment

This exercise can be difficult. It asks you to bring to the surface ways of acting as a social worker or volunteer that are often unspoken, assumed rather than overtly done. However, it is important that you become aware of what influences you to respond in the ways that you do and how this might be perceived by others. It is this reflection on practice that can help you to change and adapt to circumstances.

Everyday practices

It is with the family theorist David Morgan (1996, 1999) that the clearest articulation of practices is given, in which he introduces difference and diversity as core to understanding; this is especially helpful when working with marginalised people. He challenges the uncritical usage of the term 'family' as potentially rigidifying and normalising; we may perhaps recognise the same problems in respect of terms such as 'person in need', 'abused child', or 'person with mental health problems'. Seeing 'family' as a verb rather than noun helps us to understand how we might respond to it in society because we understand something about how this perception came about. Everyday practices draw upon common-sense, day-to-day understandings and how these are used reflexively to structure that world.

Bernades (1997) adds that they also demarcate from practices not assumed or considered to be part of that site of practice. For example, if being a rough sleeper is our site of practice, we would want to consider our experiences of rough sleepers and how that creates understandings of what this is and what it is not. This may help us understand why certain social, or indeed personal, prejudices develop when considering that someone identifying as a rough sleeper was able to sleep on the sofa of various acquaintances, or why confusion occurs in popular thinking between homelessness and rough sleeping. As social workers we want to understand and empathise with people's experiences and so need to interrogate our own practices and the beliefs that underpin them.

In general, practices are defined by the social actors (the people) involved in them, but this is not the sole criterion of definition. These definitions might not always be available to the observer. For instance, it might be possible for a member of an armed response unit in the police to interpret his or her role in a very different way to that of an observing member of the public when viewing an incident. This is perhaps what was happening in the shooting of Mark Duggan which preceded the 2011 riots in London, and subsequent inquiries into it, for instance (Taylor, 2017). Practices are concerned with cognitive constructions but also with the significance for those parties involved. They are *a way of looking at, and describing, practices which might also be described in a variety of other ways* (Morgan, 1996:199). Practices can, therefore, be described by others involved in an observational or descriptive role.

There are three sets of agencies involved in constructing practices (Morgan, 1999). Firstly, as we have mentioned above, the social actors, those individuals and groups, involved in the social entity themselves make links between activities and general notions of the practice. These linkages, activities and notions are constantly negotiated and redefined by individual experience and reflection.

Secondly, more abstract agencies are involved. These may include professionals such as social workers, teachers, police officers, moral and religious agencies, policy makers and the like. Distinctions are made in these pronouncements between the focus of practice, between positive and negative images, and between who is included and excluded. These professional accounts are influential to individuals and may build a cultural resource, which provides meaning for the individuals dependent on location and ideological positioning. There is a reflexive monitoring of one's own routine practices against some standard of normality that becomes reproductive of those standards. So this element involved in the construction of daily practices is particularly important to social workers so that we do not unwittingly reproduce the processes that lead people into marginalised and excluded positions in society.

The final agency involved in the construction of practices is the observer. It is routinely experienced that the constructions of observers should match and derive from those of the actors whose practices are being described. This is not always the case and observer effects/notions/constructions are important. So, we ourselves help to construct those representations, which is why we need to take care when discussing terrorism and terrorists.

The term 'practices' conveys a range of related themes:

1. a sense of interplay between the perspectives of the social actor, the individual whose actions are being described and accounted for and the perspectives of the observer (Morgan, 1999:17).

   The concept of practices emphasises that there are different perspectives and interpretations.

2. a sense of active rather than passive or static (Morgan, 1999:17).

   There is a sense of 'doing' which both constitutes and derives from notions of the practice being described.

3. a focus on the everyday (Morgan, 1999:17).

   There is a concern with the routine and trivial as part of how something is seen.

4. a stress on regularities (Morgan, 1999:17).

   Regularities or repeated actions constitute part of the everyday taken-for-granted worlds.

5. a sense of fluidity (Morgan, 1999:18).

   Practices are not bounded but flow into other practices that are similar or different.

6. an interplay between history and biography (Morgan, 1999:18).

   Practices have societal and historical dimensions as well as concern with the everyday and here and now.

Practices represent a way of conceptualising the fluidity of social life as a point of departure. They allow for a variety of different perspectives and to consider subjects through a variety of different lenses. External practices may reinforce or construct notions of the social entity described. They are associated with wider understandings of the world and do not necessarily take place in times and spaces that are conventionally designated to do with the entity described.

Case study

Let us return briefly to the case of James, Veronique and Robbie that we saw earlier. Veronique's understanding of daily life and family centred around working for a living, ensuring that you tried hard in everything you did and that you only get what you deserve by working for it. Robbie's 'daily practice' was to reject the conventional world because of his experiences and their interpretation, forming the assumption that nothing could change to make things better; the world was conspiring against his future, leading him not to engage with authorities, and to dismiss offers of help of support to lead him into work. These different approaches to life and the world of work led to tensions and arguments between them because they did not conform to each other's views. Veronique consigned Robbie to the marginalised position of a failure and a bad influence on James, and wanted the men's friendship to end.

Rites of passage and liminality

The processes of marginalisation are complex, as we have seen, but they can be understood through many of the unspoken processes by which life is conducted in society. This can also be seen as a ritual process through which individuals, groups and communities pass on their often fluid and difficult social journeys. One neglected but important way of conceptualising this process is to consider the notion of *rites of passage* (van Gennep, 1906) and liminality (Turner, 1969).

The concepts, taken from anthropology, are directly relevant to those people with whom social workers come into contact and work alongside and to social workers themselves. We will briefly explore the concepts. Rites of passage represent those rituals that accompany all our social interactions and states and are marked by three phases – separation, marginalisation or liminality, and aggregation (van Gennep, 1906). Separation involves symbolic behaviours that signify the separation or detachment from a particular social or cultural state. This separation creates ambiguity in the person as the marginalisation removes those people from what has served as a known or constant state beforehand. In order to move through this process and become a part of the stable state again, the person must move through certain behaviours and behave appropriately in respect of cultural and social norms and standards. This process lends itself to analysis from both functionalist and critical sociology and this is where social workers require a degree of reflexivity.

If social workers move people from a marginalised state of separation and ambiguity towards a socially acceptable place in society, they are 'fixing' the broken social functioning of those people, bringing them into an agreed and legitimate social system (Howe, 2009). Of course, this immediately suggests that people on the margins of society are in need of 'changing', or 'making right'. This may not be the case. A more critical approach is needed in which the ritual passage from one state to another involves a *dialectic*. What this means is that the problem, situation or position that led to contact with a social worker will be tested against a range of alternatives, perhaps embodied by the social worker or at least identified with that person, and this will lead to a synthesis of different ways of being, with the most acceptable to that individual being the end result – a synthesis rather than aggregation.

Social workers as limen: on the margins

Social workers can stand alongside those people with whom they work, taking an ethical stance towards the issues and concerns that those people experience. This can put social workers into a liminal state, removing or separating them from their legitimised positions and placing them in a liminal space in which they work alongside the displaced, seeking to move through a ritualised process towards acceptance and reduction of marginalisation and removal of social disadvantages.

This is an uncomfortable space for social workers. They are at one and the same time part of an established order, part of the system that creates disadvantage and marginalisation and placed outside it in a position alongside those people who have experienced disenfranchisement, de-legitimation and marginalisation by society (Parker, 2007). Social workers can be considered as *threshold* people occupying an ambiguous position as neither one thing nor the other.

Research summary

Parker et al. (2012b) studied the learning processes of social work students working in non-governmental organisations (NGOs) in Malaysia as part of a placement. What they found was that students were separated from their comfort zones and placed in unusual and sometimes discomforting situations. They were no longer British social work students; they were between this role and that of the workers in the NGOs, between one culture and a different one. This allowed the students to play with different experiences and understandings in order to maximise their learning and to forge new and different ways of being on their return.

People who use social work or have it imposed on them

As liminals those people who use social work services can also work with the structures of society to become an accepted part of it, performing the behaviours and actions that are required to be accepted and demonstrating compliance and humility as they are assessed as good enough to rejoin or take up position in the taken-for-granted club. This functionalist position is one that legislation, policy and procedure would indicate is something that social workers should encourage people to work towards. However, it may be that compliance and stripping out the layers of difference and separation are likely to detract from that individual's position in life, removing that person's cultural or value bases. So social workers may find themselves working to consolidate a person's marginalisation from a society that is antithetical to that person's wellbeing.

Of course, reality is not usually as clear-cut in distinguishing between a functionalist or critical binary approach. Social workers negotiate a tricky, complex path between their status as, often, government employees and morally purposeful practitioners seeking social justice on behalf of those with whom they practise. Sometimes these two positions converge, sometimes they diverge, and frequently they sit in an uncomfortable tension demanding a thoughtful, reflexive and moral approach from social workers. There are no easy answers. However, social workers need to take care that their actions, behaviours and statements do not further marginalise or disadvantage people.

Chapter summary

In this chapter we have built on our understanding of what marginalisation and disadvantage constitute and who might be in those positions. We have examined different theoretical concepts to understand the processes involved in how people become marginalised, recognising it is a complex and sometimes ambiguous process that demands constant reflection and critical questioning so that we, as social workers, do not contribute further to people's marginalisation, disadvantage and distress but that we work with that to create change. We also recognised that marginalisation may be a beneficial thing in some circumstances. This prepares the way for the next chapter's discussion of the impacts that marginalisation and disadvantage may have on the people with whom we as social workers are called to work.

Further reading

Layder, D. (2006) *Understanding Social Theory*, 2nd ed. London: SAGE.

This book provides readers with a well-written and researched text covering key social theories that have influenced sociological thinking. Layder deals with the thorny issue of the individual versus society collective in a way that shows its complex, inter-connecting arguments.

Mooney, L., Knox, D. and Schacht, C. (2016) *Understanding Social Problems*, 10th ed. Belmont, NJ: Wadsworth.

This text offers an introduction to sociological thinkers and thinking that takes its starting point from social problems; it presents applied sociology.

Parker, J., Ashencaen Crabtree, S., Baba, I., Carlo, D.P. and Azman, A. (2012) Liminality and learning: international placements as a rite of passage. *Asia Pacific Journal of Social Work and Development*, 22 (3): 146–158.

This paper explores the passage through which social work students undertaking an international placement in a different culture journey as they learn about their own cultural markers and perspectives and those of others.

4: The impact: how disadvantage and marginalisation are experienced

(Continued)

It will also introduce you to the following academic standards as set out in the social work subject benchmark statement.

5.2.iv Social work theory

5.3.iv, x Values and ethics

5.4 i–v Service users and carers

5.5.v, vi The nature of social work

Having identified what constitutes disadvantage and marginalisation together with those people and groups who may be classed as such in the previous chapters, we now begin to outline some of the ways this might be experienced by people. Here too the potential consequences of the experiences will also be outlined. Again the structure of this chapter will delineate the social impact of disadvantage and marginalisation at a societal level, at the level of communities and specific groups along with individuals and families.

Austerity: impact of this on health and social care

At the withering tail-end of Beveridge's vision of the Welfare State in Britain, the question for many still in paid work may well be not *when* but *if* they can retire, and this question is increasingly amplified depending largely on how young the interlocutor is, with a probable and grim outlook for younger generations who may struggle to foresee a time when they may be able retire at all, so uncertain is any reliance on diminishing state pensions to keep body and soul together for future pensioners.

However, for those ageing towards retirement years within the foreseeable future, the present time may not herald long-awaited golden years of leisure, where one in three people aged 65 years old plus form part of the 6.5 million carers in the UK, caring for elderly parents, grandchildren or, exhaustingly, both (Hill, 2017). Moreover, living to great old age is no longer so unusual that it is celebrated by a telegram from the Queen, but instead, given the increasing fragility of health and social care infrastructures, old age may be viewed with a high level of ambivalence, as it may be accompanied by increasing dependence on support that may no longer be adequate. Although there are attempts to reframe old age as positive in terms of 'active ageing' notions, the politicised discourse is that ageing constitutes a social problem that is exacerbated by dwindling pensions and increased need of support from public services (Gómez-Jiménez and Parker, 2014). Accordingly, in this section we consider the impact of change to the Welfare State and cuts to services on vulnerable people, exploring these in relation to older age and in terms of disability.

The turbulence of global recession has had its impact on the UK, which has seen a number of different economic arguments taken on how best the country can ride out the storm. The Conservative Government has argued for a traditional and basic 'piggy bank' understanding in its fiscal approaches and has enthusiastically applied austerity measures to public expenditure and stringent public sector wage caps. This economic argument has relied on simplistic imagery of the mass 'tightening of belts' and the metaphorical idea of forgoing butter for margarine on the public slice of bread. Keynesian economic arguments can be and are put forward to claim that austerity and cut-backs lead to outcomes that do not swell the national piggy bank but serve to deplete it further due to 'knock-on' effects and unintended consequences of enabling less money to circulate in society to grow the economy (Varoufakis, 2017).

Moreover, these basic thrift concepts that might work at a micro, individual level certainly do not work in the same way when scaled up across the complexities of national economics and employment, which are influenced by and contribute to the vast and complicated arena of the global economy. A damning report published on behalf of HM's Office of Manpower Economics (Bryson and Forth, 2017), with little government fanfare, reveals a 6% drop in the real wages of public sector workers between 2005 and 2015. This has served to support the shocking claim that nurses are turning to food banks owing to poverty, as claimed by Janet Davies, General Secretary of the Royal College of Nursing (Campbell, 2017). If such is true of nurses, it is also very likely to be true of social workers, who earn a comparative salary to nurses and teachers, as public sector workers. However, if austerity is having such an impact on professionally qualified staff in key areas of societal need, the question arises concerning the numerous repercussions this may be having on many other individuals, families and communities, as we discuss further.

Austerity and disability

There has probably never been a good time to be disabled, but in the spirit of modernity one would casually assume that social progress is, on the whole, upwards. The current political climate in the UK defies that logic in being markedly and increasingly inhospitable towards dependency caused by disability. Recently there have been major changes to the benefits system where the Personal Independent Payment has replaced the old Disability Living Allowance. In 2012 the Department of Work and Pensions outsourced work capability assessments of vulnerable people to the private French IT firm, Atos. This company's inexperienced and inefficient assessments of individuals led to a spate of cases regarding people with severe health problems such as terminal illness being found fit for work and other people being left in desperate financial straits. Unsurprisingly, abuse was heaped upon Atos staff and the company's reputation was severely damaged. Consequently Atos retracted on the deal for self-preservation and the contract has now been passed to yet another private firm, Magnus, a US company, which will now assess claimants for crucial sickness and disability benefits (Gentleman, 2015).

For those at home who are assessed as in need of health and social care support, even these hard-won rights are not inalienable. Deep dismay has been expressed by Disability United (**http://disabilityunited.co.uk/2017/01/nhs-staff-can-decide-disabled-people-live-even-choice/**), and duly picked up by the media (Brown, 2017), that under new rules National Health Service (NHS) clinical commissioning groups may now be able to remove people to a care home on the basis of cost alone, regardless of service user wishes. The question of whether forcibly removing people from their homes would violate human rights has been raised, although it is uncertain whether such a claim could be viably legally pursued in a post-Brexit UK, eager to shake off inconvenient EU human rights legislation.

The privatisation of the care of vulnerable people (including proposed privatisation of children's services) is a highly controversial political manoeuvre directly in keeping with a neoliberal approach to state responsibility. As the Atos disaster has shown, the rolling back of state intervention in key areas of welfare provision carries critically important repercussions for individuals undergoing the processing of their claims. The entire notion that such processing is merely another bureaucratic exercise is dangerously simplistic and, arguably, a serious abrogation of state responsibility. It is worth reminding ourselves that in the past assessments for disability benefits claims involved the expertise of a qualified doctor, rather than remote clerical workers ignorant of the complexities of sickness and disability and how these affect day-to-day living.

It is also important to note that delays and incompetence are not new phenomena and that such obviously occurred at times in the monolithic state-run services of the recent past. However, the key point is that these were not run for profit or as cost-cutting exercises to the public purse, but were originally set up as part of the commitment of a Welfare State to the people. Such services and procedures may have been often paternalistic, unimaginative, restrictive and bureaucratically rather than service user-driven, but state responsibility for citizens lay at the heart of the entire edifice.

Case study

Rachael is a 34-year-old single woman with multiple sclerosis. Previously working as a commercial artist and managing her own deteriorating health, Rachael was eventually admitted to hospital seriously ill and subsequently referred to social work and occupational therapy for assessment with a view to planning domiciliary support.

Now no longer able to work and confined to a wheelchair, Rachael has received social care for over four years from community care agencies. During that time she has seen over 100 different staff; 66 of these have been new primary carers who have been allocated her case. 'It's exhausting', Rachael says, 'you have to begin all over again with each one.'

The problem, as Rachael sees it, is that there is a continual rotation of care workers coming into care work and leaving the business because it is so unrewarding in terms of pay, in addition to the stress imposed on harried staff dealing with each individual on their rota within the minimum time set, before hurrying on to the next.

Rachael's care plan was 'dumped', as she calls it, by her former agency after she made complaints about the quality of the service they provided, such as carers not turning up in the morning to help her get up or being very late, leaving Rachael helpless in bed with a full bucket of urine and painful muscle spasms. On one such occasion she complained to her social worker that she felt (unsurprisingly) vulnerable being shouted at by a stressed and overworked care worker standing over her while she lay helpless in bed with the curtains drawn. 'But,' Rachael recollects, 'the social worker said: "It's only counted as vulnerability if you are without water for 24 hours."'

Reflecting on the past, Rachael notes that insecurity and anxiety about care are dominant service user experiences. In the commodification of individuals' needs, care can be threatened in the very tangible sense of agencies being able to drop packages of care if they become inconvenient or insufficiently profitable. The service user is not the customer, the local authority is; the individual is merely the recipient of care, which may be randomly good, adequate or poor.

After some miserable experiences from agencies Rachael finally succeeded in having more control over her care and life through direct payments. For Rachael this has been nothing short of a revelation in achieving a level of autonomy in her life that she thought had been forever lost. She now employs two of the best care staff that she encountered in the past and pays out a percentage of her payments for the services of a direct payment subcontractor who handles tax, human resource issues, wages and pensions on her behalf.

Austerity and mortality

Today the Welfare State notion of care from cradle to grave is dismissed as both impossibly old-fashioned and unaffordable, despite continuing examples of this being practised in various forms across continental Europe. However, the symbolism of the grave continues to have relevance to the continuing debate of how vulnerable people should be cared for. Death as a consequence of austerity appears to be becoming part of the solution to insufficient support in the new, barren Welfare State landscape in respect of people of working age with disabilities or serious illness. Moreover, it has been revealed that, unlike other regions, such as Hong Kong Special Autonomous Region (itself a highly industrialised, pressure-cooker capitalist state), increased longevity has come to a sudden halt in the UK since 2010 – an anomalous, localised human phenomenon that is being correlated with the effect of austerity measures in health and social care in Britain (Triggle, 2017b).

In respect of deaths connected to welfare systems, following a number of Freedom of Information requests, the government has allowed public access to numerical information on people who have died following claims for employment and support allowance (ESA), incapacity benefit (IB) or severe disablement allowance (SDA). The numerical data are complex and an explanation of why deaths occurred is not given in this Department for Work and Pensions reply to the Freedom of Information request, which covers data from 2010 to 2015. We learn that, of those judged 'fit for work' and thus ineligible for the ESA, IB or SDA, 2,380 people died between 2011 and 2014 (Ryan, 2015). A further 7,200 individuals died after being awarded the ESA, with the expectation of being returned to the workforce (Ryan, 2015). Film director Ken Loach's searingly angry film, *I, Daniel Blake*, offers a powerful cinematic account of how such individuals are driven to an early grave. Commensurately, given these alarming government figures in relation to draconian changes to the benefit system, convenient deaths of claimants suggest that a sharp and expedient form of state-sponsored manslaughter is a quasi-legitimised exercise in cost cutting.

The creation of vulnerability in old age: erosion of the Welfare State

As Muriel's story in Chapter 2 demonstrates, a nation state without adequate welfare safety nets, particularly in relation to health, imposes uncivilised and intolerable suffering on those without the buffer of fiscal wealth. Today the NHS has reached the point of being labelled a *humanitarian crisis*, as claimed by Dr Saleyha Ahsan, an accident and emergency physician and former British Army officer (BBC, 2017a). This assertion was strenuously refuted by the current Prime Minister, Theresa May (whose government has been embroiled in unseemly disputes over the contracts of young doctors, normally viewed as already exploited), who called the claim *irresponsible and overblown* (BBC, 2017b, c). Conservative Government stances towards the NHS have not been accepted easily in Britain, where big demonstrations have rebuked the government for failures to support the NHS sufficiently and challenged the political implication that national health care is unaffordable.

The monolithic construction of a hand-in-glove health and social care provision has been based on notions of fiscal and management efficiencies, with the outcome of attempting to subsume the subtle and autonomous master-craft of social work to prosaic 'care management'. The devising of machinery of health and social care, however, proves unable to prevent a clogging system where inadequate levels of social care lag behind the medical needs of patients being processed, such as the 'bed-blocking' case of the unfortunate Mrs Sibley.

Case study

A recent example was that of Mrs Iris Sibley, aged 89. Iris languished in hospital at the Bristol Royal Infirmary for six months after she was fit to be discharged because she was assessed as being in need of 24-hour nursing care, rather than the level of support received in her current residential home. Despite repeated attempts, no suitable nursing home could be found. Mrs Sibley's family claim that during this time her health deteriorated further, with the NHS bill for this unnecessary six months on the ward mounting to £81,000. Mrs Sibley's case was then reassessed; she was found to be no longer qualified for NHS funding, requiring the council and relatives to find the money to top up nursing home costs (Topping, 2017).

The current Conservative Government has been strongly pressed by the Labour Opposition to shore up the NHS, with concerns expressed over social care. Few constructive aims seems to have come out of these shouting matches in the House of Commons, although the Conservative MP David Mowat made headlines in February 2017 when he stated that people had the same duty to care for their parents as they do to care for their children (Swinford, 2017).

While Confucian societies, like Singapore and Malaysia, may well view this as a culturally accommodated norm (see Chapter 5), the MP's comment was not well received by critics; rather it was considered suggestive of another clumsy attempt to avoid state responsibility as well as being patently simplistic thinking. Dealing with incontinence in a toddler is not quite of the same order as the strenuous, daily work of dealing with the same in an elderly adult for reasons that should be quite obvious to any thinking individual. Furthermore, while normally children grow towards independence, the trend is the reverse in frail older relatives, while their carers are also descending into advanced years. This entire pseudo-Confucian scenario of course assumes from the outset that older people have adult children or other close relatives able to provide devoted care in the first place.[1]

The Welfare State has always been supported by a range of community-based services run by the charitable and independent sector, but Clifford (2017:3) argues that charities face a *perfect storm* during periods of austerity when there are high demands on their services but serious declines in income via donations from individuals and the public services. The range of charitable and independent services is of course very wide, including law and advocacy, community and neighbourhood development schemes, health and social care services, to name but some areas covered. While some of these have experienced a decline over time, a marked increase in demand can be noted in health and social care, for example, which covers children and family work, working with elders, mental health and disabilities. An Age UK review, however, reveals that almost 1.2 million people do not receive the care they need, representing a 48% rise in numbers since 2010 (Triggle, 2017a). This journalist argues that cuts to council budgets are blamed for the rationing of services where now 695,500 people receive no help at all, with 487,400 people receiving insufficient help to address their needs.

---

[1] An appalling example of clashing political principles relates to the forced and traumatic deportation from the UK of a Singaporean-born woman married to a Briton whose deportation was made on the grounds of her trips back to Singapore to manage the care of her dying parents, while she was also the main carer of her sick husband (Slawson, 2017).

While other vulnerable people may be in danger of losing their home and independence by being transferred to residential homes, for those who are already in homes through need and by choice, the security afforded may be highly tenuous, as the case of Mrs Alice Wood demonstrates.

Case study

Alice Wood was an 88-year-old retired academic with quadriplegia (the result of a stroke) and late-stage dementia. She was now living in her seventh care home and seemed settled, until her personal funds from her savings, private pension and the sale of her home ran out, resulting in mounting arrears in payment of the home's fees. This private nursing home consequently not only served Mrs Wood with an eviction notice but literally hung the notice right above Mrs Wood's bed and refused to remove it. Her horrified daughter, Sarah, who suffers from chronic health problems, fought to prevent yet another move as, apart from this example of rank callousness, the nursing home was viewed as providing appropriate and good care.

Mrs Wood's history with social care had been a very difficult, exhausting and demoralising one. Prior to being accommodated in this nursing home, social services had previously placed Mrs Wood in a locked, mixed elderly mentally infirm (EMI) unit. Sarah removed her mother from what she described as a foul-smelling and chaotic environment as Mrs Wood appeared to be terrified of the other residents, who exhibited a variety of distressed and challenging behaviours. Moreover, Sarah strongly suspected that one member of staff in particular was physically abusing her mother as Mrs Wood appeared very agitated in this person's presence and used the word 'clout' repeatedly to her daughter.

Prior to being placed in this EMI unit Mrs Wood had been moved from residential to nursing homes as her physical health deteriorated. One residential home took her in only to close down soon after, unable to afford renovation work required of it. A further residential home where Mrs Wood was placed could no longer accommodate her needs after her stroke, as she now required 24-hour nursing care. Social services consequently placed Mrs Wood in a nursing home where she regained some help and became more mobile, enjoying a level of independence on short trips out. The home disliked this, however, and informed Sarah they could no longer offer Mrs Wood a home because her growing independence represented a risk to her personal safety as they were situated on a busy road.

When Mrs Wood made her seventh move to the home that was now seeking to evict her, she had anxiously asked Sarah, 'Will they love me enough to keep me?' The move was a success at first. Sarah noted how the staff respected Mrs Wood's personhood and gave her back her dignity. Over time Mrs Wood's mental and physical condition deteriorated, but she remained well cared for by the ground staff who formed a good relationship with her.

Now battling to prevent her mother's eviction, Sarah wrote to social services to request their support, but was told that, owing to the £50 weekly shortfall, Mrs Wood would be moved and they had the authority to do this without Sarah's consent. Weeks were now spent while Sarah consulted solicitors about Mrs Wood's rights and researched suitable care trusts. She then wrote to each care trust to try to raise the required funds, with a complete biography of her mother's impressive professional life with accompanying photographs of her down the years to help them to see her mother's personhood and plight, rather than just another anonymous case. After an enormous struggle by her devoted daughter, the weekly £50 was secured and Mrs Wood was able to continue living at the home up to the time she died.

Marginalisation of the young

We have so far considered the needs of older people and those with disabilities, but now we turn to another significant group who are conspicuously marginalised in the country – the young. In Britain, unlike many other European countries, the state takes little overt interest in supporting families to any significant degree. As a Welfare State the UK is more akin to the US *minimal state*, as described by Nozick (1974) in reference to the classic welfare model theorisation of Gøsta Esping-Andersen (1990). Minimal states typically only offer limited benefits, which are often viewed as stigmatising and are based on strict criteria. In contrast to this model is the 'corporatist state', as characterised by France, Germany and Italy. Finally, we have the rarer 'social democratic state', featuring universal benefits designed to promote citizen equality (the current Finnish experiment in the universal wage conforms to this model) (Sodha, 2017).

Gender forms a subtheme of our discussion of children and youth as marginalised groups. As Joan Orme (2001) and other critiques have long since pointed out, care giving of the young, the old, the frail and the sick is generally viewed as a female burden. It is a *feminised* task and so, although it is one where men may of course occupy the role of carers and nurturers, there is still an assumption that male carers buck this traditional gendered trend. It is likely therefore still to be largely mothers who are the primary careers of children and children and family social work services are in turn mainly targeted at women and children. In consequence a feminist critique has been levied regarding the unequal power of women (as social workers) over women as clients/service users (Orme, 2001). This aside, the professional focus of children and family work can either indirectly or deliberately marginalise the role of fathers and, where they are considered at all, problematise them as absent or abusive fathers (Scourfield, 2001, 2006). These skewed professional frameworks may be viewed as oppressive towards male clients and service users but are also implicated in the fall in numbers of male social work students entering the profession (Ashencaen Crabtree and Parker, 2014; Parker and Ashencaen Crabtree, 2014a), with ramifications for the marginalisation of male client/service user groups across the lifespan.

Austerity as an economic policy has hit some groups much harder than others. Findings from government studies revealed by the Shadow Cabinet show that the brunt falls heaviest upon women, whether they are mothers or others. These estimates have been calculated according to payments apportioned to individuals in households (Stewart, 2017a). From these it is claimed that austerity cuts have cost women £79 billion since 2010, in comparison to £13 billion borne by men (Stewart, 2017a); in view of these figures, it can be prudently surmised that the impact felt of austerity must also fall heavily upon children in families.

In Chapter 2, we discussed the issue of child poverty, which is now exacerbated by significant cuts to child tax credits for low-income families (Williams, 2017). A truism is that the lives and plight of children are encompassed within that of the family, whether the child lives with family members, parents or kin, or is otherwise accommodated owing to family problems. Consequently the care of children does not take place in a socio-political vacuum; children are also conspicuous victims of so-called austerity measures. Indeed, what has been suspected by many has now been supported by very powerful evidence in an extensive follow-up study on poverty in Organisation for Economic Co-operation and Development and EU countries by London School of Economics academics Kerris Cooper and Kitty Stewart (2017). The findings show that there is a direct causal link between parental income levels and cognitive, social, behavioural and health factors in children, irrespective of other factors such as parental education. The significance of this finding is immense and powerfully challenges political obfuscations regarding whether low family incomes dramatically affect the outcomes and life prospects of the most vulnerable of all in society, children. The answer is, they do.

Even targeted early preventive schemes that have been shown to yield great benefits to young families, like Sure Start, are now in danger of being swept away by severe cuts in their government funds (Rigby, 2017). The Sure Start focus was on working with those families with pre-school infants who required early intervention to develop good parenting coping skills, creating greater family resilience and cohesion, diminishing the likelihood of more serious and more expensive future state intervention. One can put this government response into the balance against the huge and overwhelming numbers of children in need suffering from neglect and abuse, which the NSPCC (2016) estimated to be 58,000 in the UK. Additional costs relate to social control: between 2010 and 2016, police numbers in England and Wales fell by 18,991 owing to cuts (Eaton, 2017). Added to this, the tremendous overcrowding of prisons has already reached crisis level (Bulman, 2016), as have the soaring rates of mental illness leading to self-harm and suicide (Vize, 2017). Furthermore, a new and damning report from the chief inspector of prisons reveals that no youth offender unit or private secure training centre for children and young people is considered safe for inmate health (Travis, 2017b). Under the circumstances therefore it makes little sense to cut funding to early intervention programmes that may help to prevent later social problems

More marginalised youth

The issue of tuition fees has been another key example of the marginalisation of young people, now taken up by Labour as a *cause célèbre* in its new manifesto. University (tertiary-level)

education has been reframed in the neoliberal perspective as being solely to an individual's advantage – an argument that continues to be rehearsed by Tory politician, Michael Gove (Stewart, 2017b). From these faulty premises it is reasoned that the financial burden of university education should be carried by students themselves. Yet this stands in complete contrast to the former and now recently resurgent view that tertiary education is a social good that benefits wider society, where linguists, teachers, social workers, dentists, lawyers, artists, journalists, architects and surgeons (and most other professions) were once viewed as contributing to creating a healthily functioning civil society. In consequence, the reasoning followed that civil society should contribute to its self-perpetuation by paying students a modest grant for their socially vital education which fed into, among other benefits, vocational careers from which all citizens benefited, directly or otherwise.

Again, one can easily trace the erosion of the notion of education from social weald (wellbeing) to individual advantage in political rhetoric and policy, where the semantic shift from using the word 'vocation' (as in the vocation of social workers and doctors) to that of 'profession' sums up these changes. One word (vocation) connotes communal values, altruistic duty, social conscience and social wellbeing. The other word tends to connote individualism, prestige, privilege and personal gain.

The impact of such thinking has forced a Faustian pact on British youth. University education purportedly offers a step into well-paid professions, but mass education has devalued undergraduate degrees to the extent that graduate-entry career positions are in very short supply and other kinds of jobs (rather than careers) have been able to raise their entry requirements far above the traditional school-leaving qualifications formerly required.

School leavers may also attempt to make career progress through apprenticeships but these too are in very short supply and carry insecurities in terms of future career opportunities. To avoid future employment disadvantage most young people opting for university education are obliged to shoulder terrifyingly huge debts, with various political muddle-headed approaches towards paying them back. In turn tuition fees, and the road towards them by the loss of the student grant system, has seriously undermined higher education, which has had little choice but to buy into mass education (as opposed to wider access, a different conceptual beast altogether). With heavily diminished state financial support higher education institutions (charitable, non-profit-making organisations) are forced into quasi-capitalism by charging the highest tuition fees they can get away with, while suppressing the wage increases of academics, apart from the enormous emolliments paid to vice chancellors. The Association of University Teachers claims there has been a wage fall for academics of 40%; other figures show that academics are poorly paid compared to other comparator professional groups (Collins et al., 2007). Commensurately, academic workloads and workplace stress are noted to be very high (Berg and Seeber, 2016).

The skewing of what education is and should be has resulted in unhappy students shaped into pseudo-customers buying a degree and unhappy academics unable to offer students the intellectually stimulating education that previous generations of students experienced, but instead being obliged to create education 'products' for sale and urged to bolt on eye-catching but usually pointless 'learning' gimmicks. Ultimately this absurdly flawed, commodified thinking across the public and non-profit sector has spread across society like some pernicious cancer, distorting public perceptions and serving neither the individual nor the community well.

Political marginalisation of young people

Thanks to the Trump Administration's creative use of language, we have 'alternative facts' but in the UK we may also boast of *alternative logic*. One rhetorical question posed by alternative logic is: do politicians regard the social consequences of bad political decisions today as of any particular concern for party politics tomorrow? Even to have to pose such a question suggests that social commentators like George Monbiot (2017) may well be right: maybe the overarching crisis in our time has been a monumental loss of faith in society in the benign and progressive social power of democratic politics. This is an alarming thought given the lessons recent European history teaches us of where other socio-political ideological paths can lead.

The conclusion one must regrettably reach is that little thought is given to a future where one or another political party may not necessarily be in power. If political parties are fundamentally only self-perpetuating bodies focused on insular political gamesmanship, does this constitute gross political irresponsibility? Such conclusions have been reached by many social analysts regarding the shocking EU referendum results in June 2016, when many poorer UK regional areas who had benefited so much from EU funding appeared to be at the front of the queue to vote out of the EU! As one dismayed journalist wrote about the referendum vote among his native Welsh valleys, it seemed a case of *turkeys voting for Christmas* (Wyn Jones, 2016).

Be that as it may, the EU referendum saw a high turnout of voters, at 72% of eligible voters, with the outcome swung by a controversially small minority (Electoral Commission, 2016). Voting was not dependent on party politics but was manifested across parties, serving to highlight yawning schisms in British society. Entire regions of the country were dominated by Remain or Leave votes, with the Remain vote being the strongest in Scotland, London and the Home Counties and Northern Ireland, with some Remain pockets in the North of England and Wales as well. However, it was the Leave vote that carried the day in England and Wales, which included among others a number of Northern cities like Birmingham and Sheffield (BBC, 2016); a surprising outcome given the cosmopolitan, multicultural nature of urban Britain.

Further divisions were found in terms of age: older people were more likely to vote Leave than younger people. Education levels also played a part, with graduates more likely to vote Remain. Income was implicated in the vote, once again: those earning about £30,000 per annum and above were more likely to vote Remain. Given the apparent débâcle regarding the issues of belonging to the EU, and critically, what the impact of leaving the EU would entail for Britain, the outcome of the EU referendum seemed to speak more about British society and its deepening divisions than about EU membership or what kind of entity the EU actually is.

The question of citizen disenfranchisement of large sections of British society as part of the EU referendum process is one that has not been sufficiently driven home in public. Leaving aside the question of whether such a referendum was sufficient justification for such a monumental historical decision with such huge social repercussions, the facts are that the majority vote was a very slim one, at 48.1% Remain versus 51.9% Leave (Electoral Commission, 2016). Since then Theresa May, the current Prime Minister (who played her cards ambiguously before former Prime Minister David Cameron resigned, although in all fairness, so did Jeremy Corbyn), has, along with the rest of the triumphant Leave campaign, continually referred to the *British people* as having spoken. This oppressive rhetoric strongly implies to the nation that firstly, the vote was swung by a much larger majority than it was or that otherwise the millions of people who voted to remain EU citizens are not included in the term 'British people'. The clear suggestion is that they do not really count and can be told to stop moaning or discarded on the 'red, white and blue' march away from Europe into an uncertain future of national isolationism in a world that has long forgotten the former hegemonic power of the British Empire or its pivotal Cold War influences.

Regardless of the triumphalist propaganda, having cast aside its main trading partners, Britain will need to fight extremely hard not to be reduced to anything other than an obscure, impoverished and marginalised nation, unless the fantasies of new, global markets to exploit are substantiated, for which there is as yet no real evidence. As we write, the huge economic ramifications of leaving the EU are becoming clearer as the dismayed responses of the business community become more audible.

Among those who did not count as the post-referendum voice of Britain are the young. Here we speak of the 16- and 17-year-olds (as well as their younger counterparts) who were ineligible to vote on the grounds of age. It is nonetheless they and younger generations who will carry the heavy burden of this unknown future of curtailed international mobility influencing their broader education, their qualifications, their careers, future adult relationships and their ability to compete in a world where it is most likely that they will be greatly disadvantaged by the decisions that older citizens have made on their behalf, as articulated by the underage blogger, Niklaus McKerrell (2016).

It would also be wrong to forget that older voters benefited from all the EU gave, including many protective rights offered to employees, women and people with disabilities, which are now jeopardised by the political pull away from Europe. The question of morality versus legality comes to the fore here, regarding such handicapping of young people, whose legal disenfranchisement could have been waived on moral and pragmatic grounds, given that they were so close in age to vote and were among the generation in the vanguard of receiving the first real impact on leaving. Had they been allowed to vote and had the voting patterns been borne out, the EU referendum would have swung towards remaining. A year on from the referendum a new poll indicates that 60% of UK citizens would actually hand over a good deal of hard cash to maintain the right to remain EU citizens (Farand, 2017). Rich irony indeed!

What the future may hold for young citizens will fall out in due course and will be the subject of much analysis and critique by future historians. It may well be that today's young Britons will eventually weigh up the consequences of recent history and choose to return Britain to the EU alliance, as Jean-Claude Juncker has suggested, or the UK may not leave the EU at all, as Vince Cable has since suggested. In the meantime the young will be the product of and inherit an educational system that has been subject to continual, random political experimentation for years in the form of curriculum interference, endless testing of young children, bombastic and elitist pronouncements of what education should be, taught by a heavily over-burdened and deskilled, demoralised teaching profession.

The issue of non-state-run 'free schools' represents such political experimentation: money that could be diverted to cash-starved state schools contines to be lavished upon such schools. Many faith schools have been set up on very doubtful notions that do little to engage with and enhance a European, multiculturalist agenda of inclusion or broader education; while the evidence is equivocal, with some outstanding examples, many free schools seem to be proving to be inadequate to the task before them (Bolton, 2016; Schools Week, 2016). In the meantime finance-pinched state schools are reaching critical breaking point, to the extent of proposing to shorten the school day because they cannot afford sufficient teaching cover (for more information on teaching cuts, see the National Union of Teachers: **https://www.teachers.org.uk/education-policies/funding**).

In the recent Conservative manifesto, plans were announced to remove free school lunches from families on low incomes and replace them with a cheaper breakfast (a subsidised meal that is already often provided to such children at schools). Jamie Oliver, the celebrity chef at the forefront of campaigns for decent school meals, launched a vigorous media attack on these plans (Richardson, 2017). Predictable bad publicity around this idea means that there has been a rapid government *volte face* on this ugly measure, as there has been on the party's so-called 'dementia tax'. The imposition of greater inequity on the least privileged groups in society has thus been narrowly averted on this occasion.

Marginalisation in context

The NHS, as we have seen, is a victim of the tragic saga of political incompetence and starvation of adequate funds, combined with zealous ideological dogma. So too with the rest of public services that have been kicked about by political parties like a shabby, unloved and deflating football, to end up decaying in the long grass and forgotten by those who are meant to serve the public interest first and foremost. The lives and needs of individuals have equally been subject to politicised discourses that are both degrading and dehumanising, depicted as resource-hungry consumers of commodities that are offered by privatised community care agencies competing in a market economy of reducing overheads and maximising profits. It is this worrying socio-political context that younger social work graduates entering the professions will already have much personal and social experiences of, not least in their journey through social work education, as outlined in Chapter 2.

Fortunately social work still provides a reasonably intact, critically intellectual terrain from which to survey the impact of political ideologies and social policies on communities. From this vantage point we can consider the familiar social work concept of 'learned helplessness'. This refers to the feeling and associated behaviours by which an individual 'learns' that over time actions/behaviour do not seem to lead to a change in circumstances; therefore there is nothing they can do to effect changes. This can be seen as a psychological response in people and families who become trapped in the perpetuation of unhealthy, dysfunctional behaviours – which by the nature of things often do not tend to remain static, but spiral downwards. In dealing with learned helplessness the social worker/therapist's aim is to facilitate new ways of thinking by helping individuals/groups to take effective steps that challenge previous thinking and are seen to lead to changes, thus creating a virtuous circle of perceived action leading to rewarding changes.

With this in mind it is worth exploring whether society, composed of individuals, also suffers from a degree of learned helplessness, as epitomised in the suspicious, jaundiced post-Second World War saying, 'Whoever you vote for, the government gets in.' It is certainly interesting to note that, while the sales of Orwell's (1949) dystopic novel *1984* have rocketed in the USA and the UK once again, this has lately been counterbalanced by ripe nostalgia for a Britain that never was, along with frank and belligerent jingoism. The vote against the EU was largely interpreted by social analysts at the time as a vote against the selfish hegemony of the British elite, symbolised by London-centric myopia (for London, read 'Westminster'). The terrible irony of how this electoral reactionism will rebound on regional communities that view themselves as ignored has already been discussed.

However, how should social workers respond to these socio-political developments that impact upon their work, and where and with whom such work is carried out? Such questions demand a level of serious engagement by the profession as marginalised communities are made up of those marginal groups and individuals with whom social workers often works directly. Political attempts to embed *apoliticisation* in social work, in what has been in general a highly politicised profession, damages a social work paradigm that is fundamentally reflective, proactive and dynamic rather than merely reactive (a topic we revisit in Chapter 9). Further than this, however, such understandings of the profession directly link to social work as an international profession, as articulated in the *Global Definition of Social Work* by the International Federation of Social Workers (IFSW, 2014). While the IFSW aims to create an agenda of social work solidarity, at national levels how well social work is supported at home is instrumental to the profession's level of confidence and coherence – and thus effective work.

Political agendas that play on collective learned helplessness and scapegoating of others serve to deflect the public's attention from problems within society. Yet tackling these at grassroot levels in ways that enable social workers actively to side with beleaguered communities is one of the dominant challenges facing UK social work today and returns us to the spirit of the radical social work of the 1970s (Ferguson, 2015).

Chapter summary

The impact of every experience we have as an individual differs from person to person. It depends on our prior life experiences, our psychological and physical make-up and our social supports. However, we have seen in this chapter some of the effects of marginalising life experiences on the people with whom we work as social workers. What we have tried to achieve in this chapter is to map different experiences in a way that can be used to navigate the complex, shifting terrain of social work and to politicise these. This enables us, as social workers, to maintain an awareness of the various contexts in which people's experiences of marginalisation and disadvantage take place. This chapter draws to a conclusion the first part of the book and allows us now to move from the theoretical and conceptual into the knowledge and skills that we need to draw from in order to practise good social work.

Further reading

Brown, G.W. and Harris, T. (1978) *The Social Origins of Depression: A Study of Psychiatric Disorder in Women.* London: Tavistock.

This psychiatric study represents a seminal work in understanding how social pressures and divisions can affect a person's health in serious ways, and how opportunities for social contact and support can aid health. It is not a social work text but is central to our developing understanding of the world.

Varuofakis, Y. (2017) *And the Weak Must Suffer What They Must? Europe, Austerity and the Threat to Global Stability.* London: Vintage.

Again, this is not a social work text, but it details some of the wider social and political implications of current life in Britain and the rest of Europe. It is important to be aware of these wider issues (see Chapters 5 and 7).

Alongside these books you should seek to watch the Ken Loach film *I, Daniel Blake.* This film tells the story of a widowed carpenter who had to give up work because of a heart attack and his brutalising experiences of a benefit system geared to returning him to work despite medical evidence to the contrary.

Part II

Knowledge and skills

Chapters 5–7 consider the different sets of knowledge and skills that are important to develop when working in the complex world of marginalisation and disadvantage.

5: Factual and interpretive knowledge

(Continued)

Critical reflection and analysis

Inform decision making through the identification and gathering of information from multiple sources, actively seeking new sources.

With support, rigorously question and evaluate the reliability and validity of information from different sources.

It will also introduce you to the following academic standards as set out in the social work subject benchmark statement.

5.2.i, iii Social work theory
5.5.i The nature of social work practice

Introduction

The knowledge base for working with people and groups who are disadvantaged and marginalised is wide ranging. We have already explored a great deal of it throughout this book. In this chapter a range of 'factual knowledges' – knowledge that exists and is interpreted in the social world inhabited by social workers and those with whom they work – will be considered (Parker, 2017). The plural is used to convey the broad nature of understanding that social workers need. These types of knowledge range from the very practical understanding and use of legislation, of organisational policy and procedure, through understanding wider world events having an impact on people, groups and communities, to theoretical understandings of working with difference, diversity, discrimination and disadvantage. The chapter will also consider the centrality of values and ethics in social work practice. Whilst these available forms of knowledge are considered 'factual', this does not mean that they exist as realities outside our interpretation. All knowledge employed in the social world and, indeed, for social work practice, is interpreted by ourselves, our employers and those with whom we meet and interact. It is important that we keep this in mind and that we act reflexively, questioning the knowledge, its sources and the impact it may have on our practice as social workers.

Knowing the law relating to disadvantage, discrimination and what can be done is an important element of social work, and some relevant law will be considered in this chapter, although the ways in which it might be used given its underpinning by human rights legislation will be considered more deeply in Chapter 8. Legislation is always understood in particular ways within those organisations in which social workers are employed and applied accordingly. Therefore, service and organisational literacy is central. It is also helpful for social workers to find out what organisations exist in their local area and how these might help in countering disadvantage and marginalisation.

Knowledge of global, national and local politics is important for social workers to understand the structural pressures affecting people's involvement in society. In order to achieve this social workers need a basic knowledge of world events and politics and a grasp of current events that may affect groups and communities. A focus on the centrality of reflexivity in considering political and current affairs will be discussed.

After considering the wider political knowledge required for working with disadvantage and marginalisation, the importance of theoretical knowledge about working with difference and diversity and understanding the concepts and approaches to anti-oppressive, anti-discriminatory practice, cultural competences, critical race theory and anti-racist social work, super-diversity and intersectionality will be revisited for practice, advancing on their introduction in earlier chapters.

The last part of the chapter will examine social work ethics and values and how these connect with practice for social justice, dignity and wellbeing and act as a backdrop for Chapter 9 and the exploration of ethical dilemmas. In this section, we will consider the complexities of absolute versus relative belief systems in which social workers practise.

What legislation and policy knowledge do you need to work with people who are marginalised or unfairly treated?

As we write, we in the UK are still members of the European Union (EU) and, as a country, bound by over 40 years of important legislation that has driven the creation and adoption of understandings and practices in social and health care, about communities, equalities and rights. We are uncertain, and not a little concerned, how the legislative base of our society will change as the UK moves towards leaving the EU. However, what we will rehearse here is existing legislation that is important to have knowledge of as a social worker, remembering that legislation concerning social work, welfare and safeguarding tends to be amended fairly frequently (Brammer, 2015; Johns, 2017). What is also important is that you have an understanding of the court structures in which social workers operate and the legislative structures from which the law and policy emanate.

The courts are extremely important in social work practice as the fora in which key decisions affecting people's lives are made, rights are determined, and in which social work reports and evidence are central to outcomes. The courts are separated hierarchically and most social workers will appear in magistrates', county and high courts concerning family and civil proceedings. If working in youth justice you may also appear in magistrates' and crown court for criminal proceedings. Above these courts are courts of appeal, the Supreme Court and, currently, the European Court of Human Rights. An important way of getting to know the courts and their structures and operations is to visit and to talk to the clerks to the court. It is worthwhile making time to do so during your qualifying education.

The range of specific legislation and guidance you will need to be aware of as a social worker depends to a large extent on your field of practice. However, it is important to have a grasp of legislation relating to children and young people, mental health, capacity, care, health and criminal law – especially that relating to violence and offences against the person.

Activity 5.1

What legislation do you think you will need to have at least a basic awareness of as a practising social worker? Make a list and then identify what you already know about and what you need to know.

Comment

There are many excellent textbooks that detail law for social workers. Some of the most used are those by Brammer (2015) and Brayne et al. (2015), both written by law academics, Johns (2017) and Braye and Preston-Shoot (2016), who offer readily accessible texts for beginning and more experienced social workers from the perspective of the discipline. These texts are often updated because legislation changes and new precedents are set as case law develops. As you move through your education and on into practice it will be important to keep up to date in these areas as the law changes.

Alongside law dealing with the specific areas social workers find themselves practising, it is central to good practice to be well versed in those aspects of policy and legislation that relate to people's exclusion on specific traits and characteristics. Anti-discriminatory legislation has a fairly long history in the UK, as explicit laws dealing with specific aspects of discrimination in social life came to people's attention during the turbulent and changing times of the 1960s (see Chapter 1). This was influenced by many diverse events and shifts, such as the Notting Hill riots in 1958, where race and ethnicity surfaced with disaffected White youths attacking African-Caribbean men, leading to the murder of Kelso Cochrane in 1959 (Warwick Digital Collections, n.d.), the Dagenham car dispute in which women machinists campaigned for equal pay for equal work (Friedman and Meredeen, 1980), campaigns to change anti-abortion and anti-homosexuality legislation in the late 1960s, alongside civil rights protests in the USA and in Northern Ireland (Parker, 2007). By the early 1970s we had race relations, sex discrimination and equal pay legislation, some stemming from the mid-1960s. Whilst legislation does not immediately change behaviour or attitudes, it does set a pathway to change in society (Baier, 2016).

The Equality Act has pulled together our anti-discrimination legislation, making it much easier to consider a consistent approach to practice. However, the history of the development of specific laws relating to those with whom social workers engage is still central to our knowledge base. We do not need to cover the legislation in any detail here but it is important to ensure that you have an understanding of the principles underpinning the legislation and the key elements as this will have a tremendous effect on how you approach the social work role with marginalised people. A good place to start in examining the history is Thane (2010), and we will explore more contemporary uses in Chapter 8.

What do you need to know about politics, history and the ways the world works?

Although we have already enjoyed a short historical excursion in Chapter 2 in examining care in the community, let us start this section with three questions that we have heard from students over many years.

Why is history important to social workers?

The twentieth-century sociologist who coined the enduring phrase *the sociological imagination*, C. Wright Mills (1959) stated clearly that you cannot understand your place in the world, or in society, without seeing your life (your biography) in the context of wider history. In this sense he was writing as a historical sociologist. This is something that social workers often take on themselves, although it is unlikely that many would make that claim. Social workers seek to understand why people have trod the pathway through life that they have and in order to do so effectively consider structural factors that create and deny opportunities for individuals, criminalise or legitimate their behaviours and support or marginalise them. It is within this messy context that social workers practise to find ways in which individuals can take their place in society or, where appropriate and necessary, challenge that society.

Why should social workers be interested in and informed by politics and political events?

When we became social workers people in the profession were politically engaged, often taking a left-of-centre stance, as a means of effecting positive change. Of course, not everyone was politically active, nor did everyone follow the same views, but there was greater interest and, seemingly, faith in political action. Over recent years engagement and interest in politics appear to have waned (White et al., 2000). Partly, this can be understood as growing cynicism towards the perceived corruption and power-seeking behaviours of politicians, the convergence of centrist positions in parties gaining power in the UK and a concomitant feeling of powerlessness amongst the electorate.

In social work this has been compounded by increased political interest (or interference) in social work education and practice as a means of regulating people and responding to popular pressures or criticisms. Some of these changes are well rehearsed but it is important to remember the overt political involvement of the (then) Education Minister, Ed Balls, when the report of the inquiry into the death of Peter Connelly (Baby P) was released in 2009 (Jones, 2014; Shoesmith, 2016). A furore erupted following the report in which social workers were pilloried and education was found wanting in what appeared to be a means of responding to popularism and became a deflection from the excellent work that social workers were doing every day; it was, in effect, a marginalisation of the social work discipline. This has left social work, and education, in England weakened and more subject to political influence. It is something that we as social workers must strive to take back and ensure that we can understand these processes so they are not allowed to damage our work with service users and carers in the future.

What has the state of the world got to do with social work?

For some readers the answers may appear obvious, whilst for others the urgency of individual practice situations and the immediacy of the 'local' cloud the issue somewhat. The intensity of social work on a daily basis often concerns the management of too many cases, too many targets and too much bureaucracy, say many social workers (Munro, 2011). However, it is imperative that we do not lose sight of the biographies of individuals, that we hear their narratives. Elsewhere we have talked about social work as a kind of ethnographic practice (Parker and Ashencaen Crabtree, 2016; Parker, 2017). This involves a deep immersion into the lives and lived experiences of those with whom you are working which necessitates interest in individual biographies and the contexts in which they have developed, the wider histories.

Ways in which you can gain knowledge of the world, current issues and its politics and history are varied and, of course, dependent on the bias of those who present them. For instance, it is helpful, and important, to read a newspaper but if you read the *Guardian*, *Independent*, *Telegraph*, *Times*, *Daily Mirror*, *Daily Mail* or the *Sun* you will get a different point of view. Most of the British press takes a centre to right-wing perspective; some attempt to be more balanced or are slightly left of centre. When reading the news these political perspectives need to be taken into account as they influence the type of 'truths' you are being introduced to. Also, the centrality of social work values are key and should play a part in determining the approach you take to your news reading.

Printed media, and the online versions of newspapers, are not the only ways in which you can keep up to date with current affairs. Television, radio, online and social media sources are replete with items of interest. Again, it is important to identify the biases of each source so you can interpret them accordingly.

Activity 5.2

Choose a news item relating to social work or social care that you are aware of and search the internet for two different reports of the same story. Consider what perspective each report is taking, what meanings are being constructed and what the impact of each might be on the general public, on the people who are the focus of the reports and on your practice as a social worker. How do the news items relate to the context of world affairs? What are the implications for social work values?

Comment

Different approaches may be taken to each news item and your perspectives will be influenced by a combination of your own experiences in life, your personal values and beliefs. However, you will no doubt have been able to identify some of the ways in which political biases influence reporting, reading and the actions you are more likely to take having read the news stories. What is important in this, in particular, is to identify the impact the reports may have on people in similar situations and on the general public. Such reports can often lead to the formation of assumptions and beliefs that influence the ways in which those events, circumstances and situations are approached in the future and the moral analysis made of them.

So, having introduced these three questions we can ask: what do we need to know about history, politics and international affairs in order to practise with people who are marginalised in society? Firstly, it is important to remember that Britain, like many other European nations, has a history as a colonial power, which continues to have important implications for contemporary practice. Not only did Britain administer many colonies, some well into the twentieth century, but it was a nation intimately involved in the slave trade until the first half of the nineteenth century. Of course, it may be said that this was a long time ago and that times have changed. This is true. However, the ways in which international relations take place, the distribution of wealth and wellbeing and the effects of conflicts in the world are, to an extent, influenced by these past events, amongst others. Therefore, it is important that social workers have an awareness when practising with, for instance, a refugee from a war-torn country, an African-Caribbean British man with health problems or a victim of forced marriage.

Contemporary historical events also have an impact on people's lives that require some understanding. For instance, the experiences of a former member of the armed forces in Bosnia in the 1990s or in Afghanistan in the 2000s may well have influenced that person's behaviours, thoughts and emotions. It may help to explain some of the difficulties the individual is experiencing and, although not an excuse, it can help understand someone's engagement in anti-social and violent behaviours.

In respect of politics social workers need an awareness of the political views of parties and how these would affect, often differentially, the care and support offered to different people and groups. Policies are part of the pathway to marginalisation and social workers are often the agents of the state who are charged with enacting them. Therefore, it is important that alternative perspectives are sought, that the values of social work are maintained and that people are not disadvantaged and marginalised by your actions. Having a knowledge of the political system, and being politically involved as a citizen, are two distinct and important ways that social workers use and develop their knowledge of politics.

Anti-oppressive, anti-discriminatory practice and knowledge for addressing unfair treatment

In Chapter 1 we introduced some of the core concepts relating to understanding people who are marginalised within or from society. Here we need to consider how these translate into workable models for practice. The core questions here concern how we work anti-discriminatorily and anti-oppressively. Thompson (2016) identifies seven positive steps that we can take towards practising in an anti-discriminatory way:

1. Undertaking awareness training can develop a personal understanding of the implications of our practice and, when undertaken as a group, allows teams to address some of the cultural perspectives that develop.

2. Valuing diversity and exploring the positive elements of diversity in the world, in points of view and practices. Thompson warns that this remains somewhat undeveloped but it does allow for self-reflection, questioning and challenge.

3. Raising collective awareness of problems can lead to collective action against our own marginalisation. For instance, where women recognise a gender gap in pay it can lead to a collective action to demand parity. This kind of collective action can be facilitated by social workers who have enhanced their awareness of discrimination and its effects and are able to pass this on to marginalised people and groups to take action themselves.

4. Thompson argues for the overt integration of theory into practice to prevent 'common-sense' understandings permeating. This is because it is those common-sense perspectives that so often underpin stereotypical approaches to the 'other' and permit discrimination and oppression.

5. The principles of equality and social justice should be placed at the forefront of practice and not seen as an add-on extra. This may bring you into conflict with your employer organisation, whose targets and demands may be seen as taking precedence. However, it is important as a social worker to hold dear these core principles.

6. We have stressed throughout the book the need for critical, challenging and reflective questioning of one's self and this forms the basis of Thompson's sixth positive step.

7. Finally, and similarly to the previous step, it is recommended that you develop your self-reflective critical approach by internalising good practice as a whole.

Let's now turn to the following case study to see how these steps may be followed in practice.

Case study

The Greenwood team was a children and families team in a local authority that had recently rehoused a number of refugee families. The local authority and the social workers in the team were committed to providing appropriate support to these families. However, the team were unsure how to respond, what customs they needed to be mindful of and how to balance the complexities of culture and protection for the families coming into the area.

Two of the social workers were asked to consider what the team needed in order to prepare for supporting these families. They discussed with the team their own needs and the philosophy from which they approached the task – social justice and human rights. This led to the development of awareness raising and reflection on personal and team needs. They also sought assistance directly from the families rehoused in their area and, with translation support, encouraged and enabled members of that community to offer training sessions directly to the team and to join a community liaison group.

It is often useful to have some understanding of the groups and individuals with whom you work. However, criticism has been levelled against the concept of cultural competence (Laird, 2008; Ashencaen Crabtree et al., 2016). It has been suggested that a little knowledge can be a dangerous thing, leading to 'essentialising' of the characteristics of another. The same charge may be made in respect of having a little knowledge of history, politics and world affairs. However, this need not be the case. Keeping in mind a reflexive approach in which you question your understanding and allow it to be challenged by asking those with whom you are working to offer their stories or biographies, views and understandings, it is possible to stay close to those people. The concept sits uneasily with critical race theory, which may suggest that racism represents a normal art of everyday life embedded within its structures and not diminished by equality legislation (Crenshaw et al., 1995). However, when we take a critical self-reflexive stance and are honest enough to recognise our own prejudices and positions, a beginning stance is reached in which change and development become possible. This is how the Greenwood team (see above) began to address their needs in supporting the new community.

What will also help here is to bring to mind your knowledge of theoretical positions and concepts. For instance, in Chapter 1 we introduced intersectionality and super-diversity. These concepts help us to see the multiple social characteristics and divisions that make up our complex lives and to understand that knowledge of a 'culture' or a 'people' is a homogenised view that does not portray the individuals who make up those groups. These approaches insist that we recognise individuals' experiences within a political world and that we abandon our assumptions in favour of the 'lived experiences' of those individuals. This is important because, when people are a refugees, they are also a woman or a man, of a certain age, with friends and relatives who may or may not be with them or even alive; they have different experiences of education, of work and of home. Social work itself is complex and can work with the complexity of people's lives. One of the interesting, and contested, aspects of intersectionality and super-diversity is the replacement of a hierarchy of oppressive experience with a multiple one. Some people will privilege one aspect of their make-up and/or experience and this should be accepted, but imposing a hierarchy to diminish the experiences of others should be resisted, leading as it does to differential treatment and access to resources that may be equally needed.

What knowledge do you need about values and ethics in social work?

You will come into contact with some core elements of Western philosophy when considering values and ethics in social work. An obvious gap here is where other philosophies and approaches to axiology (the study of ethics) sit. The three types of approach that you are most likely to study are deontological or absolutist approaches to social life, utilitarian or consequentialist ones and probably Aristotelian virtue ethics. The latter may be couched in post-modern terms. However, we are going to consider some non-Western approaches, including Confucianism (which we have already referred to in Chapter 4), important as we work within a more fluid and global world, before examining the place of 'situation ethics', concepts stemming from theological debates, within the context of social work practice. The musts, shoulds and oughts of practice are explored within different approaches to values and ethics and are key elements of our knowledge base when dealing with people who are marginalised in and from society.

Deontology

Deontology concerns given and accepted rules that must be followed. Deontological approaches to social work ethics do not concern themselves with the motives of the individuals acting, their intention, or what happens as a result of the actions or behaviours that are undertaken. They are only concerned with the rules being followed to the letter. This kind of approach seems to remove the person or subject from the actions or context and to promote an instrumentalism that we can see in procedural and bureaucratic practice.

Deontology has its place in social work practice. Consider, for instance, if ethical procedures and rules concerning confidentiality are not followed and one of the people you are working with is identified in her community, possibly leading to greater stigmatisation. Even if your intentions were for the good of that person you are liable to be in 'hot water'.

The British Association of Social Workers (BASW) code of ethics (2012) sets out three core principles – human rights, social justice and professional integrity – which carry additional prescriptions. A deontological approach to these would be to see them as 'musts' which have to be completed regardless of context, circumstances or resources. However, BASW recognises there are complex circumstances in practice, sometimes tensions between employing organisations and practitioners or a lack of resources that put the completion of some prescriptions at risk. Human beings and interactions between people do not fit neatly into rule-bound behaviours and sometimes we need to consider the results of our actions. It is to utilitarian or consequentialist ethical positions that we now turn.

Utilitarian/consequentialist approaches

Utilitarian ethics is often promoted as quite a benign ethic, something that can be encapsulated in the maxim stating that actions are good if they maximise happiness, a good outcome, for the many rather than the few. The rightness of an action is judged by its consequences. At face value this seems to be democratic and quite appropriate. When we dig deeper there are complicating factors associated with this model.

Historically, utilitarian approaches developed towards the end of the eighteenth and into the nineteenth century in a context of political debate and uncertainty in which the age-old question of how much involvement the state should have in people's everyday lives was hotly discussed. Jeremy Bentham, one of the originators of this type of thinking, believed the state should have, at most, a minimal involvement and this influenced a number of people's understanding of poor relief (Harris, 2004). Most of us value our privacy and do not want our lives restricted by external entities. Indeed, privacy is enshrined in human rights and underpins much of data protection laws, emphasis on confidentiality and freedom from surveillance. However, there are times when people require assistance. There are times when people are not in a position, no matter how hard we try, to make decisions on their own behalf. At these times the state and, often, social workers need to intervene. So, whilst the greatest happiness of the greatest number may be achieved by protecting us from state interference, there are, at least, residual situations that require involvement.

Previously one of us wrote about the attractions and pitfalls of employing utilitarian ethics when working with people living with dementia (Parker, 2001). At that time, even more so than today, people with dementia were marginalised from everyday living and considered in a very negative light with very little future other than a slow decline towards an ignominious death. Capacity issues were often overlooked and certainly not encouraged. The ways in which social work and social care could maximise the happiness or best outcome for the many were liable, therefore, to focus on those included in society, having an accepted voice and citizenship or entitlement. Excluding people with dementia to focus on other needs, on carers who potentially had differing needs, represented a utilitarian approach but left out a growing marginalised group. When people with dementia were the focus, an assumed, taken-for-granted approach was considered: day care, nursing home care and homogeneous support were likely to be offered that might work for most people but would not offer tailor-made care to individuals who each had a unique biography and history. More ominously was the focus on the best outcome for the many, which included options that controlled and restricted to enable a better life for those who remained – for instance, moving someone into residential or nursing home care to meet the needs of carers, not the person with dementia. Moves towards personalised care through the personalisation agenda and enshrined in the Care Act 2014 have shifted the emphasis, although political complexities demand that we approach these changes with caution (Gardner, 2014; Parker, 2017).

A utilitarian approach can, therefore, further marginalise the excluded whilst supporting the many. This may be seen as inevitable in a financially constrained and imperfect world where the messiness of human lives, need and social work care operate. However, it is important to reflect on the reasons for our actions and the processes involved as well as their consequences. We must also note that consequences are valued differently by different people with different agendas, which again makes the utilitarian approach more complex. This was shown in the 2017 Conservative election manifesto (Conservative Party, 2017) focus on social policy and welfare issues. To reiterate, the manifesto suggested that free school meals would be removed from infants to pay for breakfasts for nursery school children, saving money but removing an important source of nourishment for many disadvantaged children. In respect of social care and older people the Conservative manifesto proposed that older people requiring social care, a group marginalised by age, need and number, would be required to use their assets to fund that care. Whilst these positions were adapted, they raise questions. The arguments about the moral rightness of paying for social care needs is a complex one and there are many positions to be taken into account. However, the focus is again on the many (citizens not requiring social care) and not the few (those in need). Thus, in social work we need to be aware of the ethical maxims driving what we do and how we do it, and to consider other models of right behaviour. Let us turn, first of all, to an exploration of what is right and good – virtue ethics.

Virtue ethics

Aristotle accepted that people approach the concept of a good life in different ways, reflecting their different characteristics and needs. This approach demands experimentation and deep observation, reflecting social work's imperative to 'walk alongside' people on the margins and to immerse themselves in their society. Whilst Aristotle spoke of moderation between extremes relative to the needs of situation and individual, he did identify a range of virtues that are necessary to achieve within oneself to conduct a good life, a life of happiness. It is from this thinking that virtue ethics stems. This approach to ethics takes the person and his or her moral character as central rather than searching for an overarching model of ethical life, unlike deontology and consequentialism (Baron et al., 1997). The approach requires us to ask questions about what constitutes a morally worthwhile or good life and has been used to delineate an ethics of care and nurture important in feminist and social work settings (Gilligan, 1982, 1988; Halwani, 2003).

Virtue ethics represents a relativistic ethic, however, and does not give any instrumental guidance as to how one should behave. This has been used as a critique but perhaps belies a point for critical reflection by social workers that challenges a regimented and categorising approach to people and groups, something that necessarily marginalises and disadvantages those who fall outside accepted parameters. Rather, social work stands with those at the edges and beyond and walks with them. It needs to answer the question, nonetheless, how other people are protected from those whose 'good life' and ethic increase the needs of others. Virtue ethics, as an approach to social work, raises important issues in determining what we do, when and how we do it. These are questions that aid critical self-reflection and determine, contextually, why we take a certain position or not in our practice. The relativism of virtue ethics may cause some difficulties and it is useful also to find an anchor. We will now turn to situation ethics which, through social justice and human rights, may begin to provide such a grounding.

Situation ethics and the 'post-post-modern'

An important perspective, known as 'situation ethics', derived from theological debate, was taken up in feminist thinking and has developed in social research and practice. Situation ethics demands respect for the requirements of ethical codes and prescriptions but interrogates them for contextual appropriateness, asking whether it is always 'right' to follow rules to the letter. Indeed, situation ethics is prepared to set aside certain ethical rules in given situations when it is considered that the benefits outweigh the possible harms (Parker and Ashencaen Crabtree, 2014b). In social work research this has been referred to as 'principled relativism' (Hardwick and Worsley, 2011). Critics of this approach suggest it sits within a relativistic or antinomian framework, somewhere without laws or rules (Kainer, 2012). However, an approach using situation ethics believes it is important to recognise the centrality of norms, rules and standards but emphasises the need to select flexible application according to the context in which one finds oneself. Joseph Fletcher, the theologian who developed this understanding of ethics, states:

> *The situationist enters into every decision-making situation fully armed with the ethical maxims of his community and its heritage, and he treats them with respect as illuminators of his problems. Just the same he is prepared in any situation to compromise them or set them aside in the situation if love seems better served by doing so.*

(Fletcher, 1966:26)

This is important for social work practice. We have certainly discussed the broad acceptance of globally developed ethical prescriptions concerning social justice and human rights from which more specific ethical codes have been derived. Evidence in practice, however, is often fluid, contingent and contextual and the need for self-reflexive criticality in each social worker comes to the fore. So, when the 'rule' demands further marginalisation of an individual or leads directly to that person's disadvantage, whereas transgressing that rule does not but leads to a positive outcome, the social worker faces an important dilemma in making a decision. This decision needs to be based partly on outcomes, as a consequentialist would suggest, partly on respect for the values and ethics of social work, as espoused by a deontologist, and partly on the 'love' that Fletcher describes or, in social work terms, on the service of social justice and human rights for that individual or group. Situation ethics can be described as being *'post-*post-modern' in its contextual and contingent specificity but in its inclusion of a reference point which is important for social work practice. It allows human rights and social justice to take centre stage.

Confucianism and non-Western philosophical approaches to ethics

The approaches to ethics that we have considered have come from Western philosophy. It is important, in our global and mobile world, to recognise there are other sources of moral and ethical codes which will be accepted and promoted by some social workers and often by those with whom we work. We do not have the space to review these different perspectives adequately but want to draw attention to important concepts that may drive some people's approach to social and family life. Acknowledging there are many moral and ethical belief systems, we will focus on Confucianism and filial piety.

Confucian philosophy in its classical and more modern forms is multi-faceted and difficult to describe in ways that do justice to it (Berthrong, 1998). However, it is recognised that it is axiological, or concerned with social and interpersonal ethics. This particular ethical way is called 'concern consciousness'. In a sense this relates to a continuing commitment to seeking, reflecting on and following social ethics and practices that encourage human flourishing (Berthrong, 1998; Berthrong and Berthrong, 2000). In many ways this echoes much of the positive aspects of virtue ethics and situational approaches. It is certainly something that social workers can bear in mind when reflecting on their practices in a complex and imperfect social and political context (Houston, 2009).

One key element of this care and concern is 'filial piety'. The family has a unique position in Chinese and Confucian thought, acting as a semiotic (something that acts as a sign for something wider than its surface definition) for understanding social relations. It is a broader concept than the Judaeo-Christian *Honour thy father and thy mother* (Exodus 20:12; Ephesians 6:2) but does emphasise duty, concern and obedience hierarchically from younger to older generations as a means of continuing the family line. The duty stems from younger generations being cared for and nurtured by their parents and therefore having an obligation to do the same when their parents are older. It is clear how this belief may have a significant impact on those following it if social work services become involved in their care. The following case study exemplifies some of the issues that can arise.

Case study

Chang had worked hard to ensure his father's grocer's shop survived when his father retired some years ago. He was proud of his achievements. Chang's father, a widower, had become increasingly frail and his GP had suggested that social services visit to see if they could offer some support. Chang was often busy with the shop and his father was on his own for some time. However, when talking to the social worker who visited, Chang was adamant that it was his responsibility to care for his father and he would do so without outside help. The social worker thought his reaction was hostile but on talking with her line manager was helped to contextualise this in terms of Chang's commitment to filial piety.

Towards ethical practice

It is the social worker who must negotiate these tricky pathways within human lives and do so in a way that ensures an ethical approach to practice. Therefore, knowledge of ethics is central. However, it must be remembered that knowledge will remain partial, somewhat removed from individual experiences, and a questioning self-reflective approach is needed to ensure that assumptions are not made without rigorously testing your thoughts and relying on the voice of those with whom you are working to understand the perspectives they are reflecting.

You may ask how you can gain or enhance your knowledge of social work values and ethics with marginalised people. As with your knowledge of the wider world, there are many different ways this can be achieved in addition to critical self-reflection on practice. The range of social work texts concerning ethics and values is important, given that these are often grounded in the real, everyday experiences of people who themselves are often at the edges of society. Some of the most popular books to consult, not only during qualifying education but into practice and beyond, are Banks (2012), Ahktar (2013), Dickens (2013), Parrott (2014) and Beckett et al. (2017), dealing specifically with the UK context. Wider perspectives are found within Gray and Webb (2010) and Reamer (2013), although it is sobering to note that the most popular texts are from Western or Global North authors.

It is important to bear in mind the plurality of perspectives, beliefs and cultural values that individuals bring to human life as well as the wider group perspectives that may be more widely known. In seeking to work ethically as a social worker, you can ask those individuals to share their positions, values and beliefs so that you can practise in an appropriate and authentic way, acknowledging difference but having a clear, honest and well-communicated stance on certain lines of behaviour and action.

Activity 5.3

Think of the brief review of core ethical approaches set out above. Note down the ones you most identify with and ask yourself why. Where does your understanding come from and how has it developed during your life? Are there alternative perspectives that might be useful to your practice?

Comment

What is particularly important when considering ethics is not to make the mistake of aligning uncritically with one approach to the exclusion of others. Houston (2009), in an elegant piece, summarises this well by referring to a syncretistic turn in which the rigidity of ethical schools is challenged and key thoughts are synthesised. To do so, Houston employs Habermas's discourse ethics, which sees three types of claim for ethical validity being made from objective rules, subjective rules and community norms, and Honneth's theory of recognition in social and interpersonal contexts that gives weight to identity. What Houston achieves is a synthesis of ethical approaches that is unbound, context-related and concerned. This is something that social workers need to achieve in negotiating the rough terrains of contemporary practice.

Chapter summary

This chapter has outlined some of the knowledge that social workers need in developing their practice with marginalised and disadvantaged people. We have covered 'factual' knowledge such as the law and political or historical events, but we recognised that all knowledge is interpreted by those experiencing it as members of the public, employers, policy makers or social workers and those who use their services. Indeed, the perspectives we adopt in interpreting and applying knowledge are affected by the multiple characteristics and social positions we inhabit. Being true to ourselves and honest in our dealings, and being prepared to reflect deeply and critically on our beliefs, understandings and practices will help us to ensure our practice works alongside people rather than imposing external perspectives upon them. In the next chapter we will consider the skills that social workers need to develop in order to apply their knowledge fruitfully and constructively.

Further reading

Banks, S. (2012) *Ethics and Values in Social Work*, 4th ed. Basingstoke: Palgrave.

This popular volume is at one and the same time erudite and accessible. It covers real-world dilemmas that social workers, community and youth workers and others are likely to face as it takes readers through core aspects of various positions in values and ethics.

Johns, R. (2017) *Using the Law in Social Work*, 7th ed. London: SAGE.

This popular book continues to offer students an all-round introduction to using the law in social work practice, covering aspects of relevant legislation and accompanying knowledge.

Thompson, N. (2016) *Anti-Discriminatory Practice*, 6th ed. Basingstoke: Palgrave.

This seminal work explicates the personal/cultural/social model and then applies it to a range of different areas of practice relating to the social divisions and characteristics we share.

6: Skills

The knowledge base for practice with people and groups who have been disadvantaged and/or marginalised provides the underpinning social workers need and from which they can exploit their skills in order to work constructively alongside people towards change. The skills that will be explored within this chapter include interpersonal skills, negotiating and bargaining, arguing and defending, skills which use social work knowledge in order to assist people and groups in challenging unfair discrimination, routes into disadvantage and marginalisation as well as working directly with people experiencing the distress and lack of dignity associated with such. The role of social workers in developing and enhancing their organisational policies and practices will also be considered.

What is 'good practice'?

What is it to be a good social worker? That is both apparently easy and very difficult to answer. It all depends from which position you tackle this deceptively simple question. Is a good social worker one who opens cases, sets prompt goals with service users, works swiftly towards these and rapidly closes cases, moving on to the next case in quick succession? Such a professional may well be viewed as a highly efficient and therefore a good social worker from a managerial perspective. Another social worker may work at a different tempo, preferring to take time exploring options with service users, monitoring and evaluating services and generally staying in touch with service users until it is clear that the services identified are appropriate for their needs and acceptable to them. Such a social worker may well be regarded as effective from a service user point of view thanks to this thorough and cautious approach.

In between these two approaches will lie many others that gravitate towards one style or another, depending on a whole range of factors, including (but certainly not exclusive to) social work specialisms and service user groups, waiting lists of cases requiring allocation, the number of team mates available, the team work culture, managerial support, potential resourcing and referral to other professionals, as well as the individual's work pressures, levels of emotional resilience, the personal domain of wellbeing involving one's family, health, financial and/or job security, not forgetting personal attitudes towards particular cases and those individuals at the receiving end of social work services. The personal element of practitioners' attitudes of attraction towards or aversion to particular service users and their problems may well accelerate or slow down the pace of social work, all other issues in the workplace being equal. This may not sound a very professional consideration but social workers, like those they serve, are first and foremost human beings.

Case study

Bridget was a newly qualified, young social worker who joined a hospital-based social work team at a large NHS trust. She was given the task of providing social work services to a geriatric ward with a more experienced colleague. Bridget learned to work with many different levels of need and capacity in this elderly patient group. She felt valued and learned how to make contributions viewed as useful at the consultant-led weekly ward meetings. A year later Bridget was allocated the case of Edith, an 85-year-old woman who lived independently in the local neighbourhood and had been admitted following a fall, which caused some physical injuries and later complications, which meant that her hospital stay was extended to some weeks.

This situation had damaged Edith's confidence about managing at home and she welcomed being allocated to Bridget, to discuss her situation. During the course of these conversations Bridget learned that Edith had enjoyed a very interesting and eventful life, and she in turn loved to tell recollections to her attentive listener. Eventually Edith was discharged home with a package of domiciliary care and minor modifications to her home, as recommended by occupational therapists. But, having made a monitoring home visit, Bridget felt reluctant to close the case, although the number of cases requiring allocation created pressure to do so. It was not difficult for Bridget to find reasons why yet more time was required before the case could be closed. Finally, in supervision Bridget was able to gather insights into her deep reluctance to say goodbye to this particularly charming and charismatic client for whom she had developed much personal admiration and affection.

The context of social work

New social workers often report on the perceived differences between the realities of practice and the expectations they have developed undertaking social work education (Higgins and Goodyer, 2015). Too often it is difficult for social workers to feel sufficiently empowered to flex their professional autonomy in developing intervention strategies, whether well-established or innovative. Commonly the rhetoric of service user 'choice' does not translate into realities for service users, where choice is relegated to the ideal rather than the feasible. Where service users are in need of more time or therapeutic approaches that require this, such needs may be viewed as a luxury that cannot be accommodated under the forced tempo of contemporary social services, where allocation is under severe threat owing to the pressure of increasing case numbers. These and many other aspects that require recalibration of professional expectations can all lead to disappointment, and potentially a level of cynicism, of which more will be said later.

The gulfs between expectations and realities in the context of social work are open to a number of different interpretations, but notably it has also been politically exploited in arguments seeking to undermine both the quality of social work education and the skills of the social work profession (Ring, 2014; Taylor and Bogo, 2014). Such criticisms have in turn forced a significant sea change in regulatory bodies for social work, now brought under the same control as health via the Health and Care Professions Council (for the time being); and the education and assessment of social workers, with the introduction of the PCF model (Burgess et al., 2014).

The rationale for the PCF, as described, was to move from an assumed instrumental and 'atomised' approach of the 'tick-box' mentality towards a capacity model (Burgess et al., 2014:2069). This has been claimed to offer a more holistic, adaptive and inclusive model of skills and knowledge, encouraging a developmental approach to professional expertise. However, there is also the implication that the PCF provides strong encouragement to retain professional *soft skills and other complex achievements that employers value, such as teamwork, collaboration across boundaries, problem solving and ethical practice* (Taylor and Bogo, 2014:1414).

These skills may be viewed as 'soft' because they are either difficult to assess or are simply implicit in what social workers do. Problem solving, however, can and does require careful deliberation and often, delicate and sensitive intervention work, none of which can be a rushed or forced process.

Despite the profession now being armoured with the PCF, some might argue that social work is still stepping into the realm of the ideal rather than the actual and the PCF does not prepare social workers for the realities of practice. Yet this is not to say that these so-called ideals should be jettisoned and the latter privileged – rather that the idealism that led to many joining the profession initially must not be sacrificed as an inevitable loss of innocence in the face of fire. In fact, ideals should be cultivated and preserved, holding that purer power as a moral driver that leads towards personal self-actualisation to becoming a qualified and practising social worker. The earlier, liminal identity of a social work novice does not need to be shed on the road towards now becoming a professional veteran, but instead could valuably be enveloped as an important part of self in the process of becoming.

Higgins and Goodyer (2015) approach the issue of *dissonance* between aspiration and the everyday realities of practice by reframing the use of *irony*. This is a novel idea that acts as a sticking plaster over the wound of disillusion in an attempt to prevent the infection of ulceration into cynicism. Irony, in this authorial usage, provides the space between evaluating the philosophical, deontological Kantian position of what *should* be with what *is*. One or the other is not jettisoned in so doing but both positions are kept in suspension, from which one can examine each. This could be construed as a form of dialectical tension, where two competing discourses may be juxtaposed to construct new meanings or a new paradigm (model or approach); or perhaps only to spring back to a possible starting point of polarisation upon the conceptual continuum of change.

Skills: the practicalities

Learning how to undertake a good assessment is a key skill. This is particularly the case when the social remit is expanding drastically to cover areas that were previously not expected of social work, while other interdisciplinary experts, such as occupational therapy, are reducing in availability. A good assessment is a complex and holistic process, drawing on practice experience, theoretical perspectives, good communication and interpersonal skills as well as a genuine interest in people. A bad assessment is quickly spotted in the files. It is frequently brief and routine in detail, with usually only the sketchiest picture of the individual provided, where little is said and that may be repeated often, and where individual needs and the resources required to meet these may be uncannily similar. A good assessment requires lateral thinking along with a certain level of literal identification of specific facets of need and hopefully some creative thinking in how to meet them.

Those wishing to develop or refine their assessment skills can be referred to Parker's (2017) comprehensive explication of assessment, along with the knowledge needed for effective intervention and reviewing of services. It is worth adding here, however, that ethnography, which we have already mentioned and which is the pre-eminent qualitative methodology for studying groups and cultures, has been used to examine the 'culture' of social service teams (Ferguson, 2016). It is also an innovative approach for social workers to develop their ethnographic eye and to improve their biographic knowledge of their clients through in-depth exploration of and insight into the lives of service users and their families (Ashencaen Crabtree et al., 2016).

Empathy, as a social work value, obviously has a very important part to play, but of itself is not a means of excavating the life story of those we work with. Thus, familiarisation with ethnographic techniques is proposed as a way of developing deep understanding of the circumstances of service users and describing those effectively. To illustrate, as you read the case study of 'the mensch' in this chapter, consider Mrs Blumenthal's case. Here is a woman with dementia, but her circumstances are fortunate in many ways: materially finances are secure, she has a devoted husband by her side, appropriate services nearby and a beautiful family home. Can such a person be viewed as a tragic case or should such notions be confined solely to those far less privileged than her? For a fuller explanation of the power and use of ethnography for social work, readers are referred to Ashencaen Crabtree (2013).

Other essential skills

Report and assessment writing is another important skill, where no service is done to the profession if poor literacy skills are regarded as comparatively unimportant compared to practical skills. This is far from the case, where, for example, a high level of literacy is required to convey vital information to other professionals or courts. Poorly written reports and unclear information can actually serve to dissuade other professionals from taking seriously the social work recommendations, as unfortunately assumptions will often be made about the professional capabilities and judgement of the author. So if your skills are somewhat lacking in this area it is well worth trying to polish them up. There are many popular books on grammar and punctuation that will help in this regard.

Time management is another skill to acquire. It would be frankly duplicitous to fall into the neoliberal corporate rhetoric that most work pressures and associated stressors can be alleviated by improved personal time management. Many cannot because they are integral to the job or embedded in dysfunctional or ineffective systems that trap employees in vicious cycles.

However, certainly where there is latitude to manage your time more effectively you would be wise to do so, for example, through allocating a realistic amount of time to tasks and ensuring that the various components of your work are fairly accurately calculated (particularly where there is personal or management tendency to regard some tasks as the 'real job' and other tasks, also demanded, as trivia). Time management is therefore an important skill to develop, whilst acknowledging that the tempo of work in the particular context is not likely to be individually mastered or easily altered. That, of itself, usually requires a stronger collective team response and management support committed to change.

Using self: the first and best tool

There is perhaps no greater necessity to deploy and skilfully use self in any other profession compared to social work. The 'bedside manner' may bring out the best in the doctor–patient relationship but one could conceivably be a fairly effective physician without much in the way of personal skills. However, in social work, it is harder to imagine a good social worker with weak empathy for others, or bad interpersonal skills or with little insight, given how integral the working relationship is to the service user–social worker dyad. Reflective practice is viewed as the essential means of gaining self-insight, but this requires that time and space are set aside for it, which may not always be the case in the fire-fighting atmosphere of too many social services offices (see Chapter 9 for more on reflective practice).

Creating the necessary relationship with service users begins from the outset before the first physical encounter, whether that is by telephone or face to face. Most veteran social workers have learned their 'people skills' through trial and error, but today there are a number of textbooks (such as Wilson et al., 2008) that seek to 'walk' novice social workers through the business of writing a good explanatory letter to service users and/or their families. This could also be the task of making an introductory telephone call (which can be surprisingly tricky) or that first home visit where you are not quite sure where you are going and what you will find.

On most social work courses, the issue of appearance may arise in terms of how we present to service users and family/caregivers. For example, the following list, by no means exhaustive, are all signifiers that project a certain message to others. This includes clothing, hairstyle and facial hair. Make-up and body adornment, shoes, bags, hats/scarves, gadgets and preferred transport or walking aids may all speak volumes to others about us, our background, gender, ethnicity and class. Sometimes these may be externalised aspects that we wish to project about ourselves and sometimes these may be alien to how we perceive ourselves. For instance, heavy Cleopatra-style eyeliner may carry a certain type of message about the wearer to one generation and quite another to an older one. Similarly, hair ornamentation or the covering of head hair (and the types of cover thereof) may convey a wealth of meaning about ethnicity and/or faith to onlookers.

Activity 6.1

Thinking about your personal style, what do you feel it says about you? How do you feel that fits in with any social work persona you would like to project?

Comment

We all wear different 'hats' in life relating to the different roles we need to play every day. Sometimes our personal and professional personas are quite similar and sometimes we choose them to portray very different aspects of ourselves. What aspects of yourself do you wish to project in your professional practice and how far do you think your style enables this to be presented to others?

Accent and vernacular speech can also create strong impressions in the minds of others about who we are and what we seem to be. We can use these to our advantage if we are aware of them, but the opposite can occur if we remain unaware of how we convey ourselves to those who do not know us. To give a topical example, although it is now common to pronounce the letter 'h' as *haitch*, until the relatively recent past this was always viewed as denoting an under-privileged London Cockney background and was often the butt of many a joke.

The prevalence of the *haitch* pronunciation has only been around for the past two decades or so. It has probably arisen due to the heavy increase in telephone rather than face-to-face business interactions, where the digit 8 can be confused for the letter 'h', leading to the rise of the exaggerated pronunciation of the letter. The issue of pronunciation and enunciation, while it may sound snobbish and elitist to many readers, is useful for social workers to recognise these perceived generational and class differences in our work with diverse service user groups.

You, reader, will be judged on how you present yourself as well as what you say and do, just as you probably judge others similarly, so it is best to recognise this fully and to work it to your advantage, if and when you can. Accordingly it is always worth bearing in mind and exploring how we project ourselves, both deliberately and accidentally, perhaps by checking with people we trust but who may not be among our most loyal and closest friends, to ensure that what we wish to project about our professional intentions is being reasonably accurately conveyed. This is particularly important in those early but critical encounters with new service users and families.

The downside of this self-revealing strategy is that it requires opening ourselves to vulnerability in the critical gaze of others, which inevitably is not always a comfortable experience. Accordingly a genuine level of reciprocal trust (so far as that can be established) is a key element to such a personal exercise. It is also well worth thinking about keeping a few clothing props to hand in the back of the car, or office drawer, with the aim of projecting the right image at times. This is an old trick of social workers and thus a formal tie and suit can be replaced quickly with an open-necked shirt look and an informal/older jacket, for example. A pair of high heels can be quickly replaced by 'sensible shoes' and tight/low tops softened by a big, decorative scarf or cardigan.

Such suggestions may be open to the accusation that we are proposing that social workers need to be willing to be 'inauthentic' to an essential core self – a debatable philosophical notion in itself, as people are endlessly adaptive to a variety of roles played every day in their lives. Accordingly, it is a personal matter whether one feels that it is a constraint or just good sense in hiding aspects which might be misinterpreted by others, including, maybe, facial and tongue piercings, for instance, or multiple tattoos.

Some social workers will feel that service user groups need to try and accept practitioners whatever their appearance and background, much as social workers may attempt to do with service users. However, it is a truism to assert that many value judgements are made not only in everyday situations, but also in terms of how we perceive others in our work as practitioners – indeed, we are *trained* to develop an observant eye for tell-tale clues about the other. Consider then a service user who wears unkempt, dirty clothing and smells of stale urine. Such a person will offer a number of different clues to a social worker depending on whether that service user is elderly and infirm, living alone or living with a relative/carer; or whether this is a single man living in insecure digs or in his own home, to give but a few examples.

It would therefore be disingenuous at best, or arrogant at worst, to assume that value judgements are not similarly being made of us as practitioners in terms of our appearance, speech and conduct. The fact that many of these assumptions may be wildly inaccurate does not invalidate that observation; for sadly, not all service users and their families will be pleased to see a social worker on their doorstep and not all have had good experiences of social workers in the past. It is up to us to learn to use ourselves to best effect as the keen, adaptable and precision tool of our work.

Communication skills

Much has been written about communication in social work and the intrinsic place it carries in relationship building with service users and their families. Some people seem naturally to have very fluid, sociable and graceful interaction skills that simultaneously convey information and put others at ease. Then again, we all know of certain people who are gauche and clumsy or shrill and strident with others, serving only to create tense, anxious, confused and uncooperative atmospheres. Along this continuum will be a myriad of other styles that are to a large extent the product of our culture and upbringing, and shaped to a personal fit by our education and experiences of living in a diverse society. So whether to make frank eye contact or lower our eyes in respect; whether to shake hands or not; whether to keep our shoes on or off in someone's home; whether to accept the hospitality of food or drink or make our excuses – these are all part of the small but crucial decisions that we negotiate daily as a matter of course.

Commensurately, communication is a hugely important topic in social work, where communication courtesies in relation to preferred forms of address are considered by Koprowska (2014); while Egan (1998) explores communication in micro-skills and Hargie (1997) devotes an entire edited volume to the subject. Hanna and Nash (2012:486) explore paralanguage – tone, volume, pitch and intonation – while Lefevre (2015) notes the neglect of communication with children in the UK social work curriculum.

Language is adept and fluid in creating the foundation for good work. For example, communication that reflects local or adopted vernacular can pay generous dividends in practice; however, the opposite can create disharmony and distrust. The following two case studies demonstrate how powerful the use of language can be in creating an impression and smoothing the ground towards establishing a sound working relationship with service users. Language and its relationship to semantics (meaning) is all-important and can make or mar the helping professional relationship. The goal is to form a 'virtuous' dynamic of empathy and mutual understanding, leading to better identification of problems and solutions.

Case study

Louis is a social work student on placement in an elderly mentally infirm (EMI) day care unit in North London. His practice teacher, Sally, wishes him to take on a new service user, an elderly Jewish woman (Mrs Blumenthal), suffering from advancing dementia, whose husband has been very reluctant to engage with services, although he is evidently struggling at home with his wife's care.

Louis contacts Mr Blumenthal by telephone and manages to persuade him to permit him to make a home visit together with Sally. The couple's house is a large Victorian terrace composed of elegant rooms with an impressive grand piano and crystal chandeliers, now some-what cloaked in dust. Mr Blumenthal explains the problems his wife is having remembering things, coping and getting dressed. With much emotion in his voice he describes his wife as a former concert-level pianist who has not been able to play the piano for the last few years. Mrs Blumenthal is said to have been a very elegant and cultivated woman who was always beautifully dressed, but is now reduced to wearing elasticated, pull-up trousers. This thought seems to sadden Mr Blumenthal terribly, who appears to be struggling with deep grief as much as with care-giving responsibilities.

'My wife is a "mensch", do you know what I mean when I say that?' he asks Louis earnestly.

Fortunately Louis, although of an Afro-Caribbean evangelical Christian background, replies, 'I *do* understand and I am so sorry to hear that your wife is no longer able to be as she was.'

Mr Blumenthal seems very relieved to be understood. By the end of a warm interview Mr Blumenthal has agreed to allow his wife to attend EMI day care.

Back in the office later, Sally confesses that she could not follow all the conversation between Mr Blumenthal and Louis. For example, she does not understand what was meant by 'mensch'. Louis explains that this is Yiddish and refers to a well-brought-up Jew: someone cultured with gentlemanly manners, but in this case, applied to a lady. Louis goes on to say that he picked up some Yiddish phrases reading satirical American twentieth-century novels and these seem to be very handy to his current placement where there is a large minority of Jewish families living locally.

The next case study considers the question of language and meaning, but in this case in a more damaging dynamic, where the issue of cultural normativity is highlighted as being closely (indeed, very often intimately) tied to language. The question of difference here relates to that of super-diversity, a concept that has already been discussed in reference to multiple differences that are combined in individuals as construed in complex modern societies (Vertovec, 2007a; Ashencaen Crabtree et al., 2016). In this case a number of factors come into play, and include disability, ethnicity, gender, class, age and regional familiarity.

Case study

Maeve, a social worker from Northern Ireland, works in a team for adults with physical disabilities in the southeast Home Counties. She is in the process of passing on one of her cases to new team member Amelia, who has recently relocated from London. The case refers to Sam, who has cerebral palsy and lives in a small supported-living unit. His father, Mr Harrison, is his nearest next of kin and visits his son virtually daily. Mr Harrison presents as a small bantam of a man, formerly from the East End of London, with down-to-earth, buoyant mannerisms. Although he seems to have a loving and playful relationship with his son, Maeve expresses reservations about Mr Harrison's behaviour to Amelia, which concerned care staff have described as being physically rough and inappropriate.

$\longrightarrow$

A meeting is set up where Maeve firstly introduces Amelia to Sam and Mr Harrison. Amelia then sits in on the following interview with Mr Harrison and Sam's care worker to discuss Mr Harrison's interactions with Sam, which are described as involving the punching and smacking of a vulnerable person. Maeve says bluntly that this is open to being construed as 'abuse'. Mr Harrison seems completely taken aback and shocked at this suggestion, asserting with much indignation that he loves his son very much and would never abuse him. The atmosphere of the meeting becomes very strained and the meeting concludes with Maeve's formal handover of the case to Amelia in front of Mr Harrison, now brooding darkly and silently.

Aware of this very bad start to a new working relationship, Amelia ponders how to improve communication with Mr Harrison. She is aware that, for many men of his generation and working-class background, affection for sons is expressed through physicality, with pretend playfights of punches and feints, rather than hugs and kisses. Mr Harrison seems clearly devoted to his son but his expression of love needs some modification owing to Sam's disabilities and inability to respond in the way expected. Yet there also needs to be open professional acknowledgement that parental love and concern fully exist.

At the next meeting Amelia talks privately with Mr Harrison away from the care worker, saying she can see how well loved Sam is, but goes on to explain gently how frail the young man is and maybe that he is not well enough to enjoy fully his father's light-hearted 'larking about' like a normal lad would.

Mr Harrison immediately lights up with delight at this explanation that relocates the issue away from a personal accusation of abuse, exclaiming, 'Now you are talking my language!'

From this point onwards Amelia is able gently to steer a much-relieved and happier Mr Harrison towards interactions that are more appropriate for Sam's abilities, while being compatible with Mr Harrison's culturally, generationally and class-informed ideas of gender norms and what constitutes natural and appropriate affection between a man and his son.

Hostility and aggression

Encountering aggressiveness in practice is always disconcerting and can be very frightening. Thankfully, few people enjoy conflict, whether that is at passive-aggressive level, or openly belligerent and/or violent. The experience of aggressiveness can lead to trauma with the potential loss of otherwise talented practitioners from the profession. Perceived aggression can range from the implied threat of 'I know where you live' or 'I know what car you drive', to a tirade of verbal abuse on the telephone, to threatening or actually setting dogs on visiting social workers, to direct physical assault by the individual. In some rare cases, social workers have even been killed in the line of duty. However, most aggression, fortunately, is at a lower pitch, but even that runs the risk of compromising the emotional wellbeing of practitioners, whether this ultimately results in leaving the profession or staying in but developing a hard carapace of personal armour.

A comprehensive discussion of aggression encountered in social work is beyond the scope of this book. However, Koprowska (2014) offers some useful points on violence and aggression in terms of recognising what it constitutes (although that may seem self-evident in extreme cases) by noticing trigger warnings of impending violence, a list of dos-and-don'ts and de-escalating the possibility of violence.

Bullying and harassment in the work environment constitute another form of personal violence and, sadly, social work contexts are no more above reproducing the dynamics of victimisation than in the corporate sector. Indeed, it might be said that the moral high ground occupied by arrogance in social work can be the breeding ground for dismissal of other people and perspectives, and this is an issue that is beginning to emerge in terms of the victimisation of male social workers and male service users through the pejorative essentialisation of masculinities (Ashencaen Crabtree and Parker, 2014; Parker and Ashencaen Crabtree, 2014a).

It is to be hoped that the days of expecting an unsuspecting female social worker or social work assistant to visit, drive or deal with a clearly potentially dangerous individual all alone have now gone. One of the authors recalls how as a young novitiate she was told by a senior social worker to take an unknown man home who appeared to be at least the worst for wear for drink and emotionally excitable. This person had apparently entered the local social work office arbitrarily to seek some petty cash to tide him over until his next giro. His demeanour and level of rationality appeared questionable. With some anxieties, she dutifully drove him back to his rented digs, while he loudly drummed his fingers on the dashboard and kept up a non-stop flow of erratic and angry conversation. She declined his invitation to enter his digs with him and drove off with some relief. She heard soon after that, apparently within minutes of entering his home, this individual launched into an orgy of noisy destruction of his digs, resulting in a police arrest.

Today there are a number of health and safety protocols designed to keep staff safe; nonetheless, attuned instinct is usually the best and first warning, and in these authors' opinion, should always be heeded. However, there are times when, despite our best intentions and careful preparation, service users (and/or their families) seem to be determined not to see us in the way we would like to be seen or willing to work positively with the help that we can offer as professionals. It is only fair to add that past negative experiences of working with social services or other perceived bodies of authority can rebound on unsuspecting future social workers. In all events it is a wise social worker who reads through all the past case notes available with thorough diligence to get an accurate picture of the circumstances before taking the next step of making contact.

This said, however much care is taken, social workers cannot always hit the right note all the time. There are times when, for service users and their families, the affronts and injuries of experience, including those of previous generations within the collective memory, are played out harmfully. If these are not constructively addressed on both sides they can result in some very bruising encounters for both service users and social workers.

Case study

Jo is a White, middle-class female social worker. A referral has come in regarding a request for respite care for Desiree, an 18-year-old young woman of Afro-Caribbean descent with complex needs who lives with her mother, Mrs Abel and younger brother. Desiree's two elder married sisters live nearby and the family seems to be close-knit. Apparently Desiree's entire family plan to take a six-month holiday in the West Indies and wish her to be cared for locally in residential care during this period.

Jo's first interview with Mrs Abel and Desiree, a pleasant and cheerful young woman, appears to go well and it is agreed that Jo will seek out suitable residential care for Desiree for the family to consider. This is confirmed in a letter to Mrs Abel but from this point onwards matters rapidly deteriorate. Desiree's sisters ask for a meeting with Jo at her office and say they are acting on Mrs Abel's instructions to discuss Desiree's needs in more detail.

Once in the interview room the sisters suddenly begin to berate Jo, pointing to all sorts of offences they have read into her letter to Mrs Abel, and implying that they need to protect their sister from the institutional racism of social services and people like Jo. The atmosphere feels very hostile to Jo, who feels increasingly threatened by the unexpectedness of what seems to be a completely irrational attack and the increasing belligerence of their tone. Not being able to discuss matters with the sisters she consequently terminates the interview and leaves the room.

While the search for suitable respite care continues, Mrs Abel delegates communication with social services to her elder daughters, leaving Jo with little option but to continue to deal with the sisters. This results in further aggressive phone calls and meetings that seem to make no progress, resulting in a formal complaint against Jo over the way she has pursued finding research care. This is duly investigated by social services and dismissed as unfounded. However, by this stage Jo is feeling very stressed by her encounters with the sisters, who seem constantly on the offensive, thus requiring the additional, reassuring presence of her Asian senior social worker in her meetings with them.

Suitable but reluctantly accepted respite care is finally found for Desiree. Yet the tensions in the professional working relationship with the family have communicated themselves to Desiree, for she is withdrawn and unwilling to communicate with Jo on her monitoring visits, although otherwise Desiree seems well looked after and contented. Upon their return from holiday Jo hears that a quarrel between the family and the respite care manager has resulted in a refusal to offer further care for Desiree in the future.

Activity 6.2

How do you think you might have felt and reacted in Jo's shoes? Is there anything you feel she could have done to have improved the situation?

> **Comment**
>
> Jo seems to have been forced on to the back foot from the first by the unexpectedness of the sisters' hostile attitude and verbal abuse. Consequently she seems to have been unable to get the relationship back to a normal, functioning working relationship and the respite manager's later problems seem to confirm that this is a very difficult family to work with constructively. What about Desiree though, who is the central individual as the service user? How does the family's protectiveness impact on her life?

Dialogue and non-verbal communication

Speech

An implicit assumption made in this book is that the social work encounter with service users is about creating dialogue, as a crucial part of forming good working relationships (Trevithick, 2014). Dialogue should be a shared engagement in discussing solutions and constructing meanings; therefore imbalances of power, hegemonic or dominant discourses, assumptions and hidden agendas are not likely to be successful ways of developing constructive dialogues. 'Dialogue' is therefore not to be confused with a conversation as such, but rather refers to a theoretical view of the laying out of positions and engaging with the realities of the other person (this connects with the ethnographic approach and with empathy as well).

Accordingly, Natland (2015) explores dialogue as leading to a new level of understanding between parties, in turn permitting new action. In paraphrasing the words of the persecuted Soviet philosopher cum literary critic, Mikhail Bakhtin, we learn that there is nothing more terrible than a lack of dialogical response touching on the essence of what it is to be human and the status of humanisation.

We know, from personal experience, that to find our words, however much reiterated, falling on deaf ears (as in the case of Jo, the social worker) is both immensely frustrating and ultimately completely demoralising. This situation is of course one that is likely to be often experienced by service users and their families in their encounters with all kinds of professionals. Nonetheless there remains the hope of liberation through being heard and understood. In this respect Stan Houston (2009) offers the concept of discourse ethics as developed by the German sociologist and philosopher, Jürgen Habermas. This creates specific 'rules of engagement' for dialogue that ensure that one party's discourse cannot dominate proceedings, as follows:

1. *Every subject with the competence to speak and act is allowed to take part in a discourse.*

2. *Everyone is allowed to question any assertion whatsoever.*

3.   *Everyone is allowed to express his attitudes, desires, and needs.*

4.   *No speaker may be prevented, by internal or external coercion, from exercising his right as laid down in 1. and 2.*

(Houston, 2009:1277)

Where the evidence and words of experts override the voice of others, for example, in case reviews and other formalised situations, Houston (2009) claims that Habermas would argue that these discourse rules are being transgressed.

Body language

Body language conveys more than words ever can. For instance, much can be divined from an otherwise composed professional whose upper body is still with gently folded arms or pen held with dainty attentiveness, while beneath the desk that person's foot is tapping an erratic message of distress or discomfort. So too, observing someone leaning far back in a chair in a meeting or leaning away from another person is a clear indication of internal attitudes.

Body language has been considered in a number of social work texts. Perhaps one of the best-known *aide-mémoires* to good body language is Egan's (1998:64) mnemonic SOLER:

S: facing the client *squarely*;

O: adopting an *open* posture;

L: *leaning* towards the other;

E: maintaining good *eye* contact (bearing in mind any cultural differences that inhibit this);

R: being *relaxed*.

There are a number of devices that social workers may use to check that their body language is congruent with their verbal messages and here learning tools such as video recordings of mock interviews can be useful for students. Reflecting the body postures of the other person has been used to good effect in creating empathy by social workers at times, provided that this does not sink into physical parody.

Again, most people are well attuned intuitively to 'read' body language signs and we can normally tell who are 'best friends' by their mirrored body language with heads close together. The confiding nature of such relationships is beautifully conjured up in the French phrase *tête-à-tête*. Equally we can usually quickly recognise cold antipathy, embarrassment, hot anger or belligerence, love (filial, parental, platonic), love (amorous and erotic), as well as compassion, concern, contempt, narcissism and vanity – and a host of other complex emotions – simply by observing body language. Take time to note your own as a fun and informative exercise and ask for friendly feedback on it if you feel comfortable with this idea. Use this self-insight in your practice deliberately to seek to create better rapport with others and reduce the chances of miscommunication.

Touch

Finally, we explore the use of touch. There has tended to be a general caveat offered to novitiate social workers to avoid physical touch as potentially unwise. It can be viewed in ways that were never intended, runs the argument, and is therefore best avoided. All this of course may be true. Touch, however, is the first and most powerful means of communication towards people and animals alike, conveying reassurance, protection, concern, fear and joy. Should touch be studiously avoided or should the matter be left to personal judgement? This is a difficult question to answer in conclusive fashion, as there are so many circumstances when it is either the best or worst thing to do.

Some people, as we know, are naturally inclined towards touch as part of their repertoire of communication; they are usually easy to spot. Other people are more physically inhibited and disinclined towards touch and they too are noticeable – often sensed rather than spotted. Some are quite happy to reach out and touch an acquaintance in the spontaneity of a good conversation, but dislike being touched by those whose professional work obliges this: doctors, hairdressers, dentists, masseurs, usually because the touch is not connected to human warmth as such but to being reduced to an object to be worked on.

There are times too when it could be viewed as almost inhuman and inhumane to refrain from physical touch, particularly when under other circumstances it would be natural to do so, beyond that of the romantic or sexual encounter. Male social workers often experience the worst dilemmas in this matter, as they fear their touch may be misconstrued in its innocent intentions (Parker and Ashencaen Crabtree, 2014a).

So the conundrum remains, to touch or not to touch? How do we manage this? One of the authors is naturally inclined towards spontaneous touch and uses this as an extension of verbal communication much of the time. For example, once a big, warm reciprocated hug was given to a service user with learning disabilities, after much work had helped to get him to a good place in his life where the case could now be safely closed. The hand of a terminally ill service user was held and stroked during a particularly difficult time in hospice care. A gentle, reassuring touch on the arm was given when working with a young refugee with little English who was in turn mothering her younger, disabled brother.

The other author is less inclined to reach out and touch, but prefers the clarity of verbal eloquence to convey support. Neither way is wrong; both are right. However, this is where individual judgement is of paramount importance. Here we use the term 'judgement' as applied to the retrospective reasoning we may use following the first instinctive and immediate response – a response where words may not be required to feel (albeit sometimes fallibly) the right way forward in each encounter and circumstance.

Chapter summary

The use of communication and interpersonal skills is critical in social work practice and the individual is often said to be his or her most useful resource or tool. In this chapter we have considered the importance of the context in which social work is practised and what key skills are needed, including assessment, written skills and communication (both verbal and non-verbal). The importance of reflexivity in respect of the skills you use and wish to develop is central and helping you to identify these has permeated this chapter. In Chapter 7 we will now turn to some of the ways in which the development of practice wisdom can assist you in developing that use of self still further within a professional context, and how your social work skills can also help you foster resilience.

Further reading

Egan, G. (2014) *The Skilled Helper: A Problem-Management and Opportunity-Development Approach to Helping*, 10th ed. Belmont, CA: Brooks/Cole.

This classic book, concerning interpersonal skills and developing a problem-solving and collaborative approach to helping work, stems from the world of business and organisational development rather than social work. However, it has stood the test of time and represents an important work in the lexicon of skills texts.

Hennessey, R. (2011) *Relationship Skills in Social Work.* London: SAGE.

This book is important as it focuses on the relationship aspect of social work, something of increasing interest and a counter to some of the more instrumental and impersonal approaches to practice that we encounter today.

Koprowska, J. (2014) *Communication and Interpersonal Skills in Social Work*, 4th ed. London: SAGE.

This book provides a comprehensive and accessible introduction to a range of interpersonal and groupwork skills that are useful within the working environment with colleagues and other professionals, as well as with members of the general public.

7: Professional knowledge and skills

Achieving a social work degree

This chapter will help you to develop the following capabilities, to the appropriate level, from the Professional Capabilities Framework (PCF).

Professionalism

Demonstrate professionalism in terms of presentation, demeanour, reliability, honesty and respectfulness.

Critical reflection and analysis

Apply imagination, creativity and curiosity to practice.

Maintain accurate, comprehensible, succinct and timely records and reports in accordance with applicable legislation, protocols and guidelines, to support professional judgement and organisational responsibilities.

Demonstrate skills in sharing information appropriately and respectfully.

Contexts and organisations

Understand the roles and responsibilities of social workers in a range of organisations, lines of accountability and the boundaries of professional autonomy and discretion.

(Continued)

(Continued)

It will also introduce you to the following academic standards as set out in the social work subject benchmark statement.

5.7 Subject-specific skills
5.10 Problem-solving skills
5.15 Communication skills
5.16 Skills in working with others
5.17 Skills in personal and professional development
5.18 Use of technology and numerical skills

The final chapter in this second part draws together the knowledge and skills discussed in Chapters 5 and 6 by looking at developing social workers. Developing through their practice, social workers build practice wisdom, an intuitive and 'felt' way of responding to people, groups, situations and events. We will examine this and set it within the context of learning from those with whom social workers practise – clients, service users or experts by experience. The final part of this chapter will focus on vulnerability, resilience and looking after yourself as a social worker, developing the skills and emotional hardiness to deal with complex, emotionally draining and traumatic events and stories in others. Before considering these core issues, however, we need to examine in some detail what professionalism means in contemporary practice and what we mean by it in this chapter as it represents a fraught and contested concept.

What is professional social work practice?

When we discuss concepts of intuitive, practice wisdom and professional knowledge it is important that we clarify, as far as we can, the complex and disputed notions of profession, professional and professional practice. We have considered some of these issues elsewhere (Parker and Doel, 2013a) but need to examine the different and changing meanings of profession, professional and *being* a professional and to discuss some of the dilemmas arising from these debates.

In that earlier work we rehearsed the playwright George Bernard Shaw's oft-quoted witticism from *The Doctor's Dilemma* that *all professions are conspiracies against the laity* (Parker and Doel, 2013b). Whilst meant to be comical, in a somewhat acerbic way it also reveals a truth. The phrase has resonance for social work and we must consider its meaning; indeed, social work may, for some people, represent a means of regulating, controlling and policing people rather than an assisting, supporting and encouraging participatory activity. This view may suggest that social work and social workers are responsible for marginalising people and creating disadvantage. Think of the uproar that often occurs when a tragedy happens. An example of such is evident in the reaction to the inquiry into the death of Baby P, which we discussed earlier in Chapter 5 (Jones, 2014; McNicoll, 2016; Shoesmith, 2016). The press preyed on and exacerbated the public perception that social workers were to blame for the tragic death of the toddler and that they were in collusion in trying to protect themselves. This view of a 'profession' as a closed and secretive body designed to look after its own members pervades. It is, surely, not a view we would wish to endorse in respect of a helping profession.

However, understanding what the terms profession, professional and professionalism mean or may be understood to convey is much contested, as we have noted above. If we are to discuss the 'professional' role of social work we need to spend some time disentangling some of the definitions before we can explore the ramifications for social workers practising with people who have been marginalised and disadvantaged in some way in society.

There are a range of definitions of profession and professional which must also, to an extent, be intertwined with the current PCF (British Association of Social Workers, 2015), which by its title alone indicates the importance of trying to understand what the terms mean. The PCF, of course, attempts to underpin social work careers in England from student to the most senior positions, including those of educators and to delineate the knowledge and skills needed at each stage of one's career. Two specific domains of this approach relate explicitly to the concept of professional practice or professionalism in practice: domain 1: professionalism and domain 9: professional leadership. Considering these two domains assists us in our search to understand these terms and in exploring the professional role of social work.

Given its name as a 'Professional' Capabilities Framework, the PCF suggests that professional social work must also involve an appreciation of values and ethics, diversity, rights and justice, specific knowledge, the ability to reflect critically, being able to intervene and use skills and to understand the organisational context of social work. These relate to the other domains. However, looking specifically at the domain 'professionalism', it is acknowledged that social work is international but it focuses on the responsibility of social workers for their conduct, for continuing their development and learning and seeking appropriate support. Importantly, it aligns with some of the traits or characteristics identified for professions – safeguarding the reputation of social work and being accountable to the regulator – that we will cover later in this chapter. The focus on professional leadership in domain 9 indicates the self (re)creation of social work, its autopoiesis, through individual responsibilities for research and development of practice. Whilst this begins to give us some idea of what might be meant, it does seem to remain at the level of a list of particular traits or competencies. It is also indicative of a changing use of the term to represent key characteristics expected of a profession.

Looking a little further and more abstractly, the role of *professional* social work suggests there is such an entity as 'professional' social work, and, in turn, this implies that it must be distinct from 'unprofessional' social work. Moreover, this indicates there is a clear and undisputed understanding of what social work itself entails. Even if we restrict ourselves to Western models of social work or individual countries such as those within the UK, we find fraught and complex definitions, practices and understandings (Hutchings and Taylor, 2007), as we have seen in Chapter 1. When we prefix the word 'professional' to social work we extend that complexity and ambiguity to enter into an enduring quagmire of sociological argument, pertinent and necessary, to try to illuminate the concept and its multiple uses.

It is important to adopt a critical approach to such terms and definitions and the history of their development so that we can explore what the professional role of social work in contemporary society might mean. As social work is practised across the world, albeit in diverse ways, it is important also that we take an international perspective to ensure that our discussions of social work do not become so localised that they become divorced from the wider context. If it were to remain localised we would only need to understand what social work services and agencies are expected to do in that setting and we would, perhaps, find that social work could be understood simply as an instrumental job aimed at regulating the individual and family behaviour. The terms 'profession' or 'professional' would carry a very different meaning if that were the case. Indeed, the meanings made of the PCF for practice would be construed simply as an operations manual, a list of what social workers should do or know at various stages of their career. Thus, we need to explore some of the contested meanings and developments. Let us, therefore, briefly examine some of the history and sociology of professions and professionalism, considering their particular technical use through to one that turns the tables on established meanings.

We have heard much about the closing of ranks within professions, protecting their own members, and equally about good, open practice representing 'professional' approaches. For instance, the Francis inquiry (Francis, 2013) into the Mid Staffordshire NHS Foundation Trust has led to calls for a change in rules of reporting perceived poor practice (Lamb, 2013). In one of our own careers as a social worker (Parker), there was a situation in which a colleague 'redacted' her social work notes to protect herself from blame after a child went missing, and although this was brought to the attention of managers and investigated, it was 'dealt with quietly' so as not to damage the reputation of the profession – a 'whitewash'. Taking another perspective, we have witnessed the inexorable rise in bureaucracy and managerialism, especially since the 1980s, as a means of both ensuring accountability in practice and controlling those practices, and a concern that this in itself is causing poor outcomes (Catchpole, 2013). Does this rather unsavoury collection of examples signify what we mean by 'professionalism'? Perhaps it is this common interpretation of professionalism that raises people's suspicions and evokes comments that professionalism tends to exclude the human – that it is more concerned with the completion of impersonal targets and goals than with the creation and maintenance of relationships in difficult circumstances. However, it can be argued that such an interpretation reflects confusion between managerialist and professional practices, when the former concerns impersonalised standards and targets, whilst the latter focuses on best practice and outcomes for those to whom social workers are accountable. These questions lead to another and we must return briefly to questions of social work that we considered in the introductory chapter.

A brief history of profession and professionalism in social work

Social work, even if it were to be considered a localised activity, is practised in a globalised world (British Association of Social Workers, 2015). This is increasingly the case whether in exporter or importer migration countries in which the needs of migrants and indigenous people differ fundamentally. The rise of the 'professional', however, is set also within a context of historical adaptation. Using Rostow's (1960) model of social modernisation from traditional, corporate societies to technological and mass consumption societies and Pfeffer and Salancik's (1978) dependency theory critique that suggests these socio-political changes may maintain social strife in dependent, often former colonial nations, we may position contemporary social workers in a context of increased alienation. They apply balm to social and individual troubles affected by these developments over time, whilst also acting as 'professionals' in their role as an integral part of that evolving social structure.

In our earlier work, we suggested that when we think of a professional, we may think of a footballer, who is a 'professional' because he (usually a man) plays football as a paid job, suggesting it is simply about being paid for doing something rather than doing it voluntarily (Parker and Doel, 2013b). We also said that a footballer may be said to be acting 'unprofessionally' if he swears at the referee over a decision made. This does not mean, however, that the footballer is no longer a professional one. What it does imply is that a professional is paid a wage or fee for his or her practice and that certain prescribed rules have to be followed when engaged in that professional activity. Taking the example still further, it becomes more complex when one starts to consider such things as the 'professional foul', where as part of the game it is encouraged to commit an offence, to break the rules, in order to achieve a desired outcome. The 'professional foul' concept perhaps aligns with a view that corporate life may be associated with corruption (Brown, 2013), something that links back to the perception that professions seek to protect members from public scrutiny by 'whitewashing' difficult situations, as we suggested above.

Having considered a popular use of the term, let us now turn again to the sociology of the professions which looks more deeply at the ways in which a professional and professionalism are constructed and operate. This again is a highly contested area of study.

The sociology of the professions has an interesting history, with a critical approach gaining traction in the 1970s following Johnson's (1972) scathing critique of professions as representing an institutionalised means of controlling an occupation. This construction demonstrates a conceptual indissolubility of power and control within the concept of a profession. This critique, however, stemmed from an earlier twentieth-century dominance of functionalist and trait approaches, which were drawn predominantly from Weberian and Marxian perspectives.

Functionalist approaches to the professions emphasised the distinctiveness that professions claimed, locating them in their rationalising and positive tendencies within society, and stemming from a non-critical acceptance of Durkheim's focus on professional ethics that helped maintain and stabilise social traditions and social order through these elite occupations. However, not all functionalists accepted the benign concept of professions as arbiters and guardians of social stability. This allowed a critique around bureaucratic *eu*-function and dysfunction to develop. For example, professions could be seen as following strict rules and contributing to human good, such as in the guided application of a life-saving medical procedure, or they could be seen as protecting corrupt practices, such as hiding illegal practices within the occupation in order to continue to make money.

Rather than focus solely on the functions of professions in society, other sociologists developed trait-based approaches that attempted to discriminate the central characteristics, elements and attributes distinguishing a profession. However, Johnson (1972) considered trait-based models to be autopoietic (self-creating), bolstering professional power by using the definitions offered by the professions themselves.

Functionalist and trait-based approaches were later extended further by interactionist sociologists who examined the processes occupations went through in order to become professions. This has been important in social work's journey. Macdonald (1995) points out that these action-focused models do not ask what a profession is, but how individuals operate (the processes) and what they did to get there, assume and preserve their privilege, recognising too that the actions of professions construct the social reality in which they operate. So a profession such as social work, if we can consider it such in sociological terms, develops and creates itself through its practices, interactions with others, policy developments, and so forth.

Witz (1992), a neo-Weberian in approach, recognised that the strategies employed by professions to retain power-in-society represented strategies of social closure and *occupational imperialism* (Larkin, 1983), important concepts in the mind of the general public when trust becomes limited and helping to explain things like the public condemnation of social services following the death of Baby P. What she added to the debate, however, is particularly pertinent to our current consideration of social work and professionalism. She highlighted the relationship between gender, power and the professions, locating the *professional project* – its becoming and its maintenance – within the patriarchal, or male-dominated, structures of society. This, in itself, necessitates a critique of social and occupational closure that would privilege males in a profession favouring women, numerically at least, although this critique itself requires caution (Ashencaen Crabtree and Parker, 2014; Parker and Ashencaen Crabtree, 2014a). It is also, perhaps, a profession that could be understood as controlling the lives and social position of women. This can be seen in the child protection and safeguarding practices of social workers in which mothers generally attract greater attention than fathers. In the next section we consider social work as a profession, recognising the complex arena of definition.

The history of professionalism and the concept of 'profession' paint an especially contorted tapestry within social work. We have seen a drive and struggle towards acceptance as a profession alongside those more established or traditional professions, such as medicine and law, from which the term gained sociological meaning, as we noted above. The journey for social work has not been an easy one. Indeed, it challenges the traditional definitions we have outlined, as social work does not always conform to the accepted functionalist and trait-based characteristics of a profession. We may ask, why should it? The answer partly lies in power relations, and a wish for social work to be recognised in terms of its status.

Social work as a profession

We have already hinted that social work's journey towards professionalisation and professionalism has been and remains fraught. Social work, through its twentieth-century developments, was conceptualised as a semi-profession, 'almost but not quite' having the status of others (Payne, 2013; Thompson, 2013).

Lipsky's (1980) classic text on street-level bureaucracy helps us to explain the journey. Lipsky describes the ways in which those human service practitioners he calls *street level bureaucrats* are required to implement ambiguous public policies with inadequate resources, something which resonates with today's practice. These workers may compromise their ideals, values and ethics to negotiate this path and may develop highly individualised methods to do so (Pithouse, 1987). In addition to this the managerialist agenda in social work has changed the discipline of social work and other professions so much that the traditional definitions of a profession are no longer satisfactory (Ferguson, 2008). The culture of managerialism has increased the surveillance, control and, in the sense of curtailing autonomy, 'deprofessionalisation' of practitioners and service organisations by demanding compliance and rule-bound behaviours (Singh and Cowden, 2013).

In a coruscating and contemptuous analysis, Illich (1972) attacked what he called *disabling professions*. Professionals are those who have an acknowledged *expertise* that can be applied to *problems* that are professionally defined and legitimated. He called for a more sceptical approach to the 'diagnose and prescribe' power base of traditional professions such as medicine. This more traditional approach to the professions, which for Illich formed part of the control of the social spaces of work, created a self-perpetuating monopoly in which, for our purposes, the social worker controls, identifies and legitimates psycho-social needs, and necessarily excludes other needs by default. This may lead social workers to set agendas which meet their needs and those of their agencies, such as the completion of assessment tasks according to set timescales, rather than working at the pace that might be required for best practice and outcome. We can say that one of the dangers of understanding professional social work in this way may be that it allows practitioners to subjugate the needs of service users to their own and to act, as we noted earlier that George Bernard Shaw said, as a conspiracy against those with whom they work.

The interactionist perspective and Illich's critique oscillate around a number of concepts that can be made pertinent to social work today. *Professional power* is central to understanding the ways in which any profession can control and regulate its own work and gain dominance over others. In contemporary social work this is partly reflected in the struggles for professional body recognition gained in the four UK countries in 2002, in which English social work suffered a blow in 2012 with a move to a more generic and health-based regulatory body (the Health and Care Professions Council). This is set to change again with the creation of Social Work England, a specific body, under the Children and Social Work Act 2017. Various social work reforms and politically driven campaigns following well-publicised tragedies have questioned, challenged and curtailed social workers' powers to work autonomously and to make 'professional' judgements, whilst others have reasserted the need for such an approach (Munro, 2011). In respect of contemporary UK social work there is tension between social work and its dominance over social care, although this is further challenged by the increased dominance of health professions over social care work, diminishing the stature, perhaps, of social work still further. These examples demonstrate the contested, fluid and mutable understandings of professional work but show, also, that the actions of organisations are important in defining their position and stratification within society. Social work has struggled as a 'poor relation' when seen against medicine and law traditionally, and those newer 'professions' such as teaching, police and nursing that tend to enjoy greater public support. The actions of social work to gain acceptance as a profession have suffered somewhat because it is useful in a stratified organisational world to have a practice or discipline that is easy to blame for the ills it is created to address.

It is also the case, of course, that the state and local government tend to determine the needs of the individuals with whom social workers work, and to delineate the bureaucratic means by which services to address needs are to be delivered. This is happening despite the increased emphasis on the involvement of people who use services being involved in the planning and delivery of their services. So the power fluctuates here in ways that may not always meet the needs of individuals as assessed by social workers through application of their knowledge, values and skills. The managed bureaucratic environment in which social work is practised, as we saw above in Lipsky's (1980) work, need not, of course, disrupt social workers' own commitment to professional practice, but it does demand a revision as to what that might mean.

From a social work perspective, Hugman (1998) critiques the more traditional definitions of professional and professionalisation-based cautious, self-defined, 'expertise' which may exclude those who use services, and the concept of 'best interests' that underpins this notion of expertise. This understanding of social work as a profession is challenged by the service user and consumerist foci of recent years.

Karban and Smith (2010) recognise that health and social care professions are in a state of flux or even crisis as public confidence has been shaken by challenges, changing technologies and roles and politically motivated policy and organisational changes. They also recognise that professional working in health and social care continues to be driven by the need for interdisciplinarity which tends to homogenise the identities of each discipline, thus preventing professional distinction from developing.

As we stated earlier, the changes in the ways in which we understand or define the professions have implications for its application to social work, and necessitate asking not 'Is social work a profession?', nor 'How did it get there?', but 'What may professional social work comprise?' (Parker and Doel, 2013b).

Thompson (2009, 2013) charts the journey from more traditional approaches to professional social work, through the challenges of anti-professionalism and radical perspectives, finally arriving at an empowering 'new professionalism' based on individual commitment to enhancing one's practice.

Developing 'professional identity' in social work

Education for professional practice, which is determined by reform rather than by the profession, constructs the cultural templates and narratives for becoming a professional social worker. A process of secondary socialisation occurs as one is inculcated into the wider mind-set, tradition and practices of social work, through education and through the field education or practice placements in social work agencies. However, this is a complex and, sometimes, tense state of affairs, understandably so given the changes, demands and exigencies of contemporary practice. The current conflicts that we see from government and other bodies' statements of the alleged inadequacies of preparation for practice through the education system (Brindle, 2013) lead to role conflicts between the instrumental completion of tasks and meeting of targets, and the need for professional autonomy that relies on judgement, criticality, relationship-based and politically motivated, compassionate practice. The continuing tensions between managerialism and a value-based practice lead to a context in which being a professional social worker in today's UK may mean a variety of different things in different situations (Parker and Doel, 2013a). What remains central is that social workers adopt a critical understanding of the term to ensure that what their organisations and employers are requesting does not further marginalise or disadvantage those people with whom they practise.

Practice wisdom

The term 'practice wisdom' is sometimes employed to refer to 'clinical' or 'professional judgement' (Scott, 1990). This is not professional in the sense of being determined by the arcane knowledge and strictures of the social work profession, somewhat removed from everyday dealings with people, but refers rather to the weight of experience that allows experienced practitioners to interpret situations and act intuitively. This has been roundly criticised by those advocating an evidence-based approach (Parker, 2017), but usually without reflection on what evidence means in these circumstances and how contested it is as a concept. Indeed, Cheung (2015) suggests that it counters the limitations of technical rationality despite it being hard to define. She outlines four intertwined aspects that can be developed to progress as a social worker through her study of the ways in which practice teachers work with students. These four elements of practice wisdom comprise:

1. moral reasoning and cognitive knowledge – relating directly to the knowledge and values we have considered in this book;

2. the agential nature of knowledge – recognising that individuals interpret the world differently but relate and communicate through shared understandings;

3. the interactive nature of knowledge generation – the shared understandings are reached and constructed through relationships between people, including social workers and their service users;

4. the fluid status of knowledge – being comfortable with the changing nature of knowledge, truths and certainties.

These characteristics of practice wisdom locate it within the individual social worker drawing on her or his experiences and interactions with others in the world, understanding practice wisdom as a synthesis of these relationships and understandings. The diverse range of perspectives on the world and being comfortable with ambiguities and uncertainties as the world constantly recreates itself in the lives of social workers and those on the edges of society with whom they work is important for understanding the people with whom we work. Those who are marginalised and disenfranchised are often labelled and stigmatised, as we saw in Chapter 2, and being able to draw on selfhood, experience and intuition is an important counter to the impersonal weight in technical rationality and what it uses as evidence.

Practice wisdom represents the beginnings of an emotionally intelligent, relational approach to social work in many ways. Donald Krill, a North American social work academic, developed the concept in 1990. He suggested that learning to practise well as a social worker involved the integration of theoretical with subjective and spiritual or religious knowledge (knowledge based on belief systems). In his book, Krill outlined a range of self and other exploratory exercises that stemmed from his own pedagogical style. This began a process of deep reflection on ourselves as a tool of practice and necessarily as a human being. Much of what Krill introduced here has been developed further in discussions about reflective practice and in the resurgence of relational social work, although the focus is, at this time, very much on the spiritual self.

Dybicz (2004) focuses on the word 'wisdom', asking why this word was used instead of knowledge or experience. Using a Socratic approach he believes that, whilst these are important, wisdom illuminates practice that works first from and within the value base of social work rather than considering technical questions or efficacy. Both are, of course, important, as Klein and Bloom (1995) highlight, but it is the emphasis that is crucial.

So, it may be asked, how does it fit with a procedurally focused approach to social work, something we find in many statutory settings today? Practice wisdom does not denigrate the technical or scientific aspects of practice but attempts to re-establish the human and relational. It synthesises the art and science of social work in the individual, celebrating the intuitive knowledge, judgements and perspectives of social workers alongside the need for a systematic and structured approach (Samson, 2015; Parker, 2017). It recognises that technical rational positivistic approaches alone are not enough (Chu and Tsui, 2008).

Social workers can cultivate practice wisdom by developing a deep sense of reflexivity, by exploring their motivations for the job, their experiences and how they respond to and learn from these (Thompson and West, 2013). Recognising that we all have different ways of dealing with the stresses and tensions of the world and the distress of others, and that we all have our own experiences of disadvantage and marginalisation, is a first step in accepting differences, uncertainties and ambiguities in our professional lives. A second is drawing on how we feel, intuitively, about a situation and testing that through the relationships we are seeking to build and the perceptions or notions we are seeking to test out a little more.

Practice wisdom, as we have seen, is not an esoteric, other-worldly approach to practice. It concerns raised consciousness and awareness of situations at a deep and intuitive level and works towards change with those who find themselves at the margins of contemporary life. In this sense it is also political and it challenges the idea that has been reinforced through austerity that a procedural approach is fair, impartial and parsimonious. Indeed, the latter will often misinterpret or ignore aspects of a person's needs so that these increase and reach a higher point of intensity, demanding a more costly response in many ways. So everyday reflection, questioning and paying attention to your 'gut' feelings begin to promote your knowledge and skills, to fine tune them in ways that assist and empower those who are marginalised.

Using learning from the experience of others

Developing practice wisdom is central to your development as a thinking, reflective and moral social worker. You will have found, also, that service user and carer involvement in your education and in respect of practice is increasingly promoted as a means of ensuring the relevance and appropriateness of your work. One of the ways in which you can enhance your knowledge and skills through your everyday practice is to learn directly from the experiences of those with whom you are working. They are the experts on their own situations, on the marginalisation experienced, and can often be the ones who utilise their own capabilities to shift positions.

You will have undertaken many experiences with service users and carers, no doubt, during your qualifying programme (Stevens and Tanner, 2006). It is a requirement for qualifying programmes in social work and it seems to provide important learning and experiences (Teater and Baldwin, 2009; Agnew and Duffy, 2010; Irvine et al., 2015; Cabiati and Raineri, 2016). However, it is not entirely clear how the process works (Hatton, 2017), and it is important to take care when learning from service users and carers, because you may be assumed to hold power in relation to them (Anka and Taylor, 2016) and relationships must be collaborative (Skoura-Kirk et al., 2013). One part of the learning may be to challenge why the involvement of people who use services is involved in your education.

Activity 7.1

List the reasons why you think it is important for service users and carers to be involved in your education.

Then list some of the complex considerations that may arise through this involvement.

Finally, think about the ways in which you might learn from the experiences of and relationships with service users and carers in a way that is non-exploitational.

Comment

This will be a personal activity for you and there will be many ways of answering that are perfectly acceptable.

For us, as authors and educators, we see some of the benefits of learning from diverse situations and settings, from exploring the ways in which things go well or very badly in the delivery of social work and allied services. These encompass hearing how the experience was for those at the edges and recognising the similarities with our own lives and responses, as well as the very real differences. This can lead to the fostering of humility, which is so important when wielding such authority as social workers do.

Alongside concerns of financial exploitation or abusing people's good will, some of the complex factors arising may include a select group of marginalised people perhaps being asked to represent a homogenised group of people, as if all experiences were shared. This could, of course, reinforce the notion of people being 'othered' by sharing characteristics that perhaps we do not. It is worth thinking, also, that those service users who have been trained, supported and developed together to offer this service to students may become part of the education system and 'professional' service users and carers. Thus they may develop different relationships with the service world than they held beforehand and so may present different experiences to students.

For us, it is the honouring of the story, the experience and the building of the relationship that is central to developing trust and mutual learning.

It is important to remember that, whilst we cannot compare our experiences to those of the people we work with as colleagues or service users and carers, our individual experiences of receiving social work, care assistance or health care also offer valuable insights into how the way things are phrased, the tone of something said or a look can make us feel.

Vulnerability and resilience in emotionally challenging situations

What is vulnerability and why are social workers vulnerable?

In Chapter 2 we found that vulnerability is, like so many terms we have come in contact with, very difficult to define and is contested in its use (Penhale and Parker, 2008; Heaslip et al., 2016). If it refers to a characteristic of assumed weakness, which could be understood from earlier legislation such as the NHS and Community Care Act 1990 or the Care Standards Act 2000, this is something which can immediately be seen to stigmatise and marginalise people. Fortunately, the Care Act 2014 has removed these easily misunderstood references but the assumption still remains and needs to be guarded against. Rather we might interpret vulnerable as something created by the actions of institutions and society that makes one at risk of injury, whether that is emotional, physical or indeed social. In a sense, of course, we are all vulnerable if it refers to being at risk of harm. Perhaps social workers are made vulnerable because of their position in standing alongside those who are pushed out, disadvantaged or in some way outside of society (Parker, 2007). Being vulnerable is something that anyone can feel. Whilst it might relate to the choices and lifestyles people choose, or the experience of ill health or disability, the vulnerability to further risk of harm that we are most concerned with here is that constructed within society and by the power play between those with a vested interest in maintaining society as it is and those for whom that is debilitating.

How does knowledge of vulnerability help when working with marginalised people?

Elsewhere, we have reported the secondary trauma experienced by social workers who practise in conflict situations or where there have been terror attacks (Parker and Ashencaen Crabtree, 2014c). Knowledge of how vulnerability is created externally to the person and recognising our own limitations and potential to be vulnerable can help when working with people who are marginalised and disadvantaged. It can also help to ensure that we do not assume needs on the basis of a person's vulnerability but challenge how this has come about and seek, with the person, ways of changing that situation. The following case study helps to illuminate this.

Case study

James was 25 years old and had moderate learning disabilities. He attended a local community theatre group that brought together a range of young adults of differing abilities to write, rehearse and put on plays. James enjoyed this and made a number of friends who shared a common interest and looked out for each other. Prior to joining this group James's social worker, Evelyn, had become concerned that he was lonely and prone to be befriended by groups of people in the neighbourhood who took his money, bought beer and once that was finished moved on. Evelyn's concern was with James's ability to discern the difference between friendship and contact that became abusive. She was worried when he joined the theatre group that he would likely be used in this way again. However, his friendly and generous nature helped him to 'gel' with this group and to be supported by his new friends rather than to be taken advantage of.

The 'vulnerability' of student social workers has recently focused the attention of academics and is important to social work programmes as it has an impact on progression through the programme and on practice. Research tends to consider the emotional and psychiatric needs of social work students (Mazza, 2015), including drug and alcohol use (Lemieux et al., 2010; Prost et al., 2016) or student perceptions of vulnerability in others (Kane et al., 2009). Given the recognition that the intensity of the social work relationship begins in student days it is clearly important that ways of ameliorating its impact are developed to protect practitioners once in qualified practice.

So, knowledge of vulnerability and its construction through what we do, how we approach things and what we assume helps us to question and reflect. However, we recognised above that we as social workers may also become vulnerable. We often concern ourselves with bolstering up the psychological and emotional defences of the people we work with and focus on creating resilience. What is also central to working as a social worker is building your own resilience when faced daily with the distress and trauma of others. It is to this that we now turn.

What is resilience?

Jim Greer (2016) underlines in his important and readable book on resilience and personal effectiveness in social work that resilience is really concerned with managing the emotional demands and distresses of the work we do as social workers. It is not about putting up with more and more complex, difficult and challenging situations. He also delineates the centrality of resilience in an age of continuing austerity, fundamental changes to and attacks on public services, including social work, and increased public scrutiny in social work. Resilience concerns our capability to be flexible and adaptive in challenging situations and to reflect and interpret events in ways that help us respond constructively to them.

Activity 7.2

How do you deal with distressing or emotionally demanding situations?

Think of an example, write it down and reflect on the ways this made you feel, what you did, what help you sought from others, or what support you wished you had sought.

How might you deal with such situations better in the future?

Comment

The answers to the question 'how do you deal with distressing or emotionally demanding situations?' will differ from person to person and you may be surprised that at times you deal with things in quite a positive way whilst at others in a more negative one. If you drink alcohol, having a stiff drink may be a reasonable way of coping as a one-off. It certainly wouldn't be if it was your main way of coping. A long walk in the countryside may be your preferred way of dealing with things, or perhaps going to the gym. These are constructive coping behaviours but not always possible in a busy work schedule and often need to be planned.

Consider the different ways you cope with situations and identify which are positive, which are not so positive; which can be completed immediately and which require planning and time; which are feasible in the long term and which are not. These will help you to develop adaptive responses to emotional demands in your job – the wider the repertoire the better.

How do you as a social worker foster resilience?

Building our self-confidence and recognising limitations is important in adapting to stressful situations (Greer, 2016). You will consider wellbeing at work during staff development sessions and your employer is likely to offer a range of employee assistance programmes, supervision and occupational health measures to help cope with the intensity and stress of social work. However, it is not an endurance test and these provisions should also be working to adapt your working environment and you can ask for this so you can complete your practice more effectively. Below we identify some ways in which you can develop resilience, recognising the responsibility is not yours alone.

The *buffering hypothesis* suggests that our relationships, both personal and professional, can represent important ways of dealing with stress and regaining our composure and ability to work within distressing and demanding situations. Of course, we cannot use our relationships simply as means of bolstering our own resilience. To do so would be abusive and we would soon either lose our personal relationships and/or find work attitudes hardening towards us. However, the use of emotionally supportive supervision is important to fostering relational practice, and engaging in mutually supportive personal relationships keeps us grounded in the human side of life which we, as social workers, must never lose sight of.

The buffering hypothesis derived from social psychological research that considers the importance of social support in times of crisis but also increased distress where there is low social support (Cobb, 1976; Brown and Harris, 1978; Cohen and McKay, 1984). Seeking support for yourself, therefore, is likely to offer those people you work with a good chance of benefitting from your support – resilience can foster resilience. There are important things to consider here, however. Notably relationships and social supports may often be associated with particular personal characteristics, and poor relationships, just like poor supervision, are unlikely to help offset the deleterious effects of stress. Despite the criticisms levelled against buffering, research has continued to indicate that social capital acts as an effective buffer against stress and can thus help build resilience (Duschinsky et al., 2016; Mayer, 2017).

Including teaching and learning activities to help you develop resilience is recognised as an important part of the curriculum, even if it is only patchily embedded at present (Beddoe et al., 2013; Palma-Garcia and Hombrados-Mendieta, 2017). Farchi et al. (2014) consider *self-efficacy* as an important tool in assisting students to deal with stress and trauma. This is something we have used in our own teaching and learning with some success (Parker, 2006; Walker et al., 2008).

Crowder and Sears (2017) considered the use of *mindfulness*-based techniques as a means of preventing burnout and secondary trauma (which they term *compassion fatigue*; see also Kapoulitsas and Corcoran, 2015). Zabat-Zinn (2013) is perhaps the best-known proponent of mindfulness as a means of using quiet, reflective meditation to combat the rush, intensity and stress of our lives. This can be of particular benefit in contemporary social work. It is, however, often the case that we refuse to give ourselves the space and time to be quiet and to develop a routine in mindfulness meditation practice that embeds it within our lives. It is worth pursuing, because when we work alongside people who are disenfranchised, often distressed and excluded from full participation in our society, mindfulness can help us to deal with some of the secondary trauma we experience.

However, whilst evidence for the effectiveness of mindfulness is clear in many cases (Eberth and Sedlmeier, 2012; Greer, 2016), there are increasing anecdotal reports of problems or dangers with mindfulness for some individuals and it is first important that, as with any approach to dealing with stress and trauma, it 'feels' right to you (Marsh, 2016). Some people cannot be still-in-the-moment, focusing just on what is happening right now and emptying themselves of everything else, without filling their minds with worries and anxieties and negative thoughts that counteract the benefits others take from this approach.

Developing *resilience* demands becoming more aware of oneself (Grant and Kinman, 2012). It requires reflexive practice and an honest reflection on one's limitations as well as one's strengths. Recognising that these change in different circumstances and over time will help; none of us are constantly the same but forever acting in and reacting to the world around us. Thus being able to manage the emotional demands of social work is something that will also fluctuate and demands continued attention if we are to practise well and to challenge the structures of society and circumstances that lead to marginalisation. Resilience is not just a personal, psychological approach to our social work, or to the lives of those we work with, but it too relates to the political and the structural and can utilise the resistance and rebellion strategies of disadvantaged and marginalised groups (Guo and Tsui, 2010). It seeks an activist stance – a legitimate feature of international social work that requires recapturing in the UK.

Looking after yourself is part of a professional approach to social work practice in the sense that it helps prepare you to use your knowledge, experience and wisdom in the best ways possible to work alongside your service users. It moves beyond those negative and traditional understandings of professional practice as a conspiracy against the public to an informed engagement that is underpinned by commitment and values.

Chapter summary

This chapter brings together some of the professional knowledge and skills so necessary to contemporary practice. We explored in some detail the complex and contested notion of profession and professional, recognising that there are some unhelpful traditional understandings that serve to pit social work against those with whom they work. We suggested that a critical and reflective approach to practice is important and that you need to be committed to enhancing the knowledge, skills and values that add to working alongside people to mitigate their experiences of marginalisation and exclusion.

(Continued)

(Continued)

Following on from our discussion of professional social work we turned to consider some of those characteristics necessary to enhancing your practice. We explored the concept of practice wisdom, your own vulnerability and the importance of resilience. Whilst these represent various ways of ensuring your strength as an individual and as a social worker are maintained, they concern you as an individual social worker and that emphasis could be criticised as leaving you prone to blame if things do not go according to plan or the work becomes too much; a political approach is also crucial. We shall turn to this in the following chapter.

Further reading

Grant, L. and Kinman, G. (2014) *Developing Resilience for Social Work Practice*. Basingstoke: Palgrave.

Greer, J. (2016) *Resilience and Personal Effectiveness for Social Workers*. London: SAGE.

These two books provide an excellent introduction to the importance of looking after oneself in the complex and fraught world of contemporary social work.

Parker, J. and Doel, M. (eds) (2013) *Professional Social Work*. London: SAGE.

Thompson, N. (2009) *Understanding Social Work*, 3rd ed. Basingstoke: Palgrave.

These two works add to the understanding needed to negotiate the rough terrain of practice and the organisations in which you will work and with which you will come in contact.

Part III

Practising ethically and reflexively

The final two substantive chapters in the book bring together the conceptual understanding, knowledge and skills that we have discussed so far and set them within a context of ethical and reflexive social work practice.

8: Using the law and policy

> *(Continued)*
>
> It will also introduce you to the following academic standards as set out in the social work subject benchmark statement.
>
> 5.5 The nature of social work practice
> 5.7 Subject-specific skills
> 5.13 Problem-solving skills analysis and synthesis
> 5.16 Skills in working with others

This chapter differs from the 'knowledge' chapter in Part II (Chapter 7), given the focal change from knowledge to its application in practice, to the use of the law with individuals, groups and communities. This will include an excursus into working within the legislation as a social worker employed often in a statutory setting or operating within statutory responsibilities; making others aware of the legislation and assisting their use of it to enable change; and directly challenging the legislation. All this concerns acting politically as a social worker whether one bolsters the existing position or challenges it. A reflexive approach will be taken to such work, which asks questions of the ways in which social workers may practise and what the implications of their actions might be. This prepares the ground for the next chapter, examining the ethical dilemmas that may arise in working with people and groups who are marginalised and/or disadvantaged.

The local authority social worker

On 1 April 2005 the term 'social worker' became a protected title under section 61 of the Care Standards Act 2000. One of the unintended consequences of both this and the registration of social workers in England has been to consolidate the numbers of social workers and social work tasks in 'statutory' settings, generally in local authorities. This begins to create a particular understanding of social work as a legal, government-sponsored response to social issues in England and Wales. Social workers' actions, using this understanding, are undertaken on behalf of local and national government and under its legislative framework. This in itself creates tensions for social workers who are working with people at the social margins and who have often been disadvantaged by that particular system. It also demarcates social workers from those people, something which must be resisted.

This complex situation is not offset by seemingly antithetical moves to permit local authorities to opt out of providing child protection social work services and to allow 'for-profit' companies to manage and provide these. This was introduced in the debates surrounding the development of the Children and Social Work Bill, now the Children and Social Work Act 2017 and, although rejected, strengthened that polarisation between social workers and the people they work with. Rather than open up new, innovative ways of doing social work, the ideas seemed to entrench the position that social work is defined by its protective functions rather than its ethically charged focus on social justice and human rights. This, as we have seen, sets UK social work (in England in particular) against its counterparts elsewhere. It is important to keep these tensions in mind whilst undertaking your placement and when moving into qualified practice.

The third-sector social worker

Social workers have been a mainstay of many third-sector, community or voluntary organisations. In the past these 'social workers' may have been qualified as social workers or youth and community workers or, indeed, not qualified at all. This again relates back to that discussion at the outset of this book, where we posed the question, 'what is social work?' Whilst legally we have our answer, as set out above, we do need to keep in mind questions of social justice, humanity and wellbeing when considering this question and we need to keep our understanding of international social work at the forefront of our thinking. It is not as clear-cut as a simple legal definition would suggest and this affects your practice as beginning social workers.

Contemporary social work

Social workers in local authority, statutory settings or undertaking statutory tasks need a good grasp of the ways in which legislation can be applied, interpreted and used to work on behalf of individuals, groups and communities with whom they work. However, this is also the case for those working in voluntary, third-sector and community development organisations. It is especially important to keep in mind that law is interpreted when it is applied and that divergent interpretations are possible. This means in practice that legislation can be used to marginalise and disadvantage or discriminate as much as it can be used to help, empower and protect. Whilst social workers are not quasi-solicitors, they are required to be 'fleet of foot' when applying the law. This demands:

- knowledge of the legislation;
- a working knowledge of the guidance;
- understanding of the ways in which the social worker's employing organisation interprets and applies the legislation;
- a working knowledge of case law;
- the ability to transfer knowledge and to think critically and rapidly in complex settings.

Johns (2017) opens his discussion of using the law in social work practice to explore the notion of wanting to be a social worker, not a lawyer. This is important because it recognises that many social workers at the beginning of their career are put off by the increased emphasis on law and its application. However, as we have noted, the law is fluid and open to interpretation. Most importantly, of course, it can be used not to constrain people's lives but to open up possibilities for them within society that may have been closed off before, to argue for justice and for rights and to campaign, within the existing system, for change.

Knowledge of the legislation, guidance and beyond

The Human Rights Act 1998 and the Equality Act 2010 represent fundamental building blocks on which social workers can build their knowledge for value-based social work practice that link British, and English, social work with its international counterparts.

The Human Rights Act 1998 underpins all of the UK equality legislation and, whilst it presents a useful tool for illumination and guidance, it is in other legislation that social workers find more useable forms for everyday practice (Brammer, 2015; Ahmed and Rogers, 2016; Johns, 2017). The Equality Act 2010 is a landmark piece of legislation in drawing together previous laws aimed at tackling unfair discrimination on the basis of sex or gender, disability, race or ethnicity, as we have introduced earlier in Chapter 1. It goes further than this and covers harassment and victimisation, matters relating to gender reassignment, discrimination arising from disability, age-related matters, and so on. As such the Equality Act represents an important piece of legislation for social workers seeking to address issues of marginalisation, disadvantage and unfair discrimination.

How we, as social workers, employ the legislation is important but this is sometimes affected by the interpretations our employing organisations put upon it and 'custom and practice' may develop that is not questioned. So, when applying the law it is important to ask questions about the ways in which the law is used, what this might mean for the services offered and what this might mean for those who require services.

Case study

Max was undertaking his first complex assessment in a new team. He was aware of the time-scales demanded by his organisation, although the Care Act did not itself set rigid times for the completion of assessments. When faced with Ian, a man who, before a catastrophic motorcycle accident, had been a keen fell walker, whose anger was clear in his answers to statements such as 'I'm here to find out what you need', Max decided to put away his assessment form and the pre-determined questions that his employers required. Instead, he asked to start again and invited Ian to tell him about his life and how things were for him.

This human and relationship-based approach, that we have discussed briefly in Chapter 7, allowed a rapport to develop, permitting Ian's needs to be expressed not as physical ones or those concerned with activities of daily living but as psycho-emotional ones. After returning from hospital following his accident, Ian had succumbed to rage and thrown out his old walking boots, something he now deeply regretted. The one thing he 'needed' to improve his quality of life, he said, was to return to the mountains he used to climb. Max agreed to look into this and said he would return to complete the assessment another time.

When Max returned to his office and reported to his manager, his actions were criticised. He had failed to keep to timescales and workload pressures, he had discussed matters that were not related to a 'care package' and was said not to be doing his job.

Max's actions were criticised perhaps because the team had not allowed tangential thinking to come to the fore and had focused solely on resources. Max's knowledge of the legislation and policy was such that he knew procedures could be pliable and expectations could be managed and he followed his intuitive practice wisdom to form a relationship that established working parameters and trust. He was able to challenge practice based solely on the needs of the service and to interpret the law rather than follow the procedural interpretation his manager expected. His actions were brave because of the criticism he attracted but they took a wider perspective concerned with values, the primary intention of legislation and enhancing human relationships.

Activity 8.1

Write down your thoughts about the use of law in your practice. Why is the application and interpretation of law important? Why is a human rights-based approach important to good practice?

Comment

You may have linked your thinking to the international definition of social work (International Federation of Social Workers/International Association of Schools of Social Work, 2014), to the PCF (British Association of Social Workers, 2015) and to your sense of values in social work. Everyone will focus on slightly different things and will emphasise different ideas. This is important as we strive to keep human rights and social justice at the centre of our practice.

Keep these thoughts with you as you read the following section.

Knowledge about human rights and questions of justice is important to how we practise. There are 18 articles in schedule 1 of the Human Rights Act 1998, all of which have relevance and import in social work practice. When working with marginalised people, many of whom are migrants and refugees, you may work with people who have been subjected to torture (article 3), or you may be working with someone who has been the victim of modern slavery (article 4). Your organisation will have processes and procedures to assess the needs of these people and to whom a referral, to account for any assessed needs, may be made. Knowledge of the underlying human rights of people in these situations will help you argue for and secure the right outcome and as you develop your practice wisdom (see Chapter 7) in this area this will become an integral part of your social work persona.

The Deprivation of Liberty Standards in cases of mental capacity/incapacity and the Mental Health Act 1983/2007 represent important pieces of legislation for social work practice in protecting and supporting people who are vulnerable by dint of the incapacity to make certain decisions, or because of mental health problems. The Human Rights Act permits the deprivation of individuals' liberty, their detention, if they *are of unsound mind* (article 5.1.e). Article 5 predominantly relates to lawful detention when a criminal act has been, or is suspected as having been, committed. The short clause relating to mental health is ambiguous and open to interpretation. This is where, as a social worker, your knowledge of the law, guidance, policy and procedure is important when considered in the living context in which people find themselves.

The underpinning drive for social work with people who find themselves in these positions is to seek to ensure liberty and security and to protect freedoms and rights as far as possible when it is no longer feasible to allow the person to be at liberty. So, you need to apply the legislation and policy through a human rights lens.

Case study

Lawrence was 63 years old; he was an alcoholic with late-stage liver disease. He lived on his own but was supported by his sister in a small flat near to where she lived. She asked for an assessment under the Mental Health Act after he had fallen asleep with a cigarette and set alight the sleeping bag he was wrapped in. He had not been hurt; he had woken and put out the fire which had singed his sofa and carpet and produced a great deal of smoke in the flat. The approved mental health practitioner (AMHP) and his GP visited to assess Lawrence's situation. The AMHP, Helga, knew that the Mental Health Act 1983 section 1.3 was clear that dependence on alcohol did not constitute a mental disorder that allowed detention under the Act. She also knew the distress that Lawrence's sister, his neighbours and Lawrence himself had experienced.

Lawrence's sister was worried that he might kill himself and also concerned that she could not continue to offer the support she had in the past. She thought he was in need of care away from his flat. The GP said he had secured a bed for Lawrence in the general hospital but he had refused to go. Helga needed to assess Lawrence under the Mental Health Act as her primary role. The only legitimate reason for detention under the Act would be if he had a mental disorder under the Act and not just his alcoholism. He was also clearly able to make decisions about his life, even if he did choose those that might not be in his best interests in the eyes of others; he did not lack capacity.

The case of Lawrence above demonstrates some of the complexities of taking a human rights approach. For instance, Helga might ask, 'whose rights take precedence and why?' Lawrence wants to live his chosen life. We may feel his choice was not the most sensible, but a human rights approach demands that we recognise the right to liberty unless there are clear legal reasons to do otherwise and then to ensure that people have recourse to advocates and opportunities to challenge that decision. However, Lawrence's sister also has her human rights to security and protection. She felt compelled to offer him care and support because a prior assessment of needs indicated that Lawrence was not eligible for support from the local authority under the Care Act 2014 (Feldon, 2017). Sometimes working with the law can force someone to take a purely legalistic approach and to justify decisions on this basis – Lawrence, on the surface, did not meet the criteria for detention under the Mental Health Act 1983 because of his alcoholism alone. This ignores the human element and social work seeks to work alongside people who interact and have relationships and needs within families, groups and other living arrangements. Therefore social work with Lawrence not only demands following and applying the law but examining what can be done to uphold his rights and those of his sister in other ways.

In times of austerity and cutbacks, meaningful, human-focused and relational approaches to practice can be difficult and as social workers you will be pressured to complete prescribed work in time, to meet targets and not to work outside these prescriptions. Only to do what is set and not to transgress those boundaries, however, would let down those marginalised people relying on your support and traverses the core values of social work. So, it is important to have an awareness of the law and policies that have a bearing on the situations and lives of those people with whom you are working so that you can inform them of options, of means of resisting what is offered if this is inadequate in your 'professional opinion' as a social worker (see Chapter 7). Knowledge of other social services or support agencies who can provide advocacy, care and activism, self-help groups, website chat rooms and discussion groups is also important in providing the service users and carers the means to pursue their own needs and to challenge any decisions your employing organisation makes. This is important and legitimate. It can also lead to changes in the implementation of policy in practice if the needs are seen to be great enough.

The 18 articles contained in the Human Rights Act that social workers return to in respect of marginalised people include the following:

1. protection of property (contained in the first protocol);
2. right to life;
3. freedom from torture and inhuman or degrading treatment;
4. freedom from slavery and forced labour;
5. right to liberty and security;

6. right to a fair trial;

7. no punishment without law;

8. right to respect for private and family life;

9. freedom of thought, conscience and religion;

10. freedom of expression;

11. freedom of assembly and association;

12. right to marry;

14. prohibition of discrimination;

16. restrictions on political activity of aliens;

17. prohibition of abuse of rights;

18. limitation on use of restriction of rights.

There are two other rights making the 18 (note 13 and 15 are missing) in the first protocol to the Act as well as article 1. These are:

13. right to education;

15. right to free elections.

Just reading quickly through the titles of the articles will give you a flavour of the importance of the Act for practising social work and applying other legislation with people who are marginalised in some way. However, the complexities and contested debates about human rights have permeated discussions in social work (Katiuzhinsky and Okech, 2014). Respect for cultural diversity and difference and the promotion of human rights may at times be in conflict (Healy, 2008; International Federation of Social Workers, 2014). Where the protection of people made vulnerable by a society's actions and policies or the value placed on an individual's human rights fall below global social work standards, social workers face a dilemma. As Katiuzhinsky and Okech (2014) note, a conflict between universalist and relativist positions occurs. This is not a conflict that can be easily negotiated. They suggest, however, that whilst social work is noted as a human rights-based profession, social workers at the grassroots understand the need for basic survival and development overtaking the need for other rights until the basics have been achieved. They also suggest that our knowledge of human rights can assist us in educating and empowering people about rights and advocating legislative change to be rights-based. Drawing on our discussion of ethics and values in Chapter 7 can help us negotiate the universalist and relativist positions, especially if we employ a situation ethics approach.

Case study

The tragic events at Grenfell Tower block in London in June 2017 demonstrate from a legal perspective how a human rights approach can galvanise a community to seek justice and to challenge established social and political structures.

Residents from Grenfell Tower have demanded a public inquiry but, on hearing the caveats concerning the remit of the inquiry from its chair, they believed the focus would not be on the human side, concerned with the lived experiences of a diverse group of, in many cases, already marginalised people, but would be on the mechanics of the fire, its spread and the technical details of the refurbishment. The residents were further angered when a council meeting to discuss the fire held on 29 June 2017 was adjourned once journalists were allowed in, suggesting to residents that a secretive, non-participatory approach was excluding them and not acknowledging their distress.

A group of lawyers, BMELawyers4Grenfell (Black Activists Rising Against Cuts (BARAC), 2017) have, alongside residents, developed a campaign to replace the government-appointed chair, Sir Michael Moore-Bick, and to secure a range of rights-based demands. These demands included welfare-based claims concerning a 24-hour response service to deal with survivor emergencies, the creation of a central place for donations and charitable giving and a published audit of it, confirmation that any resident found to be illegally in the country is granted British citizenship within 28 days, and that interim findings from the inquiry will be made public within four months of it starting.

The group who developed these demands with the surviving residents are lawyers, not social workers. However, it shows what can be done by applying the law on behalf of and with disadvantaged and marginalised people and this touches social work concerns. It locates social activism and human rights within the context of practice with these communities.

At the time of writing focus on the human rights perspective has become increasingly complex because of Brexit negotiations in which the central role of the European Court of Human Rights is being fiercely debated. We are uncertain of the longer-term endurance of the European Court of Human Rights in British law. However, what remains important for social workers in practice is to hold the principles underpinning the Act at the forefront of their work interpreting and applying legislation to enable people to join in with society and life in the ways they choose and to challenge and agitate against policies, procedures and working practices that obstruct this objective. Using supervision and feeding back to managers in your employing organisation, being part of professional body discussions, joining a union and the British Association of Social Workers (or equivalent in other nations) and being politically active in ways that champion human rights and social justice are important means of contributing to the development of policy. These actions also continue the role of social work since its beginnings.

Maintaining a human rights-based stance may bring you into conflict with employers, especially where austerity measures or systems of performance management and target setting take precedence. So ensuring you are protected, through personal resilience, as discussed in Chapter 7, and through your work and employment protections where needed is important. The tensions between current standards and requirements for registration and practice and economic and procedurally driven services are difficult to negotiate. However, the accepted definition of social work and the standards and values expected of practitioners clearly require an approach that is politically motivated – not in terms of party politics but concerned with the right working of societies on behalf of its members (HCPC, 2012; International Federation of Social Workers, 2014; British Association of Social Workers, 2015). This means holding individual human rights and wider social justice concerns as core beacons illuminating your application of legislation and policy in your work. When discussing rights we also have to consider equality and inequalities and to identify the social work role in creating a fairer society through the application of law and policy.

The Equality Act 2010

The Equality Act 2010 is an important piece of legislation, as we have already noted, because it draws together equality law in one place. Like all our legislation, it is underpinned by the Human Rights Act 1998 and informed by the many international declarations concerning the rights of others to be treated equally whatever their differences. In social work this is important because it requires us to remember that difference and diversity are not excuses for unfair differential treatment. Whilst on the surface this may appear self-evident, it is often the case that large organisations like local authority social services departments and also large third-sector agencies create ways of working through policies and procedures that are hard to change. In itself it might be argued that this provides consistency in working with and the treatment of service users. However, in practice this can restrict social workers' opportunities to act creatively, to respond to needs as they arise, especially when these have not been foreseen by that agency.

Case study

Let's examine the case of Blandton mental health team which has prided itself on giving equal treatment to all needing it. Both Sajid and Rosa came from the same area in Blandton. They were both experiencing depression and had been referred to the team, Sajid by his GP and Rosa by her occupational health practitioner. The referrals requested group support in managing depression, something that the Blandton team were well known for and offered as a matter of course. Sajid was able to attend the Friday afternoon meeting as he was not currently in work and his children were at school. Rosa, however, was unable to do so as she worked weekdays and was unable to take the time off.

In this case the Blandton team offered everyone the same treatment but their individual circumstances were not always able to be accommodated. This created inequities in the ways in which the services could be taken up. Arguing for the development of services that didn't create a one-size-fits-all approach but tailored these to people's individual needs, as indicated under the Equality Act 2010 and the Care Act 2014, would offer equal services that could be taken up by all rather than restricting them to certain situations.

The Equality Act also helps in focusing our attention as social workers on ensuring fair play whatever social characteristics are shared by the individuals with whom you are working. As social workers, we can use our understanding of equality legislation to challenge existing services and resources that marginalise individuals and exclude them from participation because of the way such services are constructed or offered.

Case study

Michelle was the social worker for Rana, a young woman who lived with multiple sclerosis. Although Rana was in remission, she still found it difficult to negotiate the entrance to her housing association flat and her bathroom. The housing association was experiencing financial difficulties that had increased as austerity measures continued. They had convinced Rana that they could not undertake any adjustments to the property unless she paid for them.

When Michelle was informed about this she understood that the Equality Act 2010 called for reasonable adjustments to be made to ensure people's access to all aspects of society and living. She also knew that Rana should not be asked to pay. Informing Rana of this gave her the information she needed to challenge the housing association's decision and, when they still refused, she called in the support of Michelle, which led to easier access thanks to the provision of rails and supports.

Working in the courts

One of the most important roles local authority social workers can have is to act in court on behalf of their employing organisation. It is especially important to remember that it is your local authority or other employer organisation that you are representing whilst the service users you are working with may have their own legal representation, or social workers appointed by the courts to assist them. It is equally important to remember that you are not a legal representative but a social worker. These fundamental perspectives can help you in using the law to assist people in the best way possible. Whilst the local authority may have a stance in respect of the case and in respect of budgetary ramifications of particular outcomes, you, as the local authority representative, must also work according to the values, perspectives and human rights approach undergirding the profession. Courts of law are serious places and it is incumbent on you to be truthful to the situation as you see it and not to 'toe the line' unless you believe this to be right.

Your knowledge of the law and the ways in which it is understood and applied within your organisation will be central to the court's deliberations. If you are clear in your own mind about the application of the law as you understand it and how this guided your practice, you will be able to make the case more strongly on behalf of those service users you are supporting. In court settings it is usually, or at least often, the case that someone's wants and wishes are pitted against someone else's. This demands that your approach, the reasons why you practised in the way you did, and your plans for future working follow sound interpretations of the law, and are underpinned by a human rights-based stance. Consider the following case.

Case study

Malcolm was a three-year-old boy who had been beaten so badly by his mother and stepfather that he had been hospitalised. No charges were brought because the Crown Prosecution Service did not believe the evidence was enough to secure a conviction. The local authority is seeking a care order in respect of Malcolm on the grounds not only of the significant harm he experienced but because it is believed that he is in danger of future harm if returned to that situation.

The social worker recognised that the situation was serious and had worked with the mother, who had now left Malcolm's stepfather to develop more positive ways of parenting and ensuring discipline. The social worker had argued at the case conference that a planned and monitored return home rather than a care order would better serve Malcolm's needs in the long term but she had been overruled.

In court, when questioned, the social worker answered honestly from her practice experience and wisdom (see Chapter 7), using her understanding of human rights to both protection and to a family life, and drawing on her knowledge of social work research. The local authority solicitor was annoyed that the plans agreed at conference were derailed by the social worker's stance, but the social worker employed her knowledge and skills to secure what she believed was the right outcome to protect the rights and safety of those involved.

Working with individuals and communities and instilling activism

In an episode of Jimmy McGovern's 2017 TV series *Broken*, Sean Bean's priest, Father Michael Kerrigan, used the story of Jesus turning out the money changers from the temple to encourage his congregation to take sledgehammers to a local betting shop and to smash the gambling machines. Direct action indeed! Of course, such action would carry criminal charges and is not something that social workers could encourage at the present time in this country. It does, however, provide a clear message that acts of rebellion and resistance are sometimes necessary if we are standing alongside those who are marginalised and disadvantaged. There have been times when more direct action was called for and would have been justified. Social workers in Nazi Germany were often complicit with the regime (Lorenz, 1993). From today's perspective we would think that opposition was necessary. More recently, Hungarian social worker, Norbert Ferencz, campaigned against the government directive that made searching through rubbish bins for food a misdemeanour in law. He was arrested and charged with the imprisonable offence of 'incitement' (Ioakimidis, 2013). It was social workers around the world who campaigned, successfully, for his release on the basis that he was following the International Federation of Social Workers' definition of social work and its ethical demands.

We can utilise our understanding of law and policy and its application in a range of ways. When we think of slavery, most of us look back historically to times when slavery and trade in people as slaves was legal, lucrative and contested as to its virtue or otherwise. We are, one hopes, appalled by some of the despicable and inhumane practices that occurred – the raids on villages to capture, enslave and trade people, the use of slaves as labour in colonial plantations and the abominable deliberate drowning of slaves in order to claim insurance (Thomas, 1999). However, modern slavery is rife and is something with which you may come in contact in your work as a social worker. The Modern Slavery Act 2015 represents an important piece of legislation that, again, demands to be understood and applied through the lens of human rights. The Act covers those areas in which people are forced into labour, often held against their will, and in which the practice of trafficking in human beings is often implicated.

As social workers you are likely to be working with people who have been trafficked, who may be traumatised, without residence and may have children or other dependants. Knowing the workings of the Act and underpinning legislation is necessary, but knowing your way around the various agencies and organisations available to offer assistance and national helplines such as the Modern Slavery Helpline (**https://www.modernslaveryhelpline.org**) is also key to effective working. The law outlines the legitimate and illegitimate; you, as social workers, put the human flesh on this skeleton and work as human to human to secure wellbeing and to challenge the cold and instrumental application of rules. The following case study illustrates this.

Case study

Amira was 27 years old. She had fled the fighting in Syria. Her family had been part of the popular uprising in 2011 against Bashir Assad's regime but her husband, having been arrested, beaten and imprisoned, left Damascus for friendlier areas once he had been released.

→

Unfortunately, the family was caught in the fighting as ISIS advanced and her husband was killed. Amira escaped with her seven-year-old daughter and 70-year-old father. She found some men who agreed to get her and her family safely out of the country and she paid them all that she had and handed over their passports in order to do so. She was quickly separated from her daughter and father; she was later told that her father had died on the journey but that her daughter was in Munich in Germany. She was then told that she owed money to the people who organised her escape and that she would have to work for them to pay this off. She was to be sent to Britain to work as a maid for a family and she would have to do everything she is told until the debt is paid. After nine months of solid work cleaning, cooking and looking after children and not having had a day off or been allowed outside without two or three minders, she was able to evade them. As she spoke some English she managed to secure the help of a community law centre to support her and to help her establish her identity and to search for her daughter. She did not have sufficient detail of the place she was kept or the family for the police to make any arrests.

The Border Control Agency recognised Amira as an illegal immigrant and she was subject to questioning and detention whilst her case was processed. She was one of the lucky ones whose claim for asylum was assisted by the Red Cross, who found her daughter, now eight, and liaised with the authorities about reuniting them. The local social work team working with people in this position was aware that her status excluded her from social security benefits or housing support. They helped her apply for payment from the UK Visas and Immigration support and she gained £36.95 each for herself and her daughter. As well as using the law appropriately, the social worker put Amira in touch with the Refugee Council (**https://www.refugeecouncil.org.uk**) and the national welfare charity Turn 2 Us (**https://www.turn2us.org.uk**) to marshal support for her asylum claim, for emotional support for Amira and her daughter, and to challenge any unfair application of law.

Using law and policy concerns working alongside communities, groups and individuals, recognising that you are there to interpret and offer guidance and support to people to use the law and social policies to change their situation. It is one example amongst many. A further example from on-going research, the Hideaway Project, that we are completing, concerns a local authority developing a project in which a specialist social worker has been employed to work with men and women who have experienced domestic violence and abuse alongside mental health and/or drug and alcohol problems. These people have been excluded from available services either because of their unpredictable behaviour or because those services only offer help and support in one of the areas. The social worker has been specifically employed to work across boundaries and margins with these people and to help them develop confidence and the ability to engage with multiple organisations, and to assist those organisations in dealing with situations outside their usual singular focus.

Not only does the social worker need to be well versed in legislation concerning violence and abuse, mental health and care, and to know the policies and guidance associated with them, but also must have a good grasp of what is on offer from other organisations that can help address needs and fulfil the requirements of the law.

Working politically: seeking to change policy

As a social worker you are in a somewhat ambiguous position. Your employment role precludes working politically as a member of a political party when undertaking your daily role as a social worker. Whilst you cannot impose your political beliefs on those you are working with, this does not mean that you cannot be political. In fact, it is at least as important nowadays to be political and to act politically as a social worker as it has been in previous times. Considering politics with a small 'p' or a big 'P' can be one way of understanding how we can act politically as social workers. Being political is seeking to change the ways we operate in society and being Political is acting on behalf of a party or ideology. What is certain is that we must never allow a situation to develop where whole sections of society and communities are demonised as they were in Nazi Germany in the 1930s and in which social workers were implicated by either inaction or compliance (Lorenz, 1993).

You can be a political social worker in numerous ways. In a personal capacity you can join a political party that seeks the same things that you believe are important for upholding social justice and human rights, and you can campaign on that party's behalf. This is a matter of conscience and right. You may take part in demonstrations and campaigns through political activism in order to change our social policies and to influence how we should organise our society. Of course, the criteria for registration with the professional body demand that you operate within the law, but protest is one way of showing your resolve for social justice and change.

Other ways you can be political include adding to team and organisational reviews, collecting and demonstrating evidence of the ways in which your work affects people for good or for ill. You can take part in web campaigns, writing self-help materials, developing resources for people to use. You can argue within your team for values to take a central place in social work.

One crucial way of working towards political change, however, is in your practice as a social worker. The feminist adage 'the personal is political' remains important (Hanisch, 1970), despite some misunderstandings when it is taken in a literal sense (Furedi, 2017). The way you work creates a visual 'narrative', a performance that can be read. For instance, following the letter of the law and organisational procedures alone will indicate that systems rather than people are most important. It will convey a message that marginalised people do not matter. On the other hand, if you stand alongside people in distress, a message of hope, support and political will to change is sent to those who are disenfranchised and have no voice that is heard within society. Consider the following case study.

Case study

Pawel lived in a small housing estate on the outskirts of a town in the East Midlands. He had worked in Britain for ten years as a plumber and regularly returned to Poland to visit his mother. He had experienced some racism, taunts and name calling during his time in Britain but had a range of friends and enjoyed his life there. Following the referendum on EU membership in June 2016, however, his contacts for work began to slow down and by early autumn he could no longer support himself through work. He registered for job seeker's allowance whilst searching for work. Increasingly, he experienced life on his estate as hostile. He was told to go back to Poland, spat at and sworn at and was worried for his safety after threats were made against him. The police investigated what was happening and were clear he should not have to face hate crime and that it was taken very seriously.

Noting that Pawel was distressed, the police, with his permission, referred him to social services. A social worker from the mental health team visited, assessed his situation but said he did not meet the eligibility criteria for a service. Pawel felt ashamed that he was upset by what had happened to him but also marginalised by the social worker who appeared more interested in systems than in him as a person. He was given the number of a community group in which another social worker was located and contacted that person for social support and company. The social worker listened to his story, his worries and concerns and took his case up with social services under equality legislation, again with his permission, and challenged the local council to implement community integration plans to tackle hate crime. Seeing the social worker use policy in this way gave Pawel hope and energy to volunteer with the community group and to help support other Polish residents in the community who were also experiencing racist abuse and slurs. His work allowed the community to be more vocal when abused and to report concerns to the police, who were grateful for the contact.

Another important way you can enhance your political practice within social work is to build on the historical legacy of radical and critical social work that we introduced in Chapter 1. Of course, a great deal of the thinking here stems from neo-Marxist interpretations of society and this may not suit everyone. The broad base of the contemporary radical Social Work Action Network aims to promote social justice and human rights across nations and to address the attacks that neoliberal New Public Management policies have inflicted on those using social work services. This aligns with the views of many social workers concerning the needs inherent in social work today.

Chapter summary

This chapter has taken the knowledge and skills social work requires in respect of legislation and social policies and used that to examine ways in which these may be translated into practice. Some of the reasons why social workers need a good understanding of the global, national and local political world were introduced before we considered the human rights and equality base for interpreting the law in practice. A range of ways of being political, interpreting the law and campaigning as a social worker for improved social standing and benefits for marginalised people were introduced. We can now move in the final substantive chapter to consider some of the ethical dilemmas that social workers face in daily practice.

Further reading

Brammer, A. (2015) *Social Work Law*, 4th ed. London: Pearson.

This popular edition, written by a solicitor with local authority experience, represents a *tour de force* in the centrality of understanding and using legislation for good practice, as well as an understanding of its development and changes.

Ife, J. (2012) *Human Rights and Social Work: Towards Rights-Based Practice*, 3rd ed. Cambridge: Cambridge University Press.

Jim Ife's renown in the field of human rights is unsurpassed and this book is an in-depth, erudite exposition of why and how human rights are important in social work practice.

Johns, R. (2017) *Using Law in Social Work*, 7th ed. London: SAGE.

Robert John's accessible and popular work on using the law continues to give great value to social work students and practitioners. It is written in a clear transparent way that makes direct links to practice.

9: Ethical dilemmas in practice

The final substantive chapter will consider key ethical problems that may tax the social worker in developing appropriate and authentic work with individuals and groups who have been disadvantaged or marginalised. This will include exploration of the following:

- when the policies and practices act to marginalise and disadvantage people, groups and communities;
- when agency policies and procedure conflict with your moral sense;
- when the resources aren't there;
- when communities collide with each other;
- when those who use social work challenge your moral sensibilities or value base.

Marginalising and disadvantaging people

In the previous chapters a considerable amount of ground was covered in respect of questions that explore what constitutes marginalisation and disadvantage; and therefore who may be those occupying the lowest 'rungs of the ladder' in society; and, indeed, what social workers can do in their service. In terms of how people are marginalised by social structures and social policy, we have explored poverty as social exclusion, as well as the ramifications of citizen status, rights and access to services in relation to refugees and other migrants. Equally the plight of those who occupy the edges of society through lifestyle and culture, like Roma Gypsy Travellers, has also been considered as people who are excluded from mainstream society by policies that deliberately or through omission fail to accommodate difference adequately.

Disability and age (and class) influence stability or precarity in life; and so too, to a less obvious extent, does gender. This latter factor has not been explored in specific detail but gender is noteworthy in that many of the cases of elders referred to here relate to older women, rather than men. Older men in their frailty are often cared for by their wives, but, owing to women's longer lifespan, albeit not necessarily better health, wives do not receive reciprocal marital support in turn (Galfe, 2014).

Changing circumstances across the lifespan give rise to tenuous, vulnerable and uncertain conditions for people, who weather them in different ways; although, as practice wisdom in relation to crisis theory also suggests, these can present opportunities to try out new ways of seeing and being – which is true for both service user and social workers as well. This process, although fundamentally optimistic, is clearly not likely to be without its difficulties and disappointments as well.

In this chapter therefore we return to some of these issues and characters mentioned earlier to draw out the dilemmas that they present and how these could be addressed, recognising that some dilemmas may not be entirely resolvable.

As discussed earlier, the PCF, although designed to be holistic and to overcome the problems of atomising competences in practice (Burgess et al., 2014; Higgins, 2016), is not able to address the ramifications of austerity in UK society given the shortfall in essential services in the face of increasing social and medical need in the population. In Chapter 8 we read the case study of Max, the new social worker, whose automatic processing of a quick assessment of need is put to one side when he realised the real needs of the service user: to be listened to and understood as a human being failing to come to terms with personal tragedy rather than a 'case' to be allocated a 'package of care'.

Reamer (2013) explores practice in terms of the technical, empirical and ethical dimensions of social work intervention. Max's holistic, empathic approach would be conventionally recognised by social work values as good practice, as endorsed as well by the PCF. Here the technical aspect of carrying out an assessment of need is postponed, in favour of a better understanding of the empirical situation of the service user as an ethical social work judgement. However, as Max chose to spend more time focusing on the service user rather than dealing with this case *efficiently*, if not *effectively*, he was chastised by his senior manager. *Irony*, as promoted by Higgins and Goodyer (2015), comes immediately to mind when we think about these practice conundrums. Here we may reflect upon the apparent yawning gulf that often opens between social work values and social service realities, where in this case time to do a good-enough job becomes as much a commodity in social work as are community resources.

One very powerful aspect of contemporary social work is the focus on risk. The ambiguous term 'safeguarding' is one that is prevalent in social work education and practice, which can strongly suggest that social work is too often merely about *managing risk* (Crisp and Gillingham, 2008). Stanford (2010) comments on the issue of how the term risk is used – the service user either being *at* risk or *posing* a risk to social workers. Social workers in turn can ameliorate risk or create more risk through their interventions. Risk as a term therefore becomes intimately associated with professional discomfort and fear.

A risk-aversive British society is one that we are all exposed to as employees in terms of draconian reinforcements of health and safety regimes. To be sure, this began life commendably enough, in society's need to show far greater humanitarian consideration for the welfare of people at work than formerly existed – and this lay at the heart of these earlier legislations. However, it is now questionable whether this remains the primary consideration today when the burden of responsibility has shifted from the employer to the individual employee, who can be disciplined for not observing a range of health and safety regulations to avoid the 'risk' of litigation against companies.

To illustrate this further, one of the authors was recently returning home by cross-country trains in balmy June weather. Time after time, much to the audible exasperation of travellers, there was a banal announcement made over the intercom informing passengers that the weather was 'hot' and that they should be carrying a bottle of water. The real message followed that if passengers felt unwell they should not pull the emergency cord but should alight at the next station or, better still, miss getting on the train at all. Clearly the risk management strategy here was focused on avoiding expensive delays by unwell passengers; or attempting to militate against passengers complaining about train delays and becoming unwell due to heat and dehydration. In either case, the main concern was to avoid problems for the train company rather than for the passengers.

This, we suggest, underlines the entire issue of risk aversion that curtails public and personal lives, and has seeped deeply into social work (Stanford, 2010). For while vulnerable people clearly need to be given statutory protection from exploitation and abuse, they can be and are also abused by unresponsive social care systems, inadequate or fragile services, and through being dehumanised by pressurised services and personnel.

To understand how people are made vulnerable we continue the story of Mrs Wood and her daughter Sarah from Chapter 4.

Case study

Recalling a visit to see her distressed mother in the elderly mentally infirm (EMI) ward where her daughter suspected Mrs Wood was being abused, Sarah repeats the following conversation in an interview with the authors.

Mrs Wood   I am going insane.
to Sarah:

Sarah: What makes you think you are going insane?

Mrs Wood: I have no money in my purse, my clothes have someone else's name on them and I am not allowed out unaccompanied. If that is not insanity, I don't know what it is.

As explained in Chapter 4, following her unhappy time in the EMI unit Mrs Wood was then placed in a suitable nursing home, where the next problem arose concerning the funding of her care and ensuing eviction.

Sarah seeks the active help of Mrs Wood's social worker to try to help find the funds and keep her mother in the home. Sarah believes that the difficulty has been that she has experienced a lot of difficulties trying to communicate with Jan, the social worker, and that, unfortunately, she feels that their relationship was tense and adversarial, rather than empathic and constructive. One day Sarah experiences a particularly upsetting telephone call from Jan bluntly informing her of Mrs Wood's lack of options owing to the growing funding shortfall.

Sarah: But I got to see the humanity of the social worker at a meeting when I was trying to highlight the humanity of my mother that I felt had been lost in all this process.

            You have to carry five big files around with you whenever you need to speak to some-one about care. So I had the occupational therapy file, the CHC [continuing health

$\longrightarrow$

care] file, social services paperwork, a file for trust funds, the chain of nursing homes you have contacted, all of Mum's medical paperwork and my carer's support file. All of these things have to be carried with you wherever you go, so you can quickly refer to them *if* and *when* you do manage to speak to someone in authority. I remember it was Mum's social work annual review and I was seeing what must have been her sixth social worker by then.

Sarah relates the following:

I said to Jan, the social worker, 'Would you mind if we do reflective practice?' She asked me what it was and I said, 'It's where we discuss how your practice has affected our lives, good and bad.'

It was a very helpful meeting because I just recounted the telephone conversation I had with her and how it affected me, how it had made me sob because I got so disillusioned and I lost hope. I thought the only way to reignite hope was to share the experience with Jan because I didn't believe this good social worker had meant to do that. I believe she was caught up in the system and had developed a call centre mentality, a script. She'd lost sight that these were individual human lives she was dealing with. I imagined that the pressures on her were from above, below and around – you know, management! She didn't have time to see my mother as anything more than a budget problem.

So I told her how I felt and she got it, she understood it completely. But I had to say to her, 'Your relationship style is aggressive' and she started to cry and said, 'You're the third person to say I am aggressive. Yes I am and I am so sorry.' I said to her, 'The problem is you are a social worker and you are dealing with budgets and so you are needing to be aggressive. I am a carer bringing you the person I love and I am having to put myself between you and her, and be defensive. Really we are not making any progress here, because you come with a skillset that I need and I come with the information that you need. And so instead of being aggressive and defensive, like a tug of war over my mother, why don't we look at the social care business as a complicated jigsaw puzzle and just try to work out the way together?'

She seemed really taken aback by what I said to her and went very quiet, thinking about it all I suppose, and then she said, 'I need to go back to my office and tell them what happened here because *this* has to change.' I was so relieved to hear this and I said, 'Thank you, I *really* appreciate being heard.'

In the end I felt that my mother had been 'seen' at last and her experiences recognised. I think in practice though it's like turning the Titanic. There may be one member of the crew – one social worker who stands out like a lighthouse and wants to do things differently – but it's going to take a long time to convince the others to steer this ship in a different way.

When agency policies and procedure conflict with your moral sense

This constitutes a very challenging issue for social workers that over time, if not resolved, can erode their professional commitment to their vocation. Here we look at this concept from a neutral position in exploring the idea of the social worker as a 'broker', an idea which may immediately give rise to the idea of finances, but is a concept that has been extended to embrace a wider vision of the 'middleman'. A 'support broker' is viewed as essentially the holder of information, guidance and advice that the service user/carer requires and conforms to a personalisation ethos as well as a task-centred approach (Phillips et al., 2010).

The concept of a 'cultural broker' has also been mooted in helping families from minority ethnic backgrounds or marginalised faiths to access culturally sensitive services (Lindsay et al., 2014). While these and other brokerage concepts provide useful latitude for exploring the social work role, the more sordid face of brokerage in terms of finances and financial assessments offers less scope for social work creativity. Too often this represents the uglier face of resource provision and its scarcity in the community. This is a task that may be carried out by non-social-work-qualified members of the team as well as by qualified social workers, but whoever it is allotted to, it usually carries negative connotations and is unlikely to be other than a disagreeable, even stigmatising, aspect to the workload.

Few professionals could enjoy making formal inquiries into the financial position of service users, who are either complete or comparative strangers. There may be a real concern that the likelihood is that such inquiries will either upset or embarrass service users or lead to unpleasant confrontations.

The issue of funding carries many ethical overtones. As in the case of Mrs Wood and Sarah, services may be essential to someone's wellbeing and yet remain unaffordable. The issue of using up the entire savings of an elderly person, leaving nothing for her children to inherit, is a fraught moral position. Some practitioners may argue that the savings belong entirely to the individual and not to the heirs and some would assert that the notion of inheritance is wrong in itself. Yet, depending on culture and background, certain people might regard themselves as merely guardians of the family money, which they regard as to be passed on to the next generation in order to help them as they were perhaps helped by parents in their turn; and so, based on this logic, spending it on their own needs is tantamount to robbing their family of their justified dues. Many others would certainly argue that a lifetime of paying taxes (and perhaps particularly if they have not drawn upon welfare services to an extent previously) has entitled them to a level of free care in their time of need now.

Whichever position we take up in this debate, service users or their carers who fail to show the correct documentary proof of their income in the form of bank statements and similar (which are often photographed as filed evidence – an unpleasant issue in itself) will be classified as self-funders. Clearly this may sometimes create potentially disagreeable situations or problematic ones if service users do not understand what is being asked of them or cannot comply with the request to find the correct financial evidence.

Where service users are deemed self-funding, social care staff can complete their duties with this group by simply signposting them to agencies that will provide packages of care. Some of these may be in the state-run sector but most will be found in the independent sector, which consequently has seen a mushroom growth of agencies. There are of course many reputable ones here but others may be less scrupulous or accountable agencies. Agencies of this sort may be quick to open or close and move on but, whether offering high or poor services, each is positioned to cash in on the lucrative market of care where need outstrips resources.

The neoliberal political climate in which social care operates is a less regulated and much murkier terrain than most social workers would find savoury. Agencies that open in order to cash in on care needs are a logical consequence of political drivers that promote market supply-and-demand notions with due obeisance made to the over-simplified concept of customer 'choice'. Such proponents argue in favour of the creation of market efficiencies, but equally one could point to the consequences that arise from these policies that are linked to the devolution of state responsibility down to individual resourcefulness. Service users, by the nature of their circumstances, often lack these choices or are unable to see or access them in ways that would be available in an ideal world. What choice are we actually giving someone who needs care but is not in a position to be easily able to choose how the care is managed or by whom? As we have seen, service users are often placed in positions where they are petitioners for care, which can be withheld from them if they are not seen as sufficiently compliant or profitable – for, after all, the *raison d'être* of the market economy is at the most basic level the profit motive.

When resources are not there

The fight for funding has huge ramifications for individuals and families, but is one waged higher up than at the practitioner–service user level, where it also takes place between the public service monoliths of health and social care. For many years the issue of how to fund the care of individuals with severe and chronic complex needs has been a contentious one, as each case incurs considerable financial cost to the NHS or, otherwise, social services. Thus the question of who receives CHC has often involved many tussles to establish where the main responsibility lies for funding such individuals in the community

Irony, even as a reflective tool, can take us only so far. What can we do when resources are not there to support needs, especially when we know full well that such resources were once available or where we know that the eligibility criteria may have been hoisted up another notch to exclude those who would once have received a service?

A highly important consideration is whether we believe that social work has a political role to play in the way resources are allocated in society. By extension therefore, are social workers political animals or is our practice viewed as entirely sanitised from the taint of politics? If the latter, is this a political position in itself and if so, how does that help those we work on behalf of as well as those we work with? We began thinking about such issues in Chapter 5, but these are questions that will continue to be resurrected time after time throughout one's social work career.

If we accept that social work is certainly not removed from politics – and here it is helpful to interpret the term 'politics' as not merely party politics but as also the power between people and groups that shapes or affects lives – then that is something that social work educators also have a duty to acknowledge. If essential resources are not available, how are social workers to address that in their practice according to their professional value base? If such a situation is not an act of God, then it must be of Man.[1] If so, then politics is at the root of it, but of course politics is merely composed of people and interest groups. How a society chooses to allocate its resources is a political decision and as such is open to influence by citizens and associations.

It is easy to develop a myopic vision of social work when working at the coalface of local service provision, where micro-level practice is unevenly pulled between working directly with service users and the bureaucratic demands this increasingly entails. Social work, however,

---

[1] The term 'Man' here is used rhetorically and generically to cover 'people'.

extends far further than this, encompassing meso-level intervention, whether that be at the level of community engagement or civic local government initiatives, for example – and beyond that to influencing macro-level social policy. Genuine good practice is tremendously hard for individual practitioners to achieve (and some would say, even impossible) unless there is effective professional engagement up through the vertical strata of politics to shape social structures in which social work practice is daily enacted. Thus, we argue that social work is essentially both political and politicised, and must continue to be ever more active in the democratic space to fight for its future and the futures of those who use the services.

Social workers, as is often recognised, straddle a very uncomfortable position. Classically, they advocate for the under-privileged and needy, yet they are also servants of the state, but the political vectors of influence shape the state – there is nothing static about it. Social work can therefore find itself trapped in a web of nihilistic, destructive tensions and contradictions that make social workers feel disempowered and burned out, or, by contrast, forging a dynamic, creative force that generates strength and solidarity of social workers with their client groups and with each other nationally and internationally.

With social work too comes the authority the state bestows and, although professional work can often feel like an unsung and up-hill undertaking, the power of social workers can be formidable if they choose to wield it and, in contrast, negligible if they do not do so or do not know how to make their voices count. The key as ever lies in solidarity and a cohesive mission – and a strong, inclusive body that dares speak boldly and strongly in defence of the profession and its mission. Good *savoir faire* (know-how) when it comes to using the media is very important but it has been lamentably under-exploited to-date by social work bodies. The detractors and critics of social work use media to their vicious ends, yet it can as easily work to social work's advantage. So where are the good news stories about social work, one could ask? It's easy to get into a defensive rut trying to fend off blows when a better defence is to take the offensive to speak first and loudest about the good social work does and its many successes, which far, far outweigh any shortcomings and failures.

Activity 9.2

How would you like to see social work engage effectively with the media? What kind of social work stories would you like the general public to hear about?

Comment

Sometimes the best ideas for books and programmes have been created by people who were frustrated by the lack of good material in the public sphere. Arguably probably no one knows more about what social work can say to the general public about the vital role it plays in society than social workers themselves.

In the meantime, let us not forget that there is another story to tell regarding how people are failed by austerity measures, which social workers are helpless to reverse alone.

Case study

Julie works in a local social services office where the bulk of her work involves assessment of complex needs. She describes the intense competition for funding.

> If someone in poor health is in hospital, that person would be entitled to the CHC. But where the NHS used to agree with us on many cases, they are now sending bigger and bigger consultants to overrule us so we continue to pay the care. Let me give you an example. For CHC funding you have to show that the need is intense, complex, unpredictable. But the consultant can say that the need is not unpredictable enough for funding.

> The difference that decision can make to a family is enormous. They may have to sell up. I can remember one case of this man who fell at home. He hadn't needed any care before and was pretty fit, but unfortunately he stood on an upturned bucket to put a book back on a shelf, the bucket slipped, he hit his head on a table and is now a quadriplegic. He cannot even feed himself, but still a consultant argued that his care was not unpredictable, even though he will need care all his life. The consultant also said that because he didn't need a specialist nurse his condition was not intense, so they refused to pay for CHC. Yet social services should only manage social care; his needs were way beyond that.

> To make things worse, this couple were planning to get divorced at the time but hadn't started the process off legally. So now they have to sell their house to help pay for his care and she, who would have been entitled to half of the profits in a divorce case, has lost out.

> You just spend so much valuable social work time and effort arguing about who is going to pay the bills for people's care when you could be helping someone.

Conceivably there are a number of different ways one could support the unfortunate couple in this case, whose circumstances are now seriously disadvantaged in so many ways. One immediate question arises, of whether the divorce can still go ahead if this is still desired. This underpins the important principle for respect for persons. Why should a couple remain unhappily together simply because one is now severely disabled? There is the additional issue of equity, particularly gendered equality, where women are so often automatically expected to shoulder the role of carer. A divorce would probably require additional intervention in the first instance for the individuals involved, particularly in relation to the direct service user, the ex-husband, but emotional support is compatible with a social work remit as identified by the PCF and we jeopardise these important aspects of social work at our professional peril.

When communities collide

If we immediately think of the collision of communities, we can hardly escape from the immediate and urgent political turmoil that is currently engulfing and dividing the country.

As we write, infamous and cruel terrorist attacks have been indiscriminately made on passers-by, perpetuated by both Muslim extremists and an apparent White supremacist from Wales. In response to these blows President Trump deems it within his dignity to tweet taunts to Sadiq Khan, the conscientious London Mayor. In addition hundreds of London social housing tenants have just faced or experienced a terrible death in an entirely preventable fire in the Grenfell Tower block, as referred to in Chapter 8. Moreover, the political backdrop remains enveloped in the issue of Brexit, where a caustic media and a bewildered and angry population have gone through the EU referendum, the protracted political uncertainties and contradictions of the year that has followed, a deeply divided country, the callous bargaining of the lives of EU migrant settlers as merely gambling chips in the Brexit negotiations, another hastily called general election, economic woes coming home to roost and the loss of confidence in the country's future. All of this serves to spotlight and exacerbate deep-seated tensions in the UK that are too entrenched and volatile for comfort or for any quick political fixes or 'make-overs'.

If one takes a parochial and apolitical view of social work, then such concerns could be constructed as matters of no consequence to professionals in their practice, which remains aloof from such considerations. However, social work forms part of the greater ecological system of a society, where those we work with may well carry the impact of such social manifestations as overt or hidden injuries in their lives. Moreover, we do ourselves an injustice if we do not acknowledge how these affect us in our lives as well; and so to paraphrase playfully the great Renaissance, metaphysical poet, John Donne, *no social worker is an Island*, or can pretend to be.

Competition and conflict created by interest groups seeking to protect their scant resources may result in poorer care or service for service users. Yet such competitiveness is, of course, at the basis of neoliberal thinking, working on the premise that the canny customer profits. The inappropriateness of this cut-throat corporate model applied to all social care and health is one that can challenge the professionalism of most practitioners who are instead motivated to seek to identify and offer a model of 'best practice'. This professional ideal is hardly compatible with government cheese paring of public services, where the terrible fire at Grenfell Tower in London stands as a charred symbol, a victim of local council parsimony in using cheap, flammable cladding on the building. The fact that this tragedy took place in one of the richest boroughs in the land in one of the wealthiest countries in the world has rightly become a political rallying call against the harm wreaked by austerity measures and politics that hold the poor and marginalised in contempt.

The challenges to social workers' practices challenge moral sensibilities and value base

However grim and demoralising social inequities may seem at times, without any doubt social work has a richly comic side to it, and this we must not forget. Far from being inappropriate to enjoy the occasional laugh, just like a good weep or yell and desk thumping now and again, laughter acts not only as a safety valve, but allows us to see our client group as people struggling to express their humanity against the odds, just as we are also doing in an occupation that is often very difficult and frustrating.

So we should not be overly cowed by what it means to be 'professional', which too often is interpreted as meaning the donning of a uniform mentality and depersonalised mode of communication – and, if we are not careful, losing our empathy and sense of humour into the bargain. Professionalism should never mean sanctimonious po-faced tut-tutting and not experiencing fun in our work; it means knowing how to treat the people we work with, service users, their families and indeed our colleagues, in ways that are commensurate with our professional values and principles – and where we see, respect and cherish the humanity in the other – and to help them to see that in us.

The people we work with can often have lifestyles, habits, dress and communication styles that 'tickle our funny bone' – so instead of suppressing this too far and letting good humour die, use this to explore their worlds further and more deeply and in so doing understand them and social work better on the road to becoming an even more shrewd, compassionate, resilient and self-healing practitioner.

Case study

Connie lives in a caravan, or what remains of one. The caravan is packed to the collapsing roof full of her possessions as she is an inveterate hoarder, so Connie actually lives in the old awning attached to it, which is rat-infested due to hygiene problems.

Because her caravan home is effectively uninhabitable, her social worker, Wahida, has recently managed to move her into a flat run by a housing association, provided that Connie agrees to part with some of her precious hoard. As soon as the move is accomplished, though, Connie made a quick phone call to the removal service to say that they have left some of her possessions behind. So once again Connie is surrounded by her incredible hoard, which is so extensive that it is extremely difficult to get past the front door.

→

Soon after the move Wahida receives a phone call from a neighbour regarding Connie's anti-social habits and makes a home visit to find out what's going on. Once inside the flat she explains that Connie has been seen eating out of a dustbin. Connie is hugely indignant about the idea and retorts: 'The very idea is preposterous! Do you think a woman like me would eat out of a bin? I've been to Canada – that's abroad, you know!'

Wahida, knowing Connie of old, pursues the matter and explains that others have also witnessed this. Realising denial won't work, Connie decides to bluff it out.

Connie: Well, I like to recycle the stuff in the bin. I like to make it tidy, you see.

Wahida: Have you eaten or drunk something from a bin, Connie?

Connie: Oh, for goodness sake! All right then, well I may have had a swig out of a Coke bottle. The things people throw away, it's disgraceful!

Wahida: How big was the bottle?

Connie: It was a huge bottle! Fancy someone throwing away a perfectly good bottle like that! My mother always taught me, 'waste not, want not'.

Wahida: Couple of things you need to think about Connie. Firstly, you have no history of the person who drank out of it; you don't even know what's in it – it could be urine, anything!

Connie: It tasted absolutely fine.

Wahida tries to find out what Connie did with the bottle. It turns out she has an array of bottles retrieved from bins and now littered all over the flat. Connie now becomes defensive.

Connie: I'm used to gleaning. You see, I have to empty all these bins. The things people throw away! It's very lucky I am here to sort it out!

As a person Connie is always mindful of her mother's old sayings and advice and still tries to follow them closely. She was told that fresh fruit and vegetables are good for her, so she likes to find and eat potatoes – raw.

One afternoon Wahida is telephoned by a very annoyed Connie, still living at the flat surrounded by her squalid hoard.

Connie: I had a laptop here but the last social worker stole it. She befriended me and then she stole it! Can you believe it?

After a difficult search the laptop is finally found on the floor behind the washing machine that Wahida bought to help Connie keep her clothes clean, but to little avail, as it stands unused.

Upon Wahida producing the laptop Connie exclaims: 'Goodness me! But these people are so clever to get that back in my kitchen without me noticing!'

As a social worker Wahida treads a narrow path. She describes her experience of working with Connie as both 'hilarious and appalling', and finds Connie a challenge to work with at times, while admiring her intelligence and ingenuity, not least her survival toughness. Privately Wahida admits to finding Connie's scavenging habits an affront to her personal sense of hygiene and decency. Yet, however Wahida feels about Connie's dubious life choices, she does not allow this to get in the way of her work with her, whilst being aware that the general social work space for supporting and befriending individuals like Connie is fast narrowing.

Wahida's practice wisdom dictates how important it is to ensure that Connie is able to maintain her dignity and so she does not challenge too many of Connie's fabrications, unless she feels that omission to act would actively lead to Connie's harm. The fine line between Connie being able to live her life in the way she chooses and transgressing too many social norms that would lead to her being actively shunned by her neighbours or actually inadvertently self-harming through her indiscriminate scavenging habits remains a source of professional concern.

Cases like Connie's present us with genuine philosophical difficulties. On the one hand, she is clearly exercising her autonomy, but on the other hand what kind of life is this and is it really freely chosen or just imposed by her addictive behaviour and lack of insight? These considerations relate directly to Isaiah Berlin's (1969) original philosophical concept of 'negative' and 'positive' freedoms, which has since been explored by social work academics like Raymond Plant, as illuminating many of the lives and often unwise choices that client groups sometimes make (Horne, 1999).

A 'negative' freedom means being free from interference by others to pursue choices; an example of this would be Wahida not trying to prevent Connie scavenging in bins.

We often see cases of negative freedom exercised where people return to lifestyles and people that are abusive and sometimes downright dangerous, often because professionals – social workers, the police, for instance – feel they are powerless to stop people doing otherwise. A 'positive' freedom, by contrast, is one is that is enabling, one that helps people to move towards choices which are perhaps wider and better informed, and enhance choices and lives, leading to better coping and decision-making life skills.

The following case considers the dilemma of how social workers may begin to address the impact of life choices in the lives of people working with the concepts of 'negative' and 'positive' freedom of choice.

Case study

Back to our conscientious social worker, Max, who has now been referred the case of Teresa, a pleasant, intelligent, obese older woman of Irish heritage with chronic physical health problems and who is struggling to cope with daily living skills. Teresa is prone to leg ulcers,

165

necessitating community nursing, as well as psoriasis blisters on her limbs. Like Connie, Teresa is a hoarder and has filled her house to the point where she can barely move from room to room except by carefully manoeuvring herself crab-wise through toppling towers of what anyone else would deem to be mouldering rubbish.

The house is extremely hot with the heating on full blast; there are eight cats living with Teresa and the house is buzzing with flies owing to decomposing food remains. No ventilation is allowed in as none of the windows can be reached owing to Teresa's intense hoarding habit.

Max feels that the first issue to deal with is Teresa's health and in particular preventive hygiene measures, such as help with bathing. However, he cannot arrange this while the house is in the current condition, so the first step is to get the house sufficiently cleared so that Teresa can receive care.

Knowing how important Teresa's hoard is to her, Max attempts to persuade her gently to part with some of it, for reasons he carefully outlines. The idea of a regular bath and hair washing, along with clean clothes, is made to sound most enticing to Teresa, who then shrewdly shoots the question, 'Do you think I've got mental health issues?'

Max thinks about this and replies carefully and compassionately, saying,

> Well, the brain is quite a complex piece of machinery and it's not particularly circular. We all have little dents in it where life has affected us in one way or another. Now maybe you have a big dent about maintaining your home but I can help you with that.
>
> I am not really that worried about your home, but you've got these blisters on your arms and legs and they could get infected – and then it might be hospital. I know you don't want that. So I want to get a care team in to help with this nice hot bath idea. But they won't come in when your house is like this, because it's not fair, as they have to go to someone else afterwards and they can't risk carrying any germs with them that might make someone else sick.

At the end of this cautious but respectful negotiation, Max has Teresa's agreement to get the house partially cleared and cleaned so that she can be helped. Teresa's new preferences now outweigh her allegiance to old habits.

Here one can see how Max skilfully harnesses Teresa's motivation toward self-actualisation by presenting new choices that allow her to make changes to her current lifestyle, which is jeopardising her health and risking closing her options still further. The issue of hoarding is reframed in a conversation that focuses on health and wellbeing – and pleasurable contact with people who can help Teresa in appealing ways. In so doing, the same, better destination is arrived at, but from a different route – one that does not threaten Teresa's sense of security, but enhances her sense of herself as a social being with the ability to control her own future.

Chapter summary

In this chapter we have considered a number of the ethical dilemmas that may appear in practising social work with people who are pushed to the edges or excluded. We have drawn on the knowledge of values and ethics and our political understandings of the world in which we practise, drawing on the knowledge we introduced in earlier chapters. We have not attempted to be comprehensive in our discussion – an impossible task in any case – but have presented questions, circumstances and practices that you may encounter and that may offer ways of approaching similar situations.

Further reading

Banks, S. (2012) *Ethics and Values in Social Work*, 4th ed. Basingstoke: Palgrave.

This popular volume is at one and the same time erudite and accessible. It covers real-world dilemmas that social workers, community and youth workers and others are likely to face and takes readers through core aspects of various positions in values and ethics.

Beckett, C., Maynard, A. and Jordan, P. (2017) *Values and Ethics in Social Work*, 3rd ed. London: SAGE.

This popular volume explores ethical issues in a practical and engaging way that helps readers to travel through some of the dilemmas that may arise.

Parrott, L. (2014) *Values and Ethics in Social Work Practice*, 3rd ed. London: SAGE.

Parrott's book provides an excellent introduction to the thorny issues that arise in social work in which there is often no right or wrong answer to questions and dilemmas.

10: Reflections and conclusions

Walking the terrain

When the idea of writing this book was first mooted by our publisher we wondered what new approach could be brought to an area that seemed well trodden already in social work. (We presented some of the key texts in the introduction.) What we found during the process of writing, however, was that there was a great deal to say on this hugely, perhaps fundamentally, important topic, in relation to the transition of social work as a profession operating in a society riven with inequities and divisions. Furthermore, we developed a new sense of urgency about how the profession should be positioning itself in relation to these great social problems. Thus, here we speak directly to all people working within social work, but perhaps most urgently to all those of you entering social work, with your ideals, energy, freshness and hunger for change, as yet unjaded by learned professional helplessness that, if left unchecked, can permeate the workplace context. This book acts as a so-called 'reality check' to keep that enthusiasm bright. Nothing is set in tablets of stone, of course. All discourses and their underlying assumptions can be challenged, as many have done in the past. It really is up to us to challenge damaging practices and harmful rhetoric, from whichever position we occupy, whether as service users, community activists, social work students, social work veterans, social work managers – or, of course, as social work academics.

We have, therefore, written this book to offer students a topical grounding in the subject with a solid conceptual and theoretical foundation from which vital intellectual understanding can be brought to the questions raised here. Equally we offer a close 'weather eye' on what is happening in the UK right now! This of course changes daily and our ambitions cannot keep pace with national and world events. So we cannot hope to capture all the dimensions of what marginalisation and discrimination are in the current socio-political context, but we can seek to illuminate what these may mean for service users, families and communities – and indeed for social workers as well. Likewise, while current events and news items, reported here, are topical at this moment in time, other events take their place. Yet the examples and cases we use here will remain current in terms of providing a powerful illustration of how social inequities discriminate negatively, marginalise and harm people.

This harm is often invisible or made so until such a time when it can no longer be ignored. The horrors of the fire at Grenfell Tower in the summer of 2017 stand as one such monument of this, where it was primarily the marginalised and 'have nots' who inhabited the building. The public has been told that there are approximately 80 people still missing among the dead and many identities may never be known. Their anonymity in death can be viewed as only a reflection of their perceived insignificance in life and is consequently symbolic of the scale of suffering of many people, whose grinding daily oppressions are treated with casual indifference by inhumane systems. Too often, sadly, social work becomes implicated in such systems, becomes of itself such a system, and those who came into the profession with a sense of noble vocation intact too often find they are stoking the boilers of machinery they regularly deplore.

Why walk the road? The rationale

The answer to that question is implicit in the final sentence of the previous paragraph. It surely is not acceptable for social work to risk becoming just another instrument of oppression over the oppressed. There is surely something very wrong in finding social workers unable to do the work for which they were educated. Mendaciously political rhetoric could at this point suggest again that it is in fact the education social workers receive that is out of step with what local authorities want of social workers. Social workers, so the argument runs, should adapt to heavily bureaucratised, under-resourced, process-driven social work, and thus it is education, not the context of work, that must change. We acknowledge that this argument has given rise to many – largely unwelcome – changes in social work over recent years, but we entirely disagree that social work education should be diluted to become mere training packages for uncritical mass consumption of local authority workers and the prevalence of limited in-house training schemes. Hence this book and hence the position taken within it.

Instead we argue from a very different position. Social work always has been and is still a political animal. It operates within the interstices of politicised discourses, within societies shaped by socio-political and economic forces, on behalf of those whose lives are influenced by social policies and political decisions. Social work is of itself politicised and consequently we believe that politicisation is its own best weapon to defend the profession and those with whom its works. Writing this book has made us angry at times, rightly so. Anger can be futile but it can serve a good purpose as well. Righteous anger, as we may know, can save the sacred temple from the befoulment of moneylenders; and if we wish to, we can apply this New Testament story as a parable for social work, in which the Christian element of the story can be entirely reframed as simply the rescuing of the good and noble from the defilement of the harmful and ignoble. Regardless of the oppressive practices that social work has notoriously been involved with in the past (Ioakimidis, 2013), and irrespective of the problems currently besetting social work in England and Wales, the profession is still very much worth salvaging from neoliberal ideas that threaten to devalue and dehumanise it. If for no other reason, anger can give us the courage to *speak truth to power*, to use the Quaker phrase, and in so doing delineate what is worth preserving, what is worth changing and how, and what should be abandoned. In this endeavour, the national or local and the parochial is of lesser consequence to the profession than the global and international, for while social work is enacted at local levels, its values and ethos that guide practice are universal statements. It is here, in this wider arena of identity and debate, that we believe the discussion of what social work is and should be in the UK needs to be fully explored, given (thankfully) the ephemeral nature of politics and politicians on the home front seeking to drive the shifting sands of social work.

The significance of the finds en route

All times are 'interesting' for someone somewhere, but it seems a truism that we are currently living through a time of monumental and deeply uncertain transitions in the UK that will have a decisive bearing on lives and futures. Within the country we see that public services are stretched to crisis point and that public service pay caps are plunging public sector workers and many other working people into penury. We see that poverty is increasing, incomes are falling compared to rising household costs and social welfare nets offer considerably less security than formerly.

The case studies offered here reflect some of this social chaos, although they were not chosen because of their exceptional or extreme nature, but as general examples of what the perceived realities were, as offered by social workers and service users we were privileged to speak to on the way. The social work job as hugely pressurised, time- and process-driven, and reactive, was portrayed in the case studies, where it seemed that just to be able to do a 'good enough' job seemed to require more time and resources than were usually made available to practitioners. The case of Max, the good social worker penalised for trying to do a good job (Chapter 8), spoke volumes about the blinkered and dysfunctional attitudes being imposed on social service staff through brutal neoliberal policies.

Additionally, the story of trying to break through the hardened professional carapace to find the original caring individual inside was another such revelatory case study, as offered by a thoughtful service user (Rachael, in Chapter 4). This in turn illuminated how the system jeopardises the empowerment-focused social work relationship with service users to pit practitioners unhelpfully against service users and families, when in fact the real problem is one commonly shared – the inequities of inadequate resourcing in communities.

The issue of who is marginalised is another area of contention, where in the case of Afsar, the refugee boy, it is the entire family who are made victims of the system, which fails to value and support refugee families in the UK (Chapter 2). The systematic passive-aggression of the 'help' social services offers – to split the family up and take the children into care – is a contemporary echo of the dreaded policies of the Poor Law (Reform) Act and the practices of the Victorian workhouse. Like then, such so-called help is designed to deter and prevent requests for support, rather than to offer help that is appropriate and much needed.

Where then does this leave today's social work graduates entering a beleaguered, under-funded profession? It could be that social work is living through the *worst of times*, but, maybe also one of the best, to paraphrase Dickens's (1859) *A Tale of Two Cities*. The knowledge base of social work typically constructs the concept of crisis as creating the tipping point to necessary change. We would suggest that this may be where we currently are; we certainly hope so. For while the slow and unedifying helter-skelter journey downwards has taken time, as will the spiralling journey upwards, this can occur and maybe must occur, for the profession to survive. If change does happen and the profession eases itself up to a standing position, bedraggled and in tatters maybe, it should also take matters into its own hands and refuse to serve as political 'whipping boy' any longer, in the interests of marginalised and disadvantaged individuals and families everywhere in the country. If it fails to do this then it could be that social work in England, at least, will not survive into the future as a recognisable profession that adheres to international standards and values. If such were the case, then that indeed would be counted among the greatest national tragedies of our time.

References

Agnew, A. and Duffy, J. (2010) Innovative approaches to involving service users in palliative care social work education. *Social Work Education*, 29 (7): 744–759.

Agnew, R. (2006) *Pressured into Crime: An Overview of General Strain Theory.* London: SAGE.

Ahktar, F.N. (2013) *Mastering Social Work Values and Ethics.* London: Jessica Kingsley.

Ahmed, A. and Rogers, M. (2016) Diversity and exclusion in context, in Ahmed, A. and Rogers, M. (eds.) *Working with Marginalised Groups: From Policy to Practice.* Basingstoke: Palgrave, pp. 6–20.

Ahmed, S. (2017) *Living a Feminist Life.* Durham, NC: Duke University Press.

Al-Krenawi, A., Graham, J.R. and Habobov, N. (eds.) (2016) *Diversity and Social Work in Canada.* Toronto: Oxford University Press.

Anderson, M. and Hill Collins, P. (2007) Why race, class and gender still matter, in Anderson, M. and Hill Collins, P. (eds.) *Race, Class and Gender: An Anthology*, 6th ed. Belmont, CA: Thomson Wadsworth.

Anka, A. and Taylor, I. (2016) Assessment as the site of power: a Bourdieusian interrogation of service user and carer involvement in the assessments of social work students. *Social Work Education*, 35 (2): 172–185.

Ashencaen Crabtree, S. (2013) Research ethics approval processes and the moral enterprise of ethnography. *Ethics and Social Welfare*, 7 (4): 359–378. DOI: 10.1080/17496535.2012.703683.

Ashencaen Crabtree, S. (2017a) Social work with Muslim communities: treading a critical path over the crescent moon, in Crisp, B. (ed.) *Routledge Handbook of Religion, Spirituality and Social Work.* Abingdon, Oxon: Routledge.

Ashencaen Crabtree, S. (2017b) Problematizing the context and construction of vulnerability and risk in relation to British Muslim ME groups. *Journal of Religion and Spirituality in Social Work*, 36 (1–2): http://dx.doi.org/10.1080/15426432.2017.1300080.

Ashencaen Crabtree, S. and Husain, F. (2012) Within, without: dialogical perspectives on feminism and Islam. *Religion and Gender*, 2 (1): 128–149.

Ashencaen Crabtree, S. and Parker, J. (2013) *The Kindertransport movement: an exercise in humanitarianism through British sociological history.* Available at http://blogs.bournemouth. ac.uk/research/2013/11/26/the-kindertransport-movement-an-exercise-in-humanitarianism-through-british-sociological-history-2/ (accessed 2 August 2017).

Ashencaen Crabtree, S. and Parker, J. (2014) Being male in female spaces: perceptions of masculinity amongst male social work students on a qualifying course. *Revista de Asistenţă Socială*, XIII (4): 7–26. http://www.swreview.ro.

Ashencaen Crabtree, S., Husain, F. and Spalek, B. (2016) *Islam and Social Work: Culturally Sensitive Practice in a Diverse World*, 2nd ed. Bristol: Policy Press.

Austin, M. (2014) *Social Justice and Social Work: Rediscovering a Core Value of the Profession*. Thousand Oaks, CA: SAGE.

Baier, M. (ed.) (2016) *Social and Legal Norms: Towards a Socio-legal Understanding of Normativity*. London: Routledge.

Bailey, R. and Brake, M. (eds.) (1975) *Radical Social Work*. London: Edward Arnold.

Banks, S. (2012) *Ethics and Values in Social Work*, 4th ed. Basingstoke: Palgrave.

Baron, M.W., Pettit P. and Slote, M. (1997) *Three Methods of Ethics*. Oxford: Blackwell.

Bartoli, A. (ed.) (2013) *Anti-Racism in Social Work Practice*. St. Albans: Critical Publishing.

BBC (2016) *EU referendum: the results in maps and charts*. Available at http://www.bbc.co.uk/news/uk-politics-36616028 (accessed 2 August 2017).

BBC (2017a) *Pair jailed for 'Dark Ages' murder of vulnerable man*. Available at http://www.bbc.co.uk/news/uk-england-tyne-40416578 (accessed 20 June 2017).

BBC (2017b) *Red Cross NHS description 'proportionate'*. Available at http://www.bbc.co.uk/news/av/uk-politics-38611671/dr-saleyha-ahsan-on-nhs-humanitarian-crisis-claims (accessed 17 April 2017).

BBC (2017c) *Red Cross warning 'irresponsible and overblown'*. Available at http://www.bbc.co.uk/news/av/uk-politics-38586665/pmqs-may-rejects-red-cross-nhs-humanitarian-crisis-warning (accessed 18 April 2017).

Becker, H. (1963) *Outsiders: Studies in the Sociology of Deviance*. New York: The Free Press.

Becker, H. (1967) Whose side are we on? *Social Problems,* 14 (3): 239–247.

Beckett, C., Maynard, A. and Jordan, P. (2017) *Values and Ethics in Social Work*, 3rd ed. London: SAGE.

Beddoe, L., Davys, A. and Adamson, C. (2013) Educating resilient practitioners. *Social Work Education*, 32 (1): 100–117.

Benatar, D. (2012) *The Second Sexism: Discrimination Against Men and Boys*. Chichester: Wiley-Blackwell.

Berg, M. and Seeber, B.K. (2016) *The Slow Professor*. Toronto: University of Toronto Press.

Berlin, I. (1969) *Two Concepts of Liberty*. Glasgow: Oxford University Press.

Bernades, J. (1997) *Family Studies: An Introduction*. London: Routledge.

Berthrong, J.H. (1998) *Transformations of the Confucian Way*. Boulder, CO: Westview Press.

Berthrong, J.H. and Berthrong, E.N. (2000) *Confucianism: A Short Introduction*. Oxford: Oneworld Publications.

Beveridge, W. (1942) *Social Insurance and Allied Services.* Cmnd 6404. London: HMSO.

Bhatti-Sinclair, K. (2011) *Anti-Racist Practice in Social Work.* Basingstoke: Palgrave Macmillan.

Biestek, F.P. (1961) *The Casework Relationship.* London: George Allen and Unwin.

Black, M. (1996) *Thirsty Cities: Water, Sanitation and the Urban Poor.* London: WaterAid.

Black Activists Rising Against Cuts (BARAC) (2017) *Grenfell Tower press release by leading BME organisations, lawyers and residents (BMELawyers4Grenfell)*, 3 July 2017. Available at http://blackactivistsrisingagainstcuts.blogspot.co.uk/2017/07/press-release-press-release-press.html (accessed 3 July 2017).

Blumer, H. (1969) *Symbolic Interactionism: Perspective and Method.* Englewood Cliffs, NJ: Prentice-Hall.

Bolton, P. (2016) *Free School Statistics.* Briefing paper no. 7033, 2 December 2016. London: House of Commons Library. Available at http://researchbriefings.parliament.uk/ResearchBriefing/Summary/SN07033#fullreport (accessed 19 July 2017).

Bourdieu, P. (1977) *Outline of a Theory of Practice.* Cambridge: Cambridge University Press.

Bourdieu, P. (1996) On the family as a realized category. *Theory, Culture and Society*, 13 (3): 19–26.

Bourdieu, P. and Wacquant, L. (1999) The cunning of imperialist reason. *Theory, Culture, and Society*, 16 (1): 41–57.

Brammer, A. (2015) *Social Work Law.* Basingstoke: Palgrave.

Braye, S. and Preston-Shoot, M. (2016) *Practising Social Work Law*, 4th ed. Basingstoke: Palgrave.

Brayne, H., Carr, H. and Goosey, D. (2015) *Law for Social Workers*, 13th ed. Oxford: Oxford University Press.

Brindle, D. (2013) Social work training reforms: it takes five weeks to create a social worker? *The Guardian*, 21 May 2013. Available at http://www.guardian.co.uk/society/2013/may/21/asocial-work-training-reforms (accessed 2 July 2013).

British Association of Social Workers (2012) *The Code of Ethics for Social Work: Statement of Principles*. Available at http://cdn.basw.co.uk/upload/basw_95243-9.pdf (accessed 17 May 2017).

British Association of Social Workers (2015) *The Professional Capabilities Framework*. Available at https://www.basw.co.uk/pcf/ (accessed 1 October 2016).

Brown, G.W. and Harris, T. (1978) *The Social Origins of Depression: A Study of Psychiatric Disorder in Women.* London: Tavistock.

Brown, J. (2013) Scandal: just how corrupt is Britain? Rotten banks, dodgy cops, MPs on the fiddle. A conference on public life has evidence to topple long-held assumptions. *The Independent*, 10 May 2013. Available at http://www.independent.co.uk/news/uk/crime/scandal-just-how-corrupt-is-britain-8610095.html (accessed 2 August 2017).

Brown, M. (2017) Disabled people are to be 'warehoused'. We should be livid. *The Guardian*. Available at https://www.theguardian.com/commentisfree/2017/jan/25/disabled-people-disabilities-health-care-homes (accessed 25 January 2017).

Bryson, A. and Forth, J. (2017) Wage growth in pay review body. Report to the Office of Manpower Economics. Available at https://www.gov.uk/government/uploads/system/uploads/attachment_data/file/623810/Wage_Growth_in_PRB_Occupations_-_final_report__3_.pdf (accessed 3 June 2017).

Bulman, M. (2016) Two thirds of prisons overcrowded prompting warnings UK penal system has reached 'toxic' levels. *The Independent*, 15 April 2017. Available at http://www.independent.co.uk/news/uk/home-news/prisons-overcrowding-prisoners-ministry-of-justice-howard-league-a7685641.html (accessed 30 June 2017).

Burgess, H., Barcham, C. and Kearney, P. (2014) Response to Taylor and Bogo, 'Perfect opportunity – perfect storm'. *British Journal of Social Work*, 44: 2067–2071.

Burke, P. and Parker, J. (eds.) (2007) *Social Work and Disadvantage: Addressing the Roots of Stigma Through Association*. London: Jessica Kingsley.

Cabiati, E. and Raineri, M.L. (2016) Learning from service users' involvement: a research about changing stigmatizing attitudes in social work students. *Social Work Education*, 35 (8): 982–996.

Campbell, D. (2017) Nurses will see their pay 'cut' by 12% over a decade. *The Observer*, 29 April 2017. Available at https://www.theguardian.com/society/2017/apr/29/nhs-nurses-pay-cut-12-per-cent-over-decade (accessed 5 July 2017).

Catchpole, K. (2013) Towards the monitoring of safety violations in *BMJ Quality and Safety*, doi:10.1136/bmjqs-2012-001604. Available at http://qualitysafety.bmj.com/content/early/2013/04/10/bmjqs-2012-001604.abstract (accessed 5 April 2016).

Chamberlain, J.M. (2015) *Criminological Theory in Context*. London: SAGE.

Cheung, S.O-N. (2015) Pedagogical practice wisdom in social work practice teaching: a kaleidoscopic view. *Social Work Education*, 34 (3): 258–274.

Chu, W.C.K. and Tsui, M.-S. (2008) The nature of practice wisdom in social work revisited. *International Social Work*, 51 (1): 47–54.

Clifford, D. (2017) Charitable organisations under austerity. *Journal of Social Policy*, 46 (1): 1–29.

Clifford, D. and Burke, B. (2009) *Anti-Oppressive Ethics and Values in Social Work*. Basingstoke: Palgrave.

Cobb, S. (1976) Social support as a moderator of life-stress. *Psychosomatic Medicine*, 38: 300–314.

Cohen, S. and McKay, G. (1984) Social support, stress and the buffering hypothesis: a theoretical analysis. In Baum, A., Singer, J.E. and Taylor, S.E. (eds.) *Social Psychological Aspects of Health*, vol. IV. Hillsdale, NJ: Erlbaum.

Collins, M., Vignoles, A. and Walker, J. (2007) *Higher Education Academics in the UK*. London: Centre for the Economics of Education. Available at http://cee.lse.ac.uk/ceedps/ceedp75.pdf (accessed 2 July 2017).

Conservative Party (2017) *Forward Together: The Conservative Manifesto*. Available at https://www.conservatives.com/manifesto (accessed 1 June 2017).

Cooper, K. and Stewart, K. (2017) *Does Money Affect Children's Outcomes?* CASE report. London: London School of Economics. Available at http://sticerd.lse.ac.uk/dps/case/cp/casepaper203.pdf (accessed 6 June 2017).

Corrigan, P. and Leonard, P. (1978) *Social Work under Capitalism: A Marxist Approach*. London: Macmillan.

Crenshaw, K. (1991) Mapping the margins: intersectionality, identity politics, and violence against women of color. *Stanford Law Review*, 43 (6): 1241–1299.

Crenshaw, K., Gotanda, N., Peller, G. and Thomas, K. (1995) *Critical Race Theory: The Key Writings that Formed the Movement*. New York: The New Press.

Crisis (2011) *Homelessness: A Silent Killer*. London: Crisis.

Crisp, B.R. and Gillingham, P. (2008) Some of my students are prisoners: issues and dilemmas for social work educators. *Social Work Education*, 27 (3): 307–317.

Crowder, R. and Sears, A. (2017) Building resilience in social workers: an exploratory study on the impacts of mindfulness-based intervention. *Australian Social Work*, 70 (1): 17–29.

Dalrymple, J. and Burke, B. (2006) *Anti-Oppressive Practice, Social Care and the Law*, 2nd ed. Maidenhead: Open University Press.

Dewey, J. (1935) *Liberalism and Social Action*. New York: Putnam.

Dickens, C. (1838/2003) *Oliver Twist*. London: Penguin Classics.

Dickens, C. (1843) *A Christmas Carol*. Any unabridged edition.

Dickens, C. (1858/2003) *A Tale of Two Cities*. London: Penguin Classics.

Dickens, J. (2013) *Social Work, Law and Ethics*. London: Routledge.

Dominelli, L. (2002) *Anti-Oppressive Social Work: Theory and Practice*. Basingstoke: Palgrave.

Dominelli, L. (2008) *Anti-Racist Social Work*, 3rd ed. Basingstoke: Palgrave.

Dominelli, L. (2012) *Green Social Work: From Environmental Crises to Environmental Justice*. Cambridge: Polity Press.

Dominelli, L. and McLeod, E. (1989) *Feminist Social Work*. London: Macmillan.

Durkheim, E. (1895/1982) *The Rules of Sociological Method*. New York: The Free Press.

Duschinsky, R., Lampitt, S. and Bell, S. (2016) *Sustaining Social Work: Between Power and Powerlessness*. Basingstoke: Palgrave Macmillan.

Dybicz, P. (2004) An inquiry into practice wisdom. *Families in Society*, 85 (2): 197–203.

Eaton, G. (2017) Theresa May's police cuts have returned to haunt her. *The New Statesman*, 5 June 2017. Available at http://www.newstatesman.com/politics/june2017/2017/06/theresa-mays-police-cuts-have-returned-haunt-her (accessed 30 June 2017).

Eberth, J. and Sedlmeier, P. (2012) The effects of mindfulness meditation: a meta-analysis. *Mindfulness*, 3: 174–189.

Egan, G. (1998) *The Skilled Helper*, 6th ed. Pacific Grove, CA: Brooks Cole.

Electoral Commission (2016) *2016 EU Referendum.* Available at http://www.electoralcommission.org.uk/__data/assets/pdf_file/0008/215279/2016-EU-referendum-report.pdf (accessed 11 July 2017).

Esping-Anderson, G. (1990) *The Three Worlds of Welfare Capitalism.* Cambridge: Polity Press.

Farand, C. (2017) Brexit: nearly 60% of Leave voters would now pay to retain EU citizenship. *The Independent*, 2 July 2017. Available at http://www.independent.co.uk/news/uk/home-news/leave-voters-ready-pay-to-keep-eu-citizenship-brexit-poll-lse-opinium-a7819001.html (accessed 2 July 2017).

Farchi, M., Cohen, A. and Mosek, A. (2014) Developing specific self-efficacy and resilience as first responders among students of social work and stress and trauma studies. *Journal of Teaching in Social Work*, 34 (2): 129–146.

Feldon, P. (2017) *The Social Worker's Guide to the Care Act 2014*. St Albans: Critical Publishing.

Ferguson, H. (2016) Researching social work practice close up: using ethnographic and mobile methods to understand encounters between social workers, children and families. *British Journal of Social Work*, 46 (1): 153–168.

Ferguson, I. (2008) *Reclaiming Social Work: Challenging Neo-liberalism and Promoting Social Justice.* London: SAGE.

Ferguson, S. (2015) *What does a radical model of theory and practice have to offer social work practitioners in contemporary social work with adults?* Social Work Action Network (SWAN). Available at http://www.socialworkfuture.org/articles-resources/uk-articles/77-radical-social-work-practice-adults (accessed 11 July 2017).

Fletcher, J. (1966) *Situation Ethics: The New Morality.* Philadelphia, PA: Westminster.

Fook, J. (2016) *Social Work: A Critical Approach to Practice*, 3rd ed. London: SAGE.

Foster, J. (2000) Social exclusion, crime and drugs. *Drugs: Education, Prevention and Policy*, 7 (4): 317–330.

Francis, R. (2013) *Report of the Mid Staffordshire NHS Foundation Trust Public Inquiry.* HC 947. London: The Stationery Office.

Fraser, D. (2009) *The Evolution of the British Welfare State*, 4th ed. Basingstoke: Palgrave Macmillan.

Friedman, H. and Meredeen, S. (1980) *The Dynamics of Industrial Conflict: Lessons from Ford*. London: Croom Helm.

Freire, P. (1972) *The Pedagogy of the Oppressed*. London: Penguin.

Furedi, F. (2017) *What's Happened to the University? A Sociological Exploration of Its Infantilisation*. London: Routledge.

Galfe, S. (2014) Age poverty in relation to gender issues and social problems: an analysis of the German perspective. In Ashencaen Crabtree, S. (ed.) *Diversity and the Processes of Marginalisation and Otherness*. London: Whiting and Birch, pp. 105–116.

Galvani, S. and Thurnham, A. (2014) Identifying and assessing substance use: findings from a national survey of social work and social care professionals. *British Journal of Social Work*, 44 (7): 1895–1913. DOI: https://doi.org/10.1093/bjsw/bct033.

Gardner, A. (2014) *Personalisation in Social Work*, 2nd ed. London: SAGE.

Gaskell, E. (1848/1996) *Mary Barton: A Tale of Manchester Life*. London: Penguin.

Gentleman, A. (2015) After hated Atos quits, will Maximum make work assessments less arduous? *The Guardian*, 18 January 2015. Available at https://www.theguardian.com/society/2015/jan/18/after-hated-atos-quits-will-maximus-make-work-assessments-less-arduous (accessed 20 February 2017).

Gilligan, C. (1982) *In a Different Voice*. Cambridge, MA: Harvard University Press.

Gilligan, C. (1988) *Mapping the Moral Domain: A Contribution of Women's Thinking to Psychological Theory and Education*. Cambridge, MA: Harvard University Press.

Gómez-Jiménez, M.L. and Parker, J. (eds.) (2014) *Active Ageing? Perspectives from Europe on a Vaunted Topic*. London: Whiting and Birch.

Gov.UK (2017) *Wage growth in pay review body occupations*. Office of Manpower Economics. Available at https://www.gov.uk/government/publications/wage-growth-in-pay-review-body-occupations (accessed 5 July 2017).

Grant, L. and Kinman, G. (2012) Enhancing wellbeing in social work students: building resilience in the next generation. *Social Work Education*, 31 (5): 605–621.

Gray, M. and Webb, S.A. (eds.) (2010) *Ethics and Value Perspectives in Social Work*. New York: Palgrave Macmillan.

Greer, J. (2016) *Resilience and Personal Effectiveness for Social Workers*. London: SAGE.

Guo, W.-H. and Tsui, M.-S. (2010) From resilience to resistance: a reconstruction of the strengths perspective in social work practice. *International Social Work*, 53 (2): 233–245.

Guru, S. (2012) Under siege: families of counter-terrorism. *British Journal of Social Work*, 42 (8): 1151–1173.

Habermas, J. (1987) *The Theory of Communicative Action, vol. II: Lifeworld and System*. Boston, MA: Beacon.

Halwani, R. (2003) Care ethics and virtue ethics. *Hypatia*, 18 (3): 161–192.

Hanisch, C. (1970/2006) *The Personal Is Political: The Women's Liberation Movement Classic*, with a new explanatory introduction. Avaiable at http://www.carolhanisch.org/CHwritings/PIP.html (accessed 5 July 2017).

Hanna, S. and Nash, M. (2012) 'You don't have to shout': vocal behaviour in social work communication. *Social Work Education*, 31 (4): 485–497.

Hardwick, L. and Worsley, A. (2011) *Doing Social Work Research*. London: SAGE.

Hardy, T. (1874/1993) *Far from the Madding Crowd*. London: Wordsworth Classics.

Hargie, O.D.W. (ed.) (1997) *The Handbook of Communication Skills*, 2nd ed. New York: Routledge.

Harris, B. (2004) *The Origins of the British Welfare State: Social Welfare in England and Wales, 1800–1945*. Basingstoke: Palgrave.

Hatton, K. (2017) A critical examination of the knowledge contribution service user and carer involvement brings to social work education. *Social Work Education*, 36 (2): 154–171.

HCPC (2012) *Standards of Proficiency: Social Workers in England*. London: Health and Care Professions Council. Available at www.hpc-uk.org/publications/standards/index.asp?id=569 (accessed 13 January 2014).

Healy, L.M. (2008) Exploring the history of social work as a human rights profession. *International Social Work*, 51 (6): 735–748.

Heaslip, V., Hean, S. and Parker, J. (2016) The etemic model of Gypsy Roma community vulnerability: is it time to rethink our understanding of vulnerability? *Journal of Clinical Nursing*, Early View, DOI: 10.1111/jocn.13499.

Heath, A. and Li, Y. (2014) *Reducing poverty in the UK: a collection of evidence reviews.* Joseph Rowntree Foundation. Available at https://www.jrf.org.uk/sites/default/files/jrf/migrated/files/Reducing-poverty-reviews-FULL_0.pdf (accessed 7 January 2016).

Higgins, M. (2016) How has the Professional Capabilities Framework changed social work education and practice in England? *British Journal of Social Work*, 46: 1981–1996.

Higgins, M. and Goodyer, A. (2015) The contradictions of contemporary social work: an ironic response. *British Journal of Social Work*, 45: 747–760.

Hill, A. (2017) Hidden carers: the sixty somethings looking after parents and grandchildren. *The Guardian.* Available at https://www.theguardian.com/membership/2017/feb/13/new-retirement-ageing-responsibility-carers-parents-children-care-crisis (accessed 20 March 2017).

Hill Collins, P. and Bilge, S. (2016) *Intersectionality.* Cambridge: Polity Press.

Hills, J. (2017) *Good Times, Bad Times: The Welfare Myth of Them and Us.* Bristol: Policy Press.

HM Government (2015) *Revised Prevent Duty Guidance.* Available at https://www.gov.uk/government/uploads/system/uploads/attachment_data/file/44 5977/3799_Revised_Prevent_Duty_Guidance__England_Wales_V2-Interactive.pdf. (accessed 3 November 2015).

Hodgson Burnett, F. (1905/2002) *A Little Princess*. London: Penguin Classics.

Hollis, F. (1964) *Casework: A Psycho-Social Therapy*. New York: Random House.

Horne, M. (1999) *Values in Social Work*, 2nd ed. Aldershot: Ashgate.

Houston, S. (2009) Communicating, recognition and social work: aligning the ethical theories of Habermas and Honneth. *British Journal of Social Work*, 39: 1274–1290.

Howe, D. (2009) *A Brief Introduction to Social Work Theory*. Basingstoke: Palgrave.

Hugman, R. (1998) *Social Welfare and Social Value*. Basingstoke: Macmillan.

Hugman, R. (2010) *Understanding International Social Work: A Critical Analysis*. Basingstoke: Palgrave Macmillan.

Hugo, V. (1831/1993) *The Hunchback of Notre Dame*. Hertfordshire: Wordsworth Edition.

Hutchings, A. and Taylor, I. (2007) Defining the profession? Exploring an international definition of social work in the China context. *International Journal of Social Welfare*, 16 (4): 382–390.

Ife, J. (1997) *Rethinking Social Work: Towards Critical Practice*. London: Longman.

Illich, I. (1972/2011) Disabling professions, in Illich, I., Zola, I.K., McKnight, J., Caplan, J. and Shaiken, H. (eds.) *Disabling Professions*. London: Marion Boyars.

Independent Police Complaints Commission (2011) *IPCC publishes findings into police response to incidents involving Michael Gilbert*. Available at https://www.ipcc.gov.uk/news/ipcc-publishes-findings-police-response-incidents-involving-michael-gilbert (accessed 17 November 2016).

International Federation of Social Workers/International Association of Schools of Social Work (IFSW/IASSW) (2012) *Global Standards for the Education and Training of the Social Work Profession*. Available at http://ifsw.org/policies/global-standards/ (accessed 6 June 2016).

International Federation of Social Workers (IFSW) (2014) *Global Definition of Social Work*. Available at http://ifsw.org/get-involved/global-definition-of-social-work/ (accessed 6 June 2016).

Ioakimidis, V. (2013) Beyond the dichotomies of cultural and political relativism: arguing the case for a social justice based 'global social work' definition. *Critical and Radical Social Work*, 1 (2): 183–199.

Irvine, J., Molyneux, J. and Gillman, M. (2015) 'Providing a link to the real world': learning from the student experience of service user and carer involvement in social work education. *Social Work Education*, 34 (2): 138–150.

Jackson, S. (1998) *Britain's Population: Demographic Issues in Contemporary Society*. London: Routledge.

Johns, R. (2017) *Using the Law in Social Work*, 7th ed. London: SAGE.

Johnson, T. (1972) *Professions and Power*. London: Macmillan.

Jones, R. (2014) *The Story of Baby P: Setting the Record Straight*. Bristol: Policy Press.

Jones, S. (2010) Blue Lagoon murder. *The Guardian*, 26 April 2010. Available at https://www.theguardian.com/uk/2010/apr/26/family-jailed-blue-lagoon-murder-michael-gilbert (accessed 11 January 2017).

Jones, T. (2013) The harsh reality of the forgotten rural poor. *The Guardian*, 24 January 2013. Available at https://www.theguardian.com/commentisfree/2013/feb/24/rural-poverty-invisible (accessed 18 January 2017).

Kainer, G. (2012) *Faith, Hope and Clarity: A Look at Biblical and Situation Ethics*, US: Lulu.com.

Kane, M.N., Lacey, D. and Green, D. (2009) Investigating social work students' perceptions of elders' vulnerability and resilience. *Social Work in Mental Health*, 7 (4): 307–324.

Kapoulitsas, M. and Corcoran, T. (2015) Compassion fatigue and resilience: a qualitative analysis of social work practice. *Qualitative Social Work*, 14 (1): 86–101.

Karban, K. and Smith, S. (2010) Developing critical reflection within an inter-professional learning programme, in Bradbury, H., Frost, N., Kilminster, S. and Zukas, M. (eds.) *Beyond Reflective Practice: New Approaches to Professional Lifelong Learning*. London: Routledge.

Katiuzhinsky, A. and Okech, D. (2014) Human rights, cultural practices, and state policies: implications for global social work practice and policy. *International Journal of Social Welfare*, 23 (1): 80–88.

Klein, W.C. and Bloom, M. (1995) Practice wisdom. *Social Work*, 40 (6): 799–807.

Koprowska, J. (2014) *Communication and Interpersonal Skills in Social Work*, 4th ed. London: SAGE.

Krill, D. (1990) *Practice Wisdom*. Thousand Oaks, CA: SAGE.

Laird, L.D., Amer, M.M., Barnett, E.D. and Barnes, L.L. (2007) Muslim patients and health disparities in the UK and the US. *Archives of Diseases in Childhood*, 92 (10): 922–926.

Laird, S. (2008) *Anti-Oppressive Social Work: A Guide to Developing Cultural Competence*. London: SAGE.

Lamb, N. (2013) *New rules to stop cover ups in care*. Available at http://normanlamb.org.uk/wp/2013/new-rules-to-stop-cover-ups-of-poor-care/ (accessed 3 April 2015).

Laming, H. (2003) *The Victoria Climbié Inquiry Report*. Cm 5730. London: The Stationery Office.

Langan, M. and Day, L. (eds.) (1992) *Women, Oppression and Social Work*. London: Routledge.

Larkin, G. (1983) *Occupational Monopoly and Modern Medicine*. London: Tavistock.

Lavalette, M. (ed.) (2011) *Radical Social Work Today: Social Work at the Crossroads*. Bristol: Policy Press.

Layder, D. (2006) *Understanding Social Theory*, 2nd ed. London: SAGE.

Lee, L. (1969) *As I Walked Out One Midsummer Morning*. London: André Deutsch.

Lefevre, M. (2015) Integrating the teaching, learning and assessment of communication with children within the qualifying social work curriculum. *Child and Family Social Work*, 20: 2011–2222.

Lemert, E. (1967) *Human Deviance: Social Problems and Social Control.* Englewood Cliffs, NJ: Prentice-Hall.

Lemieux, C.M., Plummer, C.A., Richardson, R., Simon, C.E. and Ai, A.L. (2010) Mental health, substance use, and adaptive coping among social work students in the aftermath of Hurricane Katrina and Rita. *Journal of Social Work Education*, 46 (3): 391–410.

Lewis, O. (1968) *A Study of Slum Culture.* New York: Random House.

Lindsay, S., Tétrault, S., Desmaris, C., King, G. and Piérart, G. (2014) Social workers as 'cultural brokers' in providing culturally sensitive care to immigrant families raising a child with a physical disability. *Health and Social Work*, 39 (2): 10–20.

Lipsky, M. (1980) *Street Level Bureaucracy: Dilemmas of the Individual in Public Services*. New York: Russell Sage Foundation.

Lorenz, W. (1993) *Social Work in a Changing Europe.* London: Routledge.

Lundy, C. (2011) *Social Work, Social Justice, and Human Rights: A Structural Approach to Practice*, 2nd ed. Toronto: University of Toronto Press.

Macdonald, K.M. (1995) *The Sociology of the Professions.* London: SAGE.

Maier, S.F. and Seligman, M.E.P. (1976) Learned helplessness: theory and evidence. *Journal of Experimental Psychology: General*, 105: 3–46.

Marsh, S. (2016) Mindfulness therapy for mental health problems? It's more useful than drugs. *The Guardian*. Available at https://www.theguardian.com/commentisfree/2016/may/18/mindfulness-therapy-mental-health-drugs (accessed 15 June 2017).

Matthies, A.-L. and Uggerhøj, L. (eds.) (2014) *Participation, Marginalization and Welfare Services: Concepts, Politics and Practices across European Countries.* Farnham: Ashgate.

Mayer, A. (2017) Social capital, economic hardship, and health: a test of the buffering hypothesis in transition and nontransition countries. *Sociological Spectrum*, 37 (2): 111–126.

Mazza, E. (2015) Experiences of social work educators working with students with psychiatric disabilities or emotional problems. *Journal of Social Work Education*, 51: 359–378.

McDuff, P. (2017) Grenfell shows us there's no north/south divide. The gap is between rich and poor. *The Guardian*, 28 June 2017. Available at https://www.theguardian.com/commentisfree/2017/jun/28/grenfell-north-south-divide-rich-poor (accessed 28 June 2017).

McKerrell, N. (2016) *A young person's perspective*. NCB. Available at https://www.ncb.org.uk/news-opinion/news-highlights/brexit-young-persons-perspective (accessed 5 July 2017).

McNicoll, A. (2016) Sharon Shoesmith on Baby P, blame and social work's climate of fear. *Community Care*, 25 August 2016. Available at http://www.communitycare.co.uk/2016/08/25/sharon-shoesmith-baby-p-blame-social-works-climate-fear/ (accessed 30 June 2017).

Mead, G.H. (1934) *Mind, Self and Society*. Chicago, IL: Chicago University Press.

Meer, N. (2014) *Key Concepts in Race and Ethnicity*. London: SAGE.

Meissner, F. and Vertovec, S. (eds.) (2015) Comparing super-diversity, special issue. *Ethnic and Racial Studies*, 38: 4.

Merton, R.K. (1938) Social structure and anomie. *American Sociological Review*, 3 (5): 672–682.

Mills, C.W. (1959) *The Sociological Imagination*. New York: Oxford University Press.

Milner, J. (2001) *Women and Social Work: Narrative Approaches*. Basingstoke: Palgrave.

Monbiot, G. (2017) Our democracy is broken, debased and distrusted, but there are ways to fix it. *The Guardian*, 25 January 2017. Available at https://www.theguardian.com/commentisfree/2017/jan/25/democracy-broken-distrusted-trump-brexit-political-system (accessed 28 January 2017).

Mooney L., Knox, D. and Schacht, C. (2016) *Understanding Social Problems*, 10th ed. Belmont, NJ: Wadsworth.

Morgan, D. (1996) *Family Connections*. Cambridge: Polity Press.

Morgan, D. (1999) Risk and family practices: accounting for change and fluidity in family life, in Silva, E.B. and Smart, C. (eds.) *The New Family*. London: SAGE.

Munro, E. (2011) *Munro Review of Child Protection: Final Report – A Child-Centred System*. CM 8062. London: The Stationery Office.

Murray, C. (1994) *Losing Ground: American Social Policy 1950–1980*. New York: Basic Books.

Muslim Council of Great Britain (MCB) (2015) *British Muslims in Numbers: A Demographic, Socio-Economic and Health Profile of Muslims in Britain Drawing on the 2011 Census*. London: Muslim Council of Great Britain.

Natland, S. (2015) Dialogical communication and empowering social work practice. *Journal of Evidence-Informed Social Work*, 12: 80–91.

Newman, D.M. (2009) *Families: A Sociological Perspective*. New York: McGraw-Hill.

Nozick, R. (1974) *Anarchy, State and Utopia*. Oxford: Basic Books.

NSPCC (2016) *Statistics on child abuse: how many children are abused or neglected in the UK?* Available at https://www.nspcc.org.uk/services-and-resources/research-and-resources/statistics/ (accessed 7 July 2017).

Orme, J. (2001) *Gender and Community Care*. Houndsmill, Basingstoke: Palgrave.

Orwell, G. (1933) *Down and Out in Paris and London*. Any unabridged edition.

Orwell, G. (1937) *The Road to Wigan Pier*. Any unabridged edition.

Orwell, G. (1949/2013) *Nineteen Eighty-Four*. London: Penguin Modern Classics.

Palma-Garcia, M. and Hombrados-Mendieta, I. (2017) Resilience and personality in social work students and social workers. *International Social Work*, 60 (1): 19–31.

Parker, J. (2001) Interrogating person-centred dementia care in social work and social care practice. *Journal of Social Work*, 1 (3): 329–345.

Parker, J. (2006) Developing perceptions of competence during practice learning. *British Journal of Social Work*, 36 (6): 1017–1036.

Parker, J. (2007) Disadvantage, stigma and anti-oppressive practice, in Burke, P. and Parker, J. (eds.) *Social Work and Disadvantage: Addressing the Roots of Stigma Through Association*. London: Jessica Kingsley, pp. 146–157.

Parker, J. (2010) *Effective Practice Learning in Social Work*, 2nd ed. London: SAGE.

Parker, J. (2017) *Social Work Practice*, 5th ed. London: SAGE.

Parker, J. and Ashencaen Crabtree, S. (2014a) Fish need bicycles: an exploration of the perceptions of male social work students on a qualifying course. *British Journal of Social Work*, 44 (2): 310–327.

Parker, J. and Ashencaen Crabtree, S. (2014b) Covert research and adult protection and safeguarding: an ethical dilemma? *Journal of Adult Protection*, 16 (1): 1–12.

Parker, J. and Ashencaen Crabtree, S. (2014c) Ripples in a pond: do social work students need to learn about terrorism? *Social Policy and Social Work in Transition*, 3 (2): 50–73. DOI: 10.1921/4704030201.

Parker, J. and Ashencaen Crabtree, S. (2016) *Ethnographic research as social work practice.* JSWEC. Open University Milton Keynes, 15 July, conference paper.

Parker, J. and Doel, M. (eds.) (2013a) *Professional Social Work*. London: SAGE.

Parker, J. and Doel, M. (2013b) Professional social work and the professional social work identity, in Parker, J. and Doel, M. (eds.) *Professional Social Work*. London: SAGE, pp. 1–18.

Parker, J. and Randall, P. (1997) *Using Social and Psychological Theories*. London: Open Learning Foundation/BASW.

Parker, J., Ashencaen Crabtree, S., Chui, W.H., Kumagai, T., Baba, I., Azman, A., Haselbacher, C., Ashkanani, H.R. and Szto, P. (2012a) WAVE: working with adults who are vulnerable – a comparison of curricula, policies and constructions. *Revista de Asistenţă Socială*, XI (3/2012): 1–18.

Parker, J., Ashencaen Crabtree, S., Baba, I., Carlo, D.P. and Azman, A. (2012b) Liminality and learning: international placements as a rite of passage. *Asia Pacific Journal of Social Work and Development*, 22 (3): 146–158.

Parker, J., Ashencaen Crabtree, S. and Azman, A. (2016a) Treading the long path: social work education in Malaysia, in Taylor, I., Bogo, M., Lefevre, M. and Teater, B. (eds.) *The Routledge International Handbook of Social Work Education*. London: Routledge, pp. 84–95.

Parker, J., Habib, N. and Brown, B. (2016b) *History and biography in the sociology of welfare: the importance of student fieldwork*. Available at http://blogs.bournemouth.ac.uk/research/2016/12/07/history-and-biography-in-the-sociology-of-welfare-the-importance-of-student-fieldwork/ (accessed 7 December 2016).

Parker, J., Ashencaen Crabtree, S., Reeks, E., Marsh, D. and Vasif, C. (forthcoming) 'River! That in silence windest.' The place of religion and spirituality in social work assessment: sociological reflections and practical implications, in Spatschek, C., Ashencaen Crabtree, S. and Parker, J. (eds.) *Methods and Methodologies of Social Work: Reflecting Professional Interventions*. London: Whiting & Birch.

Parrott, L. (2014) *Values and Ethics in Social Work Practice*, 3rd ed. London: SAGE.

Parsons, T. (1951) *The Social System*. London: Routledge.

Payne, M. (2005) *The Origins of Social Work: Continuity and Change*. Basingstoke: Palgrave.

Payne, M. (2013) Being a social work professional, in Parker, J. and Doel, M. (eds.) *Professional Social Work*. London: SAGE, pp. 19–38.

Penhale, B. and Parker, J. (2008) *Working with Vulnerable Adults*. London: Routledge.

Perlman, H. (1957) *Social Casework*. Chicago, IL: University of Chicago Press.

Pfeffer, J. and Salancik, G.R. (1978) *The External Control of Organizations: A Resource Dependence Perspective*. New York: Harper and Row.

Phillips, T., Goehing, C., Shaw, I. and Oram, J. (2010) Personalisation, support brokerage and social work – what are we teaching social work students? *Journal of Social Work Practice*, 24 (3): 335–349.

Pithouse, A. (1987) *Social Work: The Social Organisation of an Invisible Trade*. Aldershot: Ashgate.

Popple, K. (2000) *Analysing Community Work*. Maidenhead: Open University Press.

Priestley, J.B. (1945/2000) *An Inspector Call*s. London: Penguin Classics.

Prochaska, F. (2006) *Christianity and Social Services in Modern Britain*. Oxford: Oxford University Press.

Prost, S.G., Lemieux, C.M. and Ai, A.L. (2016) Social work students in the aftermath of Hurricanes Katrina and Rita: correlates of post-disaster substance use as a negative coping mechanism. *Social Work Education*, 35 (7): 825–844.

Razack, N. (2009) Decolonizing the pedagogy and practice of international social work. *International Social Work*, 52 (1): 9–21. DOI: 10.1177/0020872808097748.

Reamer, F.G. (2013) *Social Work Values and Ethics*, 4th ed. New York: Columbia University Press.

Richardson, H. (2017) Jamie Oliver: axing free school lunches a disgrace. *BBC*, 19 May 2017. Available at http://www.bbc.co.uk/news/education-39969155 (accessed 5 July 2017).

Rigby, L. (2017) Sure Start worked. So why is Theresa May out to kill it? *The Guardian*, 6 February 2017. Available at https://www.theguardian.com/commentisfree/2017/feb/06/sure-start-children-worked-why-theresa-may-out-to-kill-it (accessed 3 March 2017).

Ring, C. (2014) Social work training or social work education? An approach to curriculum design. *Social Work Education*, 35 (8): 1101–1108.

Robbins, K. (2005) Geographies of England: the north–south divide, imagined and material. *English Historical Review*, 120 (488): 1108–1110.

Robertson Elliot, F. (1996) *Gender, Families and Society*. New York: St Martin's Press.

Romero, M. (2017) *Introducing Intersectionality*. Cambridge: Polity Press.

Rosenhan, D.L. (1973) On being same in insane places. *Science*, 179: 250–258.

Rostow, W.W. (1960) *The Stage of Economic Growth: A Non-Communist Manifesto*. London: Cambridge University Press.

Rothman, D. and Morris, N. (1995) *Oxford History of the Prison: The Practice of Punishment in Western Society*. Oxford: Oxford University Press.

Runnymede Trust (1977) *Islamophobia: A Challenge for Us All*. London: Runnymede Trust.

Ryan, F. (2015) Death has become a part of Britain's welfare system. *The Guardian*, 27 August 2015. Available at https://www.theguardian.com/commentisfree/2015/aug/27/death-britains-benefits-system-fit-for-work-safety-net (accessed 20 March 2017).

Ryan, L. (2011) Muslim women negotiating collective stigmatization: 'We're just normal people'. *Sociology*, 45 (6): 1045–1060.

Samson, P.L. (2015) Practice wisdom: the art and science of social work. *Journal of Social Work Practice*, 29 (2): 119–131.

Scheff, T. (1974) The labeling theory of mental illness. *American Sociological Review*, 39 (3): 444–452.

Schofield, T. (2015) *A Sociological Approach to Health Determinants*. Port Melbourne, Australia: Cambridge University Press.

Schools Week (2016) *Free schools struggle to meet national GCSE standards*. Available at http://schoolsweek.co.uk/free-schools-struggle-to-meet-national-gcse-standards/ (accessed 1 May 2017).

Scott, A., Gilbert, A. and Gelan, A. (2007) *The Urban–Rural Divide: Myth or Reality?* Aberdeen: The Macaulay Institute.

Scott, D. (1990) Practice wisdom: the neglected source of practice research. *Social Work*, 35 (6): 564–568.

Scourfield, J.B. (2001) Constructing men in child protection work. *Men and Masculinities*, 4 (1): 70–89.

Scourfield, J.B. (2006) Placing gender in social work: the local and national dimensions of gender relations. *Social Work Education*, 25 (7): 665–679.

Scullion, L. and Brown, P. (2016) Understanding the social exclusion of Roma, in Ahmed, A. and Rogers, M. (eds.) *Working with Marginalised Groups*. London: Palgrave, pp. 70–82.

Seebohm Rowntree, B. (1901/2000) *Poverty: A Study of Town Life*, 2nd ed. Bristol: Policy Press.

Sheppard, M. (2012) *Social Work and Social Exclusion: The Idea of Practice*. Farnham: Ashgate.

Sherwood, H. (2017) Imams refuse funeral prayers to indefensible London Bridge attackers. *The Guardian*, 5 April 2017. Available at https://www.theguardian.com/uk-news/2017/jun/05/imams-refuse-funeral-prayers-to-indefensible-london-bridge-attackers (accessed 11 July 2017).

Shoesmith, S. (2016) *Learning from Baby P*. London: Jessica Kingsley.

Sibley, D. (1995) *Geographies of Exclusion*. London: Routledge.

Singh, G. and Cowden, S. (2013) The new radical social work professional, in Parker, J. and Doel, M. (eds.) *Professional Social Work*. London: SAGE, pp. 81–97.

Skoura-Kirk, E., Backhouse, B., Bennison, G., Cecil, B., Keeler, J., Talbot, D. and Watch, L. (2013) Mark my words! Service user and carer involvement in social work academic assessment. *Social Work Education*, 32 (5): 560–575.

Slawson, N. (2017) Woman deported from UK despite being married to Briton for 27 years. *The Guardian*, 26 February 2017. Available at https://www.theguardian.com/uk-news/2017/feb/26/grandmother-deported-from-uk-despite-being-married-to-briton-for-27-years (accessed 26 February 2017).

Smith, D.E. (1987) *The Everyday World as Problematic: A Feminist Sociology*. Boston, MA: Northeastern University Press

Sodha, S. (2017) Is Finland's basic universal income a solution to automation, fewer jobs and lower wages? *The Guardian*, 19 February 2017. Available at https://www.theguardian.com/society/2017/feb/19/basic-income-finland-low-wages-fewer-jobs (accessed 30 June 2017).

Stanford, S. (2010) 'Speaking back' to fear: responding to the moral dilemmas of risk in social work practice. *British Journal of Social Work*, 40: 1065–1080.

Stevens, S. and Tanner, D. (2006) Involving service users in the teaching and learning of social work students: reflections on experience. *Social Work Education*, 25 (4): 360–371.

Stewart, H. (2017a) Women bearing 86% of austerity burden, Commons figures reveal. *The Guardian*, 9 March 2017. Available at https://www.theguardian.com/world/2017/mar/09/

women-bearing-86-of-austerity-burden-labour-research-reveals?CMP=share_btn_link (accessed 2 August 2017).

Stewart, H. (2017b) Michael Gove mounts defence of university tuition fees. *The Guardian*, 2 July 2017. Available at https://www.theguardian.com/politics/2017/jul/02/michael-gove-mounts-defence-of-university-tuition-fees (accessed 2 July 2017).

Swinford, S. (2017) Parents responsible for care of their mothers and fathers as much as their own children, minister says. *The Telegraph*, 31 January 2017. Available at http://www.telegraph.co.uk/news/2017/01/31/parents-responsible-care-elderlymothers-fathers-much-children/ (accessed 4 February 2017).

Taylor, D. (2017) Mark Duggan shooting: court considers appeal against inquest verdict. *The Guardian*, 2 March 2017. Available at https://www.theguardian.com/uk-news/2017/mar/02/mark-duggan-shooting-court-considers-appeal-against-inquest-verdict (accessed 2 March 2017).

Taylor, I. and Bogo, M. (2014) Perfect opportunity – perfect storm? Raising the standards of social work education in England. *British Journal of Social Work*, 44: 1402–1418.

Teater, B. and Baldwin, M. (2009) Exploring the learning experiences of students involved in community profiling projects. *Social Work Education*, 28 (7): 778–791.

Temerlin, M.K. (1968) Suggestion effects in psychiatric diagnosis. *Journal of Mental Disorders*, 147 (4): 349–353.

Thane, P. (2010) Unequal Britain: equalities since 1945. *History and Policy.* Policy papers. Available at http://www.historyandpolicy.org/policy-papers/papers/unequal-britain-equalities-in-britain-since-1945 (accessed 12 June 2017.)

Thatcher, M. (1993) *The Downing Street Years.* London: Harper Collins.

Thomas, H. (1999) *The Slave Trade: The Story of the Atlantic Slave Trade: 1440–1870.* New York: Simon & Schuster.

Thompson, L.J. and West, D. (2013) Professional development in the contemporary educational context: encouraging practice wisdom. *Social Work Education*, 32 (1): 118–133.

Thompson, N. (2009) *Understanding Social Work*, 3rd ed. Basingstoke: Palgrave.

Thompson, N. (2013) The emotionally competent professional, in Parker, J. and Doel, M. (eds.) *Professional Social Work*. London: SAGE, pp. 68–80.

Thompson, N. (2016) *Anti-Discriminatory Practice: Equality, Diversity and Social Justice*, 6th ed. Basingstoke: Palgrave.

Thompson, S. (2005) *Age Discrimination*. Lyme Regis: Russell House.

Tolstoy, L. (1877) *Anna Karenina.* Any unabridged edition.

Topping, A. (2017) Woman, 89, trapped in hospital for six months despite being fit to leave. *The Guardian*, 6 February 2017. Available at https://www.theguardian.com/society/2017/feb/06/woman-89-trapped-hospital-six-months-despite-fit-leave-iris-sibley (accessed 6 February 2017).

Travis, A. (2017a) UK asylum seekers housing branded disgraceful by MPs. *The Guardian*, 31 January 2017. Available at https://www.theguardian.com/uk-news/2017/jan/31/uk-asylum-seekers-housing-branded-disgraceful-by-mps-yvette-cooper (accessed 1 February 2017).

Travis, A. (2017b) Prisons inspector warns of staggering declines in safety in youth jails. *The Guardian*, 18 July 2017. Available at https://www.theguardian.com/society/2017/jul/18/youth-jails-staggering-decline-standards-england-wales-peter-clarke-prisons-inspector-report (accessed 18 July 2017).

Travis, A. and Taylor, D. (2017) PM accused of closing door on child refugees as 'Dubs' scheme ends. *The Guardian*, 8 February 2017. Available at https://www.theguardian.com/world/2017/feb/08/dubs-scheme-lone-child-refugees-uk-closed-down (accessed 2 August 2017).

Trevithick, P. (2014) Humanising managerialism: reclaiming emotional reasoning, intuition, the relationship, and knowledge and skills in social work. *Journal of Social Work Practice*, 28 (3): 287–311.

Triggle, N. (2017a) Frail elderly people 'left to struggle alone'. *BBC*, 18 February 2017. Available at http://www.bbc.co.uk/news/health-38984925 (accessed 19 February 2017).

Triggle, N. (2017b) Life expectancy rises grinding to halt in England. *BBC*, 18 July 2017. Available at http://www.bbc.co.uk/news/health-40608256 (accessed 18 July 2017).

Turner, V. (1969) *The Ritual Process: Structure and Anti-Structure*. Chicago, IL: Adline.

Valadez, L. and Hirsch, D. (2016) *Child Poverty Map*. Loughborough: Centre for Research in Social Policy, Loughborough University.

van Gennep, A. (1906) *The Rites of Passage*. London: Kegan Paul.

Varoufakis, V. (2017) *And the Weak Suffer What They Must: Europe, Austerity and the Threat to Global Stability*. London: Vintage.

Vertovec, S. (2007a) Super-diversity and its implications. *Ethnic and Racial Studies*, 30 (6): 1024–1054.

Vertovec, S. (2007b) *New Complexities of Cohesion in Britain: Super-Diversity, Transnationalism ad Civil-Integration*. Wetherby: Commission on Integration and Cohesion.

Vertovec, S. (2014) *Super-Diversity*. London: Routledge.

Vize, R. (2017) Governments response to UK soaring prison suicide rate is pitiful. *The Guardian*, 5 May 2017. Available at https://www.theguardian.com/healthcare-network/2017/may/05/government-response-to-uks-soaring-prison-suicide-rate-has-been-pitiful (accessed 7 July 2017).

Wacker, R. and Dziobek, I. (2016) Preventing empathic distress and social stressors at work through nonviolent communication training: a field study with health professionals. *Journal of Occupational Health Psychology*, Advance Access http:sx.doi.org/10.1037/ocp0000058.

Walker, J., Crawford, K. and Parker, J. (2008) *Practice Education in Social Work: A Handbook for Practice Teachers, Assessors and Educators*. Exeter: Learning Matters.

Walker, P. (2011) Fiona Pilkington case: police face misconduct proceedings. *The Guardian*, 24 May 2011. Available at https://www.theguardian.com/uk/2011/may/24/fiona-pilkington-police-misconduct-proceedings (accessed 3 April 2017).

Warwick Digital Collections (n.d.) *To the Citizens of London*. Available at http://contentdm.warwick.ac.uk/cdm/ref/collection/tav/id/4921 (accessed 3 May 2017).

White, C., Bruce, S. and Ritchie, J. (2000) *Young People's Politics: Political Interest and Engagement Amongst 16–24 Year Olds*. York: Joseph Rowntree Foundation.

Wilkinson, R. and Pickett, K. (2010) *The Spirit Level: Why Equality Is Better for Everyone*. London: Penguin.

Williams, C. and Graham, M.J. (2016) *Social Work in a Diverse Society: Transformative Practice with Black and Minority Ethnic Individuals and Groups*. Bristol: Policy Press.

Williams, T. (1955/2009) *Cat on a Hot Tin Roof*. London: Penguin Classics.

Williams, Z. (2017) Cuts are a feminist issue, so what would suffragettes do? *The Guardian*, 13 March 2017. Available at https://www.theguardian.com/commentisfree/2017/mar/13/cuts-feminist-issue-suffragette-austerity?CMP=share_btn_link (accessed 2 August 2017).

Wilson, K., Ruch, G., Lymbery, M. and Cooper, A. (2008) *Social Work: An Introduction to Contemporary Practice*. Harlow: Pearson Longman.

Witz, A. (1992) *Professions and Patriacrchy*. London: Routledge.

Wyn Jones, R. (2016) Why did Wales shoot itself in the foot in this Referendum? *The Guardian*, 27 June 2016. Available at https://www.theguardian.com/commentisfree/2016/jun/27/wales-referendum-remain-leave-vote-uk-eu-membership (accessed 3 January 2017).

Zabat-Zinn, J. (2013) *Full Catastophe Living: Using the Wisdom of Your Mind and Body to Face Stress, Pain and Illness*. New York: Random House.

Žižek, S. (2011) Shoplifters of the world unite! *London Review of Books Online*, 11 August 2011. Available at https://www.lrb.co.uk/2011/08/19/slavoj-zizek/shoplifters-of-the-world-unite (accessed 13 July 2017).

Index

1984 (Orwell) 42, 77

abuse 148–9
activism 85, 131, 143, 146–9
adaptations 50–1
ageism 16
agency policies and procedure 157–9
agency and structure 9
aggregation 60
aggression 108–11
Agnew, R. 50
Ahmed, A. 13, 18
Ahsan, Saleyha 68
alcohol misuse 34, 148–9
alienation 54, 119
All Things Bright and Beautiful 26
alternative logic 74
An Inspector Calls (Priestley) 29
anger 169–70
Anna Karenina (Tolstoy) 39
anomie 49
anti-discriminatory legislation 84
anti-discriminatory practice 17, 88–90
anti-oppressive practice 16–17, 88–90
anti-psychiatry school 53
apoliticisation 77
appearance 103–4, 105
Aristotle 92–3
assessment 24
    relationship-based approach 138–9, 154
    skills 102
asylum seekers 35–7, 148
Atos 65
austerity measures 141, 161, 162–3, 170
    impacts of 64–72

Baby P (Peter Connelly) 86, 117
Baldwin, Stanley 37
Balls, Ed 86
base (substructure) 54
Becker, H. 53
Bentham, Jeremy 91
Berlin, I. 165
Bernades, J. 57
Beveridge Report 28, 30
bin-diving for food 147
Blumenthal, Mrs 102, 106–7
Blumer, H. 49
BMELawyers4Grenfell 143
body language 112–13

Booth, William 30
Bourdieu, P. 19–20, 55–6
Brexit 74–6, 77, 143, 162
British Association of Social Workers (BASW) 143
    code of ethics 91
Broken 146
broker role 157
buffering hypothesis 130
Butler, Josephine 28

Cable, Vince 76
capacity model 101
capital 19–20
Care Act 2014 31, 92, 127, 141
    care homes
        forcible removal of people to 66
        funding care in 70–1, 155–6
    care providers 158
    knowledge of 141
Care Standards Act 2000 31, 136
carers, learning from 125–7
Chalmers, Thomas 29–30
Chamberlain, J.M. 49, 52
Chamberlain, Neville 37
charities 25, 28–9, 35, 37, 69
Charities Organisation Society (COS) 29
CHC 159, 161
Cheung, S.O-N. 124
Chicago School of Sociology 48–9
    children
        asylum seekers 35–7
        impacts of austerity on 72
        labour in the Victorian era 28
        in poverty 37–8, 72
Children and Social Work Act 2017 122, 136
Climbié Inquiry 19
Cochrane, Kelso 84
collective stigmatisation 43
colonialism 87
    communication 111–14
    skills 106–8
    communities
        conflict between 162–3
        marginalised minority groups 39–43
        working with 146–9
community organisations 137
competition 162–3
concern consciousness 94–5
    conflict 54–5, 162–3
    dealing with hostility and aggression 108–11

Confucianism 94–5
Connelly, Peter (Baby P) 86, 117
consequentialist ethics 91–2
Conservative Party 2017 election manifesto 92
    context
    marginalisation in context 76–8
    of social work xii–xiii, 100–1
Cooper, K. 72
corporatist states 71
counterterrorism 56
    courts 83–4
    working in 145–6
critical race theory 89
critical theories 54–5
Crowder, R. 130
Crown Prosecution Service 33
cultural broker 157
cultural competence 89
cultural diversity 142
current affairs 86–7

Davies, Janet 65
death 67–8
dementia, people with 91–2, 102, 106–7
deontology 90–1
Deprivation of Liberty Standards 140–1
'deserving' poor 28
deviance theory 52–3
Dewey, J. 49
dialectic 58
dialogue 111–12
direct action 146–7
    disability 7
    austerity and 65–7
    people with learning disabilities 32–4
    social model of 8
Disability United 66
disabling professions 121–2
disablism 16
    disadvantage xi–xii, xv, 4–9, 20
    created by policies and practices 153–6
    disadvantaged/marginalised groups xv, 22–44
    impact of xvi, 63–78
    processes of xv, 45–62
discourse ethics 111–12
    discrimination 13, 14–16
    anti-discriminatory practice 17, 88–90
    personal/cultural/social aspects 16
domestic violence 148–9
Dominelli, L. 16
doxa (everyday practices) 20, 55, 56, 57–9
drug misuse 34, 148–9
Dublin Regulations 35, 36
Dubs, Lord Alf 36, 37
'Dubs' scheme 36–7
Duggan, Mark 58

Durkheim, E. 46, 49
Dybicz, P. 125

economic disadvantage see poverty
    education 76
    of Gypsy Roma Traveller children 41
    marginalisation of young people 72–4
Egan, G. 112
Elizabethan Poor Law 27
empathy 25, 102
employment and support allowance (ESA) 67–8
Equality Act 2010 47, 85, 138, 144–5
ethical dilemmas xvii, 152–67
ethical practice 95–6
ethics 90–6
ethnography 102
European Court of Human Rights 143
    European Union (EU) 83
    referendum 74–6, 77, 143, 162
everyday practices 55, 56, 57–9
    exclusion
    of Gypsy Roma Travellers 40–1
    social 9
experience, learning from others' 125–7
expertise 122–3

Factory Commission Report 1833 28
factual knowledge xvi, 81–97
fair play 7
family 47–8, 57
Farchi, M. 130
Ferencz, Norbert 147
field 20
filial piety 94, 95
Fletcher, Joseph 93–4
food banks 37, 38, 65
Fook, J. 17–18
Foster, J. 9, 11
foster carers UKIP row 15
Francis inquiry 118
free school meals 76, 92
free schools 76
Fry, Elizabeth 28
functionalism 46–8, 120
    funding
    care in old age 70–1, 92, 155–9
    ethical dilemmas 157–62

Galvani, S. 34
Gaskell, Elizabeth 29
    gender 12, 153
    and care-giving 71
geography 10–11
Gilbert, Michael 32, 33–4
good life 92–3
good practice 99–100

Goodyer, A. 101
Gove, Michael 73
Greer, J. 129
Grenfell Tower fire disaster 143, 162, 169
Gypsy Roma Travellers 39–41

Habermas, J. 111, 112
habitus 19, 55–6
haitch pronunciation 104
hate crimes 32–3
    health care
    Gypsy Roma Travellers 41
    impact of austerity 64–71
Health Care Professions Council 101, 122
Henry VIII 26
Hideaway Project 148
Higgins, M. 101
Hill, Octavia 28
historical materialism 54
    history
    knowledge about 85, 87
    of profession and professionalism 119–23
    of welfare provision 26–31
hoarding 163–4, 166
holistic approach 138–9, 154
Holocaust 41
Home Office 35, 36
homelessness 34–5
Hoskin, Steven 32, 33, 34
hostility 108–11
Houses of Correction 27, 28
Houston, S. 96, 111–12
Hugman, R. 122–3
Hugo, Victor 40
Human Rights Act 1998 138, 139–44
humour 163
Hunchback of Notre Dame, The (Hugo) 40
Hungary 147

I, Daniel Blake 68
idealism 101
identity, professional 123
Illich, I. 121
impact of disadvantage/marginalisation xvi, 63–78
impotent, the 27
incapacity benefit (IB) 67–8
indigeneity 39–40
inequality 6
inequity 6
institutional racism 40–1
    interactionism 120
    symbolic 49, 52
International Federation of Social Workers (IFSW) xiii–xiv, 77
intersectionality 13, 17–18, 90
irony 101, 154
Islamophobia 42

Jewish children 37
'Joe' (MENCAP campaign) 33
Johnson, T. 119–20
Juncker, Jean-Claude 76

Karban, K. 123
Katiuzhinsky, A. 142
Khan, Sadiq 162
Kindertransport 37
knowledge base, factual xvi, 81–97
Koprowska, J. 109
Krill, D. 124–5

labelling theory 51–3
language 104, 106–8
latent functions 47
leadership, professional 117
learned helplessness 9, 10, 77
learning disabilities, people with 32–4
learning from others' experience 125–7
Lee, Laurie 34
    legislation and policy xii, xvi–xvii, 135–51
    history of welfare provision 26–31
    knowledge of 83–5, 138–44
    seeking to change policy 149–50
    see also under individual Acts
Lemert, E. 52–3
life choices/decisions 33–4, 163–6
liminality 60–1
Lipsky, M. 121
local authority social workers 136–7

Magnus 65
managerialism 118–19, 121
manifest function 47
marginalia 13
    marginalisation x–xii, xv, 9–13, 20, 170–1
    in context 76–8
    impact of xvi, 63–78
    marginalised/disadvantaged groups xv, 22–44
    by policies and practices 153–6
    political 11–12, 74–6
    processes of xv, 45–62
    sexual 12
    socio-spatial 10–11
market forces 158–9
Marx, Karl 54–5
Mary Barton (Gaskell) 29
'mate crimes' 32, 33
matrix of domination 17
May, Theresa 36, 68, 75
McKerrell, Niklaus 75
Mead, G.H. 49
meaning 106–8
media 86–7, 160
Meer, N. 18

MENCAP 33
'mensch' 107
   mental health 47
   labelling theory and 53
   problems 148–9
Mental Health Act 1983/2007 140–1
Merton, R.K. 47, 49, 50
Mills, C. Wright 85
mindfulness 130–1
minimal states 71
minority groups 39–43
Modern Slavery Act 2015 147
Modern Slavery Helpline 147
modern slavery 147–8
monasteries 26
Moore-Bick, Sir M. 143
moral sensibilities, challenges to 163–6
Morgan, D. 57, 59
mortality 67–8
Mowat, David 69
Murdoch, G.K. 47–8
Muslim minority ethnic groups 39, 41–3

National Health Service (NHS) 30–1, 69
   labelled a humanitarian crisis 68
Natland, S. 111
negative freedoms 165–6
neoliberalism 66, 73, 158–9, 162, 170
new professionalism 123
news media 86–7
non-governmental organisations (NGOs) 61
non-verbal communication 112–14
norms 49
North of England 9, 11
Notting Hill riots 84
nurses 65

observers 58–9
occupational imperialism 120
Okech, D. 142
   old age
   creation of vulnerability in 68–71, 155–6
   funding of social care 70–1, 92, 155–9
   impact of austerity on health and social care in 64, 68–71
Oliver, Jamie 76
   oppression 13, 16, 169
   anti-oppressive practice 16–17, 88–90
Orme, J. 71
Orwell, George 30, 34–5, 42, 77
outdoor relief 27
outsiders 53

parish poverty relief 26
Parker, J. 61
Parsons, T. 46–8
patriarchy 120–1

paying for care see funding
people with dementia 91–2, 102, 106–7
people with learning disabilities 32–4
people trafficking 147–8
personal/cultural/social (PCS) model 16
Personal Independent Payment 65
personalisation agenda 92
Pilkington, Fiona 32
Plant, R. 165
policy see legislation and policy
political activism 85, 131, 143, 146–9
political experimentation 76
political interference 86
political intersectionality 18
   political marginalisation 11–12
   of young people 74–6
   politics 159–60, 169–70
   knowledge about 85–6, 87–8
   working politically for change 149–50
Poor Laws 27–8
populism 16
positive freedoms 165–6
potent (able-bodied) groups 27
   poverty 8, 170
   history of poor relief 26–8
   as a social work concern 37–9
   studies of 29–30
poverty line 30
power, professional 122
practice wisdom 124–5
   practices 55–9
   everyday 55, 56, 57–9
   theory of 55–7
Prevent programme 42–3, 56
Priestley, J.B. 29
primary deviance 52–3
principled relativism 93–4
prisons 72
privacy 91
privatisation of care 66
processes of marginalisation/disadvantage xv, 45–62
   profession 116–17
   history of 119–23
   social work as 121–3
   vs vocation 73
professional agencies 58
   Professional Capabilities Framework (PCF) 117, 153–4
   chapter topics and capability development 3–4, 22–3,
      45–6, 63–4, 81–2, 98, 115–16, 135–6, 152
   rationale for 101
professional development xvi, 115–32
professional identity 123
professional leadership 117
professional power 122
professional social work practice 116–19
professionalisation xii

professionalism 117, 118–19
history of 119–23
pronunciation 104
Prout, Jimmy 32, 33
public sector workers' wages 65

racism 16, 149
institutional 40–1
radical social work 16–17, 150
Raleigh, Sir Walter 38
Reamer, F.G. 154
Red Cross 35, 36, 148
reflective practice 103, 156
reflexivity 19, 89, 125
Reformation 26
Refugee Council 148
refugees 35–7, 170–1
relationship-based approach 138–9, 154
relativism 142
report writing 102–3
resilience 128–31
fostering 129–31
resource unavailability 159–62
rights, human 139–44
risk management 154–5
rites of passage 60–1
Road to Wigan Pier, The (Orwell) 30
Rogers, M. 13, 18
Roma Gypsy Travellers 39–41
Romero, M. 17
Rosenhan, D.L. 53
rough sleepers 34–5
Rowntree, Seebohm 30
rural poverty 38–9

safeguarding xii–xiii, 154
sanitation 28
scavenging 163–5
Scheff, T. 53
Sears, A. 130
secondary deviance 52–3
self-efficacy 130
self-presentation 103–5
separation 60
service users
choice rhetoric 100
creating the relationship with 103
learning from their experience 125–7
as liminals 61
severe disablement allowance (SDA) 67–8
sexism 16
sexual marginalisation 12
sexuality 12, 47–8
Shaw, George Bernard 116
Sherborne 38–9
Sibley, Iris 68–9

sick role 47
situation ethics 93–4
skills xvi, 98–114
slavery 147–8
Smith, D.E. 57
Smith, S. 123
social actors 58–9
social capital 130
social care 122
funding 70–1, 92, 155–62
impact of austerity measures 64–7, 68–71
social care agencies 158
social closure 120
social control 53, 72
social democratic states 71
social exclusion 9
social insurance 30
social model of disability 8
social welfare reforms 28
social work
changes in British social work xii–xiii, 3–5
context xii–xiii, 100–1
defining xiii–xiv
ethical practice 95–6
good practice 99–100
history of profession and professionalism in 119–23
human rights stance in 143–4
and the impact of marginalisation 77–8
importance of disadvantage and marginalisation 20
as a profession 121–3
professional practice 116–19
social workers as limen 60–1
social workers' roles 24
Social Work Action Network 150
Social Work England 122
socio-spatial marginalisation 10–11
SOLER mnemonic 112
speaking out 25
speech 104, 106–8, 111–12
Speenhamland system 27
Stanford, S. 154
Stewart, K. 72
strain theory 49–51
street-level bureaucracy 121
structural intersectionality 18
structure and agency 9
substance misuse 34, 148–9
substructure (base) 54
subversion 24
super-diversity 13, 18–20, 90, 107–8
superstructure 54
support agencies, knowledge of 141
support broker 157
Sure Start 72
symbolic interactionism 49, 52
systems thinking 46–7

terrorism 42, 56, 162
Thatcher, Margaret xi
third-sector social workers 137–8
Thompson, N. 15–16, 88–9, 123
Thurnham, A. 34
time management 103
tipping point 171
Tolstoy, L. 39
touch 113–14
trafficking of people 147–8
trait-based approaches 120
Travellers, Roma 39–41
Trump, Donald 42, 162
Trussell Trust 37
tuition fees 72–4
Turn 2 Us 148

UKIP foster parents row 15
'undeserving' poor 28
United States of America (USA) 42
universalism 142
university education 72–4
urban poverty 37–8
utilitarian ethics 91–2

values
    challenges to the value base 163–6
    knowledge about ethics and 90–6
Vertovec, S. 18–19
victimisation 32–3, 109
    violence 108–11
    domestic 148–9

virtue ethics 92–3
vocation 73
voluntary organisations 137
    vulnerability 31, 127–8
    creation of in old age 68–71, 155–6
    knowledge of and working with marginalised
        people 128
    people with learning disabilities 32–4
    of social workers 127

welfare provision, history of 26–31
    welfare state 30–1
    erosion of 68–71
    types of 71
whistle blowing 25
'whitewashing' 118, 119
Witz, A. 120–1
    women
    caring role 71
    impact of austerity measures 71–2
    Muslim 43
Wood, Alice 70–1, 155–6
work capability assessments 65
workhouse 27–8
World War I 30
World War II 30

young people, marginalisation of 71–6

Zabat-Zinn, J. 130
Zaman, Zahid 32